CONCESSIONAIRES, FINANCIERS AND COMMUNITIES

Unrelenting demands for energy, infrastructure and natural resources, and the need for developing states to augment income and signal an 'enterprise-ready' attitude, mean that transnational development projects remain a common tool for economic development. Yet little is known about the fragmented legal framework of private financial mechanisms, contractual clauses and discretionary behaviours that shape modern development projects. How do gaps and biases in formal laws cope with the might of concessionaires and financiers and their algorithmic contractual and policy technicalities negotiated in private offices? What impacts do private legal devices have for the visibility and implementation of indigenous peoples' rights to land? This original perspective on transnational development projects, explains how the patterns of poor rights recognition and implementation, power(lessness), vulnerability and, ultimately, conflict routinely seen in development projects will only be fully appreciated by acknowledging and remedying the pivotal role and priority enjoyed by private mechanisms, documentation and expertise.

KINNARI I. BHATT is a postdoctoral researcher at Erasmus University Rotterdam. She worked as a project finance lawyer with leading global law firms White & Case and Milbank, Tweed, Hadley & McCloy in London and Asia and acted as a legal adviser to the Ministry of Mineral Resources in Sierra Leone. She advises NGOs on issues of equitable natural resource management and has taught courses on legal aspects of international finance and project finance at the University of East Anglia and University College London.

CONCESSIONAIRES, FINANCIERS AND COMMUNITIES

Implementing Indigenous Peoples' Rights to Land in Transnational Development Projects

KINNARI I. BHATT

Erasmus University Rotterdam

CAMBRIDGE
UNIVERSITY PRESS

CAMBRIDGE
UNIVERSITY PRESS

University Printing House, Cambridge CB2 8BS, United Kingdom

One Liberty Plaza, 20th Floor, New York, NY 10006, USA

477 Williamstown Road, Port Melbourne, VIC 3207, Australia

314–321, 3rd Floor, Plot 3, Splendor Forum, Jasola District Centre, New Delhi – 110025, India

79 Anson Road, #06–04/06, Singapore 079906

Cambridge University Press is part of the University of Cambridge.

It furthers the University's mission by disseminating knowledge in the pursuit of education, learning, and research at the highest international levels of excellence.

www.cambridge.org
Information on this title: www.cambridge.org/9781108484657
DOI: 10.1017/9781108689106

First published 2020

Printed in the United Kingdom by TJ International Ltd., Padstow, Cornwall

A catalogue record for this publication is available from the British Library.

Library of Congress Cataloging-in-Publication Data
Names: Bhatt, Kinnari I, 1978– author.
Title: Concessionaires, financiers and communities : implementing indigenous peoples' rights to land in transnational development projects / Kinnari I. Bhatt, Erasmus Universiteit Rotterdam.
Description: Cambridge, United Kingdom ; New York, NY, USA,: Cambridge University Press, 2020. | Based on author's thesis (doctoral - University of Greenwich., 2016) issued under title: Rights to land, fragmentation and fairness : the problem of transnational legal governance for indigenous groups. | Includes bibliographical references and index.
Identifiers: LCCN 2019040369 (print) | LCCN 2019040370 (ebook) | ISBN 9781108484657 (hardback) | ISBN 9781108723459 (paperback) | ISBN 9781108689106 (epub)
Subjects: LCSH: Indigenous peoples–Land tenure–Developing countries. | Economic development projects–Law and legislation–Developing countries. | Land tenure–Law and legislation–Developing countries.
Classification: LCC K3248.L36 B48 2020 (print) | LCC K3248.L36 (ebook) | DDC 333.3089–dc23
LC record available at https://lccn.loc.gov/2019040369
LC ebook record available at https://lccn.loc.gov/2019040370

ISBN 978-1-108-48465-7 Hardback

To the memory of my inspirational mother, Pallavi,
who left too soon.

CONTENTS

PREFACE

The Bigger Picture

A few years ago (I'm not sure exactly when), I stumbled across a letter on the Internet written by a villager in Uganda describing how he had been displaced from his home to make way for the construction of the huge Bujagali hydroelectric power plant on the River Nile. The file I had downloaded was a complaint written directly to the headquarters of the African Development Bank's ombudsman and mediation service. It talked of the villager's struggle to obtain access to water and electricity despite the irony of being in sight of one of the world's largest hydroelectric plants. In it, the villager claimed a special 'indigenous' sociocultural, spiritual and economic relationship to that land and traditionally observed land rights but pointed out that the state did not recognise his indigenous status under the Ugandan constitution. I had, I suppose, become accustomed to hearing stories like these given the daily diet of global scandals in which multinational companies are implicated. This letter was different. To my surprise, the villager's letter contained a handwritten note imploring the ombudsman panel to 'please look at the margin'.

I had done some work on the Bujagali project and was broadly aware of its financial structure. On reflecting upon the letter and my experiences in practice, I was convinced that there was an interesting social and legal story to be told about what was happening inside these types of transnational development project that innately injures their ability to be drivers for the development agenda; specifically, the link between the private law financial structures, transactional terms and the behaviours that guide them and their real-world human implications. In Bujagali specifically, it meant exposing the incentives created through hefty 'micro' interest payments on asset-based lending project finance loans (as the villager so eloquently stated: its 'margin') and the impact those rates can have on communities around the project site. I was sure that the villager was making the general point about how crushing interest rates (common for projects in which lenders are highly exposed to political, commercial, legal or technical risk) are typically treated as pass-through costs under the terms of the Power Purchase Agreement (PPA) between the project company (the investors) and the government: the Ugandan Electricity Board (UEC) in this case. This means that the UEC, under the PPA, is obliged to pay sums equal to the interest on debt at actual cost, without having any control on the financing terms. As an electricity buyer, this is clearly a bad deal for the government as it is bound, through the PPA, to bear the brunt of the financing cost in the tariff. However, like all electricity providers, the UEC will then pass on these spiralling costs to its customers: local Ugandans. These linkages were made palpable in the letter. The displaced villager had hit the nail on the head, making the 'beyond border' connection between far-off financing terms and their local effects on him as a land-dependent person, so tangible within his hand-scribbled addition to the letter.

At the time, I had just finished eight years advising on the legal framework around the financing and development of all types of road, rail, port, oil, gas and mining development project in emerging markets. I had, in between the late nights, become increasingly convinced that the types of project I worked on were sites of legal interest. Reading the letter took me back to the time when the senior partner I worked with told me, with immense glee, of how, through the loan agreements and dozens of other documents required to build the supporting financial and operational structure behind a development project, we were 'legislating' in the jurisdiction of the project. Sometimes our clients were also providing private grievance mechanisms and thus a form of access to justice for communities affected by the projects. This meant inputting clauses into the debt instruments waiving the standard borrower–lender confidentiality provisions. Ombudsman panel members could then have sight of the documentation as part of any compliance investigation triggered by a community complaint lodged with that grievance mechanism. Whilst the state was visible, its voice was only heard through the concession agreements, host government guarantees or project-specific letters of comfort. Through these documents, it wore the hat of an 'enterprise-led' entity, an economic project participant, self-interested in keeping the project at full steam in order to collect taxes for the national budget and keep future donors, companies and development finance institutes interested in investing in the country, now, and in the future. States know that one development project that is successfully funded, closed, constructed and operated creates a stable and predictable precedent for reaping the fruits of future investment.

In this context of brusque deadlines and an overwilling state, I began to wonder just how rights-compatible all of these contracts actually are, and the conversations about how we were supposedly 'legislating' sent shivers down my spine. Yet, I felt that my colleague had a point. The scale of these projects, the tangible contribution to a country's gross domestic product, the level of state involvement through, for example, private law contracts and also domestic legal reforms to accommodate them, is remarkable. Many development projects are geographically situated in countries with little or no experience of the size of inward investment required to mobilise a project and subsequently require the implementation of new legislation to protect the rights of the concession-aire and the project's financiers. In some countries, this translated into new Emiri decrees or primary and secondary legislation that permitted the vast level of private land ownership, related collateral required to finance the project and altered domestic laws requiring, for instance, the public auction of assets in the event of insolvency. The latter allows lenders to exert their priority security interests by appointing a private receiver in an insolvency event to take control of their investment. An immensely clear and predictable legal framework was constructed behind closed doors that pushed the project ahead through carefully designed construction contracts, loan agreements, guarantees, offtake (sales) agreements, power purchase agreements and concession agreements, to name a few. The fact that a sacred cow of national sovereignty – law making – was being so heavily influenced by financial investors' needs gave me pause for thought. Where do the voices of communities figure in complex deal-making processes and do development projects signal a shrinking space for democratic governance?

At the same time, I saw that it was not entirely clear to practitioners exactly what binding law really says on a topic of human concern and vulnerability such as indigenous peoples' rights to land in the context of a public-private development project that interfaces with so many private agreements. I wondered about the role of so-called formal law in these projects: could it be part of the problem through the values it protects and produces in these projects? Are there gaps and uncertainties within the law itself that developers can exacerbate through their routine decision-making and use to their commercial advantage? The experi-ences I have just discussed, and others like it, started me on a trajectory of thinking about how large development projects produce power and powerlessness and impact upon the application of the rule of law today within development project contexts. This thinking continued through my work experiences and into my research trajectory as I became increasingly focused on how the projects I worked on and their contractual and policy architecture interfaced with the recognition and implementation of indigenous peoples' rights to land and the compatibility of those regimes with issues of rights and vulnerability.

After leaving private practice, I worked as a legal advisor to the Ministry of Mineral Resources in Sierra Leone on a project funded by the World Bank and the UK government's Department for International Development. I worked with the Environmental Protection Agency and a group of environmental and social experts to draft the first set of environmental and social mining regulations. Post the civil war, the government of Sierra Leone has pursued an aggressive policy of promoting large-scale investment by using the country's large land-based resources to attract investment. A number of investors are acquiring large tracts of land for mining and plantation investments of which the Addax biofuel project is, perhaps, one of the better known examples. I saw that the physical struggles between concessionaires and local communities can also, surreptitiously, be found within the state and its institutions. Whilst preparing a cabinet paper for the Minister of Mineral Resources, I recall one conversation with a lawyer in the Attorney General's Office in which he advised me to distinguish development oustees from refugees, the point being that I needed to drive home the legal difference in rights between the former subject and the latter when it came to the governance of the private sector investment regime within Sierra Leone.

I went back to my desk and thought about this. Whilst he was *factually* right to draw attention to the situational difference between communities seeking refugee status and those moved to make way for a project, I started to think about whether a state would recognise communities that observe a sociocultural, spiritual and economic relationship to that land in the context of development, and if so, how? The conversation again brought home, in a tangible way, the importance of development projects as sites of interest to practitioners, policy advisors and researchers concerned with law, vulnerability, development and practices around 'doing development' in a polarised, real-world political, economic and social context.

In the later example, concerns arose as to how development projects and the behaviours that contextualise them implicate questions of legal identity, rights and access to justice. Behind the legal question were, of course, real political and economic tensions between the state's desire to attract inward investments and new financial actors into the country, and the need to limit its sovereign role as protector of public interest in order to facilitate capital flow and prevent capital flight. The instruction to nip in the bud any possible but unlikely argument that the state owes legal rights and remedies to displaced communities as 'refugees' reflects the state turn from protecting public values towards maximising investor returns. For me, these anecdotes confirmed that the phenomenon of development projects are important living sites in which legal values are created in a setting in which the distinctions between public and private norms are so deeply fragmented and collapsed so as to be almost meaningless, on a day-to-day practical basis. They are sites in which power has become so concentrated in the hands of investors that the private mechanisms brought to bear on a project by its concessionaire and financiers will routinely overshadow formal law and break down basic rule-of-law characteristics around the clarity, predictability and fairness of the law, with long-lasting implications for indigenous peoples. In the face of such a powerful legal framework enmeshed in a behemoth political economy of economic development, can the law regulate for the recognition and, crucially, the implementation of indigenous peoples' rights to land in a clear, predictable and fair manner, and if so, how? That is the challenge.

Development projects challenge traditional international legal thinking which has struggled to move beyond the organising logic of the nation state and the provision of remedy through a purely judicial paradigm. They fully display novel and highly specialised assemblages of bits of territory, authority and rights for a particular purpose, that cut across traditional binaries of global/local, public/private and formal/informal. Aspects of these projects expose complex interdependencies and struggles between rights and obligations, unity and fragmentation, power and the law, wealth and poverty[1] and also vulnerability and strength. Development projects can constitute sites of routinely concentrated capital and power in which 'expulsions'[2] of people from land will become the norm. This book offers a complementary legal response and series of illustrations around the legal dynamics that facilitate dispossession in the context of a development project.

More specifically, I illustrate how the legal, policy and regulatory financial instruments that support a development project and are born

---

[1] Drawing on S Sassen, 'Neither Global nor National: Novel Assemblages of Territory, Authority and Rights' (2008) 1(1–2) *Ethics and Global Politics* 61–79.

[2] S Sassen, *Expulsions: Brutality and Complexity in the Global Economy* (Harvard University Press 2014).

out of rules of private contract, security and property can, without corrective actions, steadily and with algorithmic repetitiveness create benefits for their holders (as they are designed to do) but at the same time work to 'trickle out' issues of rights implementation, at the expense of communities. These benefits accrue, for example, in the form of hierarchy and priority against all competing claims which brings the quality of universality to these assets. High degrees of ring fencing, insulation and banker–client confidentiality will shield discretionary and unchecked decision-making. Creditors can also negotiate specific advantages of preferred creditor status for currency convertibility during times of domestic financial crises. My argument is not for the wholesale dismantling of these rules of contract, corporate law and property in a 'baby bathwater' mentality, but that the effect they have in the context of development projects and the implementation of indigenous peoples' rights to land requires exposure, critical discussion and reconfiguration in line with the suggestions in the final chapter.

Equally important aspects for understanding the bleak role of the law (both private and public, as I argue in Chapter 3) in these projects is the hidden institutional behaviours, incentives and culture generated through the idiosyncratic settings in which legal documentation is drafted and deals are done. As I demonstrate throughout this book, these frequently overlooked private legal rules – transactional terms and related behaviours around implementation practice – have a crucial role to play in driving inequality and expulsion. Behind them stands an international legal framework that is structurally unable to cope with these assets, legal codes and assemblages. Consequently these private legal rules and behaviours ought to be considered as important normative legal sources when examining the impact of large development projects on precarity, accountability and a broad range of social and economic outcomes.

Even though none of my experiences took place inside a shiny court-room and many of the conflicts surrounding development projects are settled through informal mechanisms, cross-border development projects pose a current legal problem for land-connected communities and rights implementation and provide insights into the role of law in creating and policing these structures. I write this study from the lens of a private law practitioner experienced in operations in which sovereign entities take a more peripheral seat. There is a name for these types of operation in the financing and development finance community, that of non-sovereign operations. To this end, this is not a study about World

Bank operations which lend directly to states, but those of the World Bank's sister organisation, the International Finance Corporation (IFC), and other similar development finance organisations. Whilst comprised of states, they have an entirely separate legal personality and enjoy a legal mandate for investing in private operations for the purposes of private sector development and in some cases, poverty alleviation, in developing countries. Those development finance institutions are important players in the globalised legal order of development. Due to their state compos- ition, they act as a comforting catalyst for commercial banks who together will blend and extend substantial amounts of debt or in some cases equity, to finance infrastructure or natural resource development in a country in which the state is considered weak in terms of having the legal and financial capacity to conduct development. In this context, development finance institutions (DFIs) will push the investment for- ward and, during this process, directly lend to the project through unique debt structures that protect commercial banks and apply social safe- guarding standards to the loan mechanics. These mechanisms, as well as the unique state-backed, private constitution of development finance institutions, provide a signal to the financial markets that a project is bankable and safe for investment. They empower and legitimise a DFI's corporate client to enter into a range of debt and project contracts. Typically confidential, those commercial contracts can have severe impacts on the recognition and implementation of the rights to land of communities claiming indigenous status.

My frame of analysis as a practitioner and researcher interested in interfaces between development, law, economics, politics and issues of vulnerability enlarges the potential interest of this book. With increasing concerns on vulnerability studies from a multidisciplinary perspective along with the quest from legal and development practitioners to finding new insights and discourse into vulnerability and inclusivity issues, with specific reference to the role of law as an addressable mechanism, this book should appeal to multiple audiences. These include scholars interested in fields of study that sit at the intersection of law, economy, institutions and vulnerability, and also practitioners including in-house lawyers, govern- ment advisors, law firms and programming officers within development agencies interested in the role of law (understood in the widest sense) for addressing issues of vulnerability and rights implementation in contexts of sustainable development, natural resource management, infrastructure development and business and human rights.

ACKNOWLEDGEMENTS

This book is the product of many years of work and study in the worlds of research and practice with a much earlier and different version having formed a doctoral thesis. The idea of writing about transnational development projects was planted in my mind as far back as 2009 when working in a law firm. It took years of further work experience and research to hone this work into its current form. Writing a book can be a taxing endeavour and I questioned this journey, especially after the passing of my mother in 2017. Fortunately, I have found an outlet in painting and input from some kind and generous people. First, heartfelt thanks to Dragana Spencer and Mehmet Ugur for supervising the thesis and being such approachable people. During the initial stages, I benefitted greatly from the support of Sarah Greer and Bill Davies. I also thank Sarah Keenan for commenting on early drafts and Ronen Shamir for the encouraging chats over tea and for reading my work. I extend my appreciation to Ilias Bantekas for his unwavering belief in this project. Many people have given up their time to answer my questions and to share their thoughts with me over the years. Hearty thanks to Anne Maryse de Soyza, Iris Krebber at the Department for International Development, Michael Meegan at Yamatji Marlpa Aboriginal Corporation, Lucy Claridge at Amnesty International, Clive Baldwin at Human Rights Watch and interlocutors at the European Bank for Reconstruction and Development. I would like to show my appreciation to Battsengel Lkhamdoorov for sharing his experiences, Oyunaa Baljir for translating our conversations and Byambajav Dalaibuyan at the Centre for Social Responsibility in Mining in Australia. I am grateful to my interlocutors at Rio Tinto – Kate Wilson, Shannara Sewell, Holly Dodd and Michelle Aeschlimann and to Malin Hillström and San Martin Orlando at Statkraft. I take this opportunity to thank all of them warmly. Thanks to Peer Zumbansen for input into the book proposal process. I am grateful to Tom Randall for taking publication and production forward and to the four anonymous reviewers who provided feedback on the book proposal. Enormous thanks to Sue Farran who read the entire book and provided helpful comments during the final push, to Celine Tan who helped me arrive at the book's main title and to Giedre Jokubauskaite for organising a wonderful workshop funded by the University of Glasgow and attended by a number of financier interlocutors.

I have been lucky enough to receive financial support throughout this project. First and foremost, thank you to the School of Law at the University of Greenwich for the full doctoral scholarship. I also thank the Transnational Law Institute at Kings College for funding my attendance at international conferences. I am grateful for the opportunities provided in my time coordinating the inter-disciplinary project 'Integrating Normative and Functional Approaches to the Rule of Law and Human Rights' between Erasmus School of Law and the International Institute of Social Studies of Erasmus University Rotterdam. In this regard, a special thanks to Sanne Taekema for welcoming me to the Netherlands and for providing me with the time and freedom in which to write this book, collaborate and find my feet – I have realised a dream in completing this. Finally, I thank Joachim for being Joachim.

Development Projects, Indigenous Peoples' Land Rights and Rights Implementation

1 Contextualising the Interface between Development Projects and Indigenous Peoples' Land Rights

The last three decades have witnessed the explosion of oil, gas, mineral and infrastructure development projects involving multiple companies, international financial institutions, transactions and financial flows from different countries. This development is taking place in diverse geographical locations, in contexts of political and social instability and, frequently, upon land that is inhabited by groups who claim indigenous status. Whilst there are historical precedents for these types of development project from colonial times which show similar characteristics,[1] the

---

[1] The emergence in the nineteenth century of John Rockefeller's Standard Oil saw the beginning of the modern oil industry. Standard Oil developed into one of the world's first and biggest multinational corporations, quickly followed by Royal Dutch Shell in the West Indies. The building of road, rail and canal projects was a feature of the colonial period with projects involving the cooperation of the government, the colonial state, individual investors and private companies – the Rothschild family were active in financing many oil and mining projects. So, in colonial Africa, the Beira Railway was built to boost trade from and to South Africa. The discovery of copper deposits provided the conditions for Tanganyika Concessions Limited, a company with extensive mining and financial interests in Central Africa, to develop the Benguela Railway. For more examples focusing on the politico-economic context of colonial era development projects see J Lunn, 'The Political Economy of Primary Railway Construction in the Rhodesias, 1890–1911' (1992) 33(2) *The Journal of African History* 239–254. From a legal dimension, scholars belonging to the field of third-world approaches to international law focus on the relationship between capital, imperialism and international law. Specifically, the creation of international financial institutions such as the World Bank Group that have replicated colonial relations through complex forms of modern development finance practices. See A Anghie, *Imperialism, Sovereignty, and the Making of International Law* (Cambridge University Press 2007). An iteration of this continuation can be seen in the creation in 1948, of the UK government's development finance institution, the Colonial Development Corporation, which continues today under the name of the CDC Group PLC. M Cowen, 'Early Years of the Colonial Development Corporation: British State Enterprise Overseas during Late Colonialism' (1984) 83(330) *African Affairs*, 63–75. For a recent and rare opinion on the relationship

modern projects I am concerned with contain some new features; for instance, in the plurality of public and private actors that fund a project from multiple locations and through a dense network of technical private contracts and policy standards and in this regulated setting, the diminished presence of the state. Many of the technical features of this network will intertwine with a larger pre-existing political-sociolegal framework which can include legacy issues over land. Another new feature of these projects is that they are taking place in a new era of increased recognition of indigenous peoples as holders of distinct rights at international and national levels. In this context, companies and their financiers seek to retrofit an economic, legal and political process to a project in the form of the contractual and policy mechanisms I analyse in this book. The result is that modern development projects often begin life with highly polarised starting points between the community, concessionaire and its financiers and the state. In this triangularity of players and the private regulatory setting, legal and social relations are reframed, community expectations can shift from the state to the private sector and the state can make decisions on issues of public interest purely on the basis of an investor's sensibilities.

In development narratives, industry and infrastructure have become indistinguishable with foreign direct investment in two areas: primary industries for natural resource development and the construction and operation of asset infrastructure.[2] Modern natural resource and infrastructure development projects are a core part of the privatisation practices within the heavily criticised Washington Consensus[3] bundle of policy prescriptions for mobilising development. Those prescriptions are aimed at opening up the market to business through policies

---

between international banking and finance, the city of London and imperialism see T Norfield, *The City: London and the Global Power of Finance* (Verso 2017).

[2] K Bhatt, 'Industry and Infrastructure', in K de Feyter, G Erdem Türkelli and S de Moerloose (eds.), *Law and Development Encyclopedia* (Edward Elgar, Forthcoming); M Sornarajah, *The International Law on Foreign Investment* (Cambridge University Press 2009).

[3] Coined by the English economist John Williamson in the 1980s, the Washington Consensus refers to a set of free market economic policies such as tax reform, financial liberalisation, privatisation practices and secure property rights that are supported by prominent international financial institutions. Leading economists Stiglitz and Chenery have, since the 1990s, criticised these policies for their disastrous impacts on inequality and their contribution to the global financial crisis. J Stiglitz, 'The Price of Inequality' (2013) 30 *New Perspectives Quarterly* 52.

promoting decreased state intervention, financial liberalisation and secure investor property rights in order to give the market free rein.[4] Under this development agenda, unlocking vast reserves of wealth would, it was believed, lead to overall increases in gross domestic product and income which will ultimately lead to a trickle-down of wealth. Increasing foreign direct investment into industry and infrastructure are therefore seen as fundamental for 'development'; providing engines along a linear path of *economic* development, progress and modernity in the host country.[5] Transnational financial transactions and their underlying documentary network are key tools for facilitating this agenda whilst also bringing international economic arrangements into closer contact with issues of land, survival and precarity.

Whilst the connection of indigenous people to land is highly diverse differing from group to group, there is a common root in this relationship to land and water that is radically different from the Western notion of property. For indigenous people, land and water are regarded as sacred, inextricably connected to their identity, culture, sense of meaning and survival. Unlike Western notions that view land and the resources within it as property rights, to be exclusively owned and enclosed for productive potential and value creation,[6] indigenous worldviews may not differentiate between the earth and the resources it supports, seeing land in a wider concept that relates to the collective right to survival as a people, for the reproduction of their culture and for their own development and plans for life.[7] Thus large development projects become major hotspots for a significant clash of worldviews

---

[4] L Minkler, *The State of Economic and Social Human Rights: A Global Overview* (Cambridge University Press 2013) 63.

[5] Although the work of Amartya Sen provides a human-centred counter-approach. See A Sen, *Development as Freedom* (Oxford University Press 2001).

[6] This of course links to the colonial premise that only enclosed, settled and intensive cultivation of land can be regarded as a 'proper' or 'effective' occupation of land. See T Flannagan, 'The Agricultural Argument and Original Appropriation: Indian Lands and Political Philosophy' (1989) 22(3) *Canadian Journal of Political Science* 589 and J Gilbert, 'Nomadic Territories: A Human Rights Approach to Nomadic Peoples' Land Rights' (2007) 7(4) *Human Rights Law Review* 681.

[7] Report of the Rapporteur, Meeting of the Working Group on the Fifth Section of the Draft Declaration with special emphasis on 'Traditional Forms of Ownership and Cultural Survival, Right to Land and Territories', Organisation of American States, Committee on Juridical and Political Affairs, OEA/Ser.K/XVI. GT/DADIN/doc.113/03 rev. 1, 20 February 2003.

and fundamentally diverging views over land as individual property and land as an individual and collective *relationship* upon which cultural and economic survival are rooted.

In this context, a state can become complicit in furthering the Western worldview of land purely as a property right by granting licences without community consent or failing to implement laws to recognise and demarcate traditional land. The social experience of dispossession can occur where a government acquires traditional land through compulsory acquisition laws and then leases a bundle of private rights to that land to a company for development reasons. A government might become involved in these projects indirectly as a minority shareholder. In that case, a dilemma will arise between the state's public law obligations to respect the property and human rights of its citizens and its role as an investor with property rights in the form of contractual royalty payments or future shareholder dividend payments, depending on the deal struck. This tension incentivises the state to ensure the timely completion of the project and to accept the social and legal consequences of its investment activity in terms of potential land displacement and related land, property and human rights violations for indigenous communities who claim breach of their customarily observed land rights.

The increase of infrastructure, extractives and even renewable projects will result in more triangular sociolegal clashes involving indigenous peoples, the state and private actors, signalling a future of systemic legal challenges in the blurring of roles, responsibilities and expectations within this modern triangularity. In the context of an enterprise-led state and the concrete and stable macroeconomic structure of contracts that are designed to push a project forward, what does the recognition and implementation of indigenous peoples' rights to land look like? Under these conditions, whether or not the state recognises traditional land rights under formal law is less important than how the state practically protects (or actively fails to protect) and implements those rights through the largely private mechanisms of a large development project which it agrees to but has limited control and influence over.

These triangular tensions can result from state and investor disregard of the social and environmental impacts of these projects, many of which do not respect the free, prior and informed consent (FPIC) of indigenous peoples. Development projects can constitute land grabbing as they run the risk of further impoverishing already marginalised communities in times of intensification of natural resource competition.[8] Whilst many land grabs are done illegally, some are done more silently through legal means within state investor private concession contracts that prioritise and protect investors' rights over all others, despite legal protection for customary rights to land, as illustrated in Papua New Guinea.[9] Through the types of contract and behaviour I will discuss, land grabbing becomes a legal action, protected and ultimately justiciable through an international arbitration mechanism typically embedded within the boilerplate provisions of a concession contract. This type of contractual and state-supported land grabbing in contexts of resource extraction is exceedingly difficult for communities and their counsel to even gain insights into, let alone regulate and discipline, casting doubt on the legal, moral and developmental assumptions supporting these projects. In 2017, Verisk Maplecroft cited the practice of banks, development finance institutions (DFIs) and corporations that finance and operate land transactions abroad as a key human rights risk area for business. This is because financiers will run an increased risk of becoming implicated in forced evictions, human rights violations, food sovereignty issues and land grabs.[10] The issue for concessionaires, financiers and communities is that land grabbing can occur legally, through the type of state-backed laws and contractual networks discussed in this book that are shaped through a mixing of confidential private contracts, policies, state laws,

---

[8] Understanding land grabbing as structures that perpetuate control, through ownership, concession, contracts or general power by any persons or entities – public or private, foreign or domestic for purposes of speculation, extraction, resource control or commodification at the expense of indigenous peoples and without sharing benefits equitably.

[9] It is estimated that in recent years, 12 per cent of Papua New Guinea, 5.5 million hectares, has been leased out to foreign corporations. Dozens of foreign companies have signed land deals under a government scheme called Special Agriculture and Business Leases despite the country's constitutional protection of customary land rights. F Mousseau, 'On Our Land: Modern Land Grabs Reversing Independence in Papua New Guinea', The Oakland Institute in collaboration with Pacific Network on Globalisation (2013) www.oaklandinstitute.org/sites/oaklandinstitute.org/files/OI_Report_On_Our_Land.pdf. Other examples of land grabbing could include the US$25.5 billion Lamu Port South Sudan Ethiopia infrastructure project that will cut across indigenous territories and the Lower Sesan II dam hydropower development project in Cambodia. In 2019, the Supreme Court of India in *Wildlife First & Ors.* v *Ministry of Forest and Environment & Ors*, Writ Petition(s)(Civil) No(s). 109/2008, ordered the eviction of millions of India's indigenous Adivasi people whose claims under the Forest Rights Act 2009 were rejected. That act recognises India's indigenous peoples' rights to their ancestral lands, with the order seen as a form of land grabbing.

[10] Verisk Maplecroft, 'Human Rights Outlook 2017'.

private actors and state actors. This means that legal and behavioural aspects of the contractual arrangements, mechanisms and behaviours surrounding development projects can also be said to support land grabbing, if done without rigorous due diligence which captures these detailed interfaces.

I have spent many hours trawling through the fantastic work of the Dutch NGO BankTrack which on its aptly titled database of 'dodgy deals'[11] presents, in a thoughtful and accessible way, profiles of projects that have damaged the environment or society around the project and because of this, constitute an investment risk to the banks financing them. Many are or have been subject to civil society campaigns and settled informally. A quick journey around this goldmine of information demonstrates the sprawling geography of these projects from North to South, East to West – India, Turkey, Brazil, Zambia and Australia are a few. If you are interested in knowing more about one of these projects, a quick click on a dodgy deal displays a list of the transnational actors involved (companies, commercial banks, national and regional development banks, the state), the social, environmental, human rights or gender-related impact of the project on local communities and the formal and informal legal network underpinning the investment. Based on BankTrack's research of a project, the latter regime might comprise a 'transnational plural' collection of state-made laws and regulations, specific international legal instruments like the United Nations Declaration on the Rights of Indigenous Peoples (UNDRIP)[12] and informal normative sources; these include relevant environmental and social performance standards of a funding DFI such as the International Finance Corporation (IFC), European Bank for Reconstruction and Development (EBRD), or a political risk insurance provider such as the World Bank's Multilateral Investment Guarantee Agency (MIGA). The website is a testament to a thirst for inward investment and governmental acceptance of the negative effects of that trend.

When things go wrong with these projects, which they invariably do, the experiences of communities living in the shadow of these projects is abysmal. The catastrophic case of the 1992 Sardar Sarovar irrigation/ hydroelectric project in India, partly financed by the World Bank,

---

[11] BankTrack website, www.banktrack.org/search#category=dodgydeals.
[12] Adopted by the United Nations General Assembly, 2 October 2007, A/RES/61/295.

displaced nearly 120,000 people including many isolated tribal Adivasi[13] indigenous communities. Following ardent local NGO advocacy, the case fuelled a bank debate on how exactly it was implementing its resettlement and indigenous peoples' policies and the way it was 'doing business'. Sardar is sadly just one of many 'development' disasters involving indigenous people. In 1995, another debacle occurred, this time involving the IFC. The bank had financed the Pangue Hydroelectric dam on the Biobío River in Chile, a project that threatened to displace and destroy the livelihoods of thousands of indigenous communities and, like Sardar, following local advocacy from environmental and indigenous organisations, pressured institutional change within the IFC. Along with these, BankTrack's website provides many recent examples of this continued trend of development project legalised land grab and dispossession.

Constituting a highly organised species of legal arrangement that conflates multiple legal norms makes development projects hard cases to regulate from a purely state-focused human rights perspective. Development projects tell us something about the general character of and values within national and international law in the context of globalisation and how that character has provided the conditions for a number of highly specialised legal disciplines that have come to challenge and unseat state power itself. My experiences, like many other practitioners, tells us that for many, the proper units of legal order are not the state or constitutional law at all, or sadly, not communities, but special highly organised subsystems of private law, such as project finance, made up of contracts, policies, decision-making and behaviours that live beyond the state. It remains a challenge for processes seeking to implement human rights in clear, predictable and fair ways to upset the apple cart of this carefully orchestrated set of arrangements.

2 Focus of the Book

The objective of this book is to highlight the phenomenon of the large transnational development project. Involving companies, financial institutions, states, non-governmental organisations and people with a special sociocultural, economic and spiritual connection to land (typically called indigenous peoples), these projects sit at a unique interface of public and

---

[13] Adivasi is the collective term for India's indigenous peoples and forest-dweller communities.

private law – state law, regulation, policy, voluntary standards and private contracts – and disciplinary thinking. More specifically, I consider how, under the conditions of a development project and its contractual framework and safeguarding policy architecture,[14] private entities and judicial and non-judicial mechanisms frame, conflict with and informally delegate out the recognition and implementation of rights to land for indigenous people. Through the lens of the development project, we can assess the interfaces between local jurisdictional, international and regulatory (in policy and contract) regimes on indigenous peoples' land rights with transnational behaviours and neoliberal values of development and financing. In doing so, we observe how the public and private actors, and mechanisms involved in large development projects can accelerate rights violations, contribute to precarity and influence rule of law values regarding fair, clear and predictable legal outcomes. The result has significant consequences for regulation (or lack thereof) of development, the protection of indigenous peoples' special relationship to land and resources and extraction of natural resources globally.

Development projects also provide an analytical lens through which to examine how different sources of indigenous rights cope with and stand up to powerful contractual and policy mechanisms and related transnational behaviours. In this way, they provide a direct lens into the

---

[14] Specifically, the use of private environmental and social performance standards dealing with issues of land and indigenous peoples, discussed in more detail in Chapter 2. Starting in the 1980s, the World Bank's in-house policy on involuntary resettlement and indigenous peoples', were shaped into Operational Directives and revised throughout the 1990s and early 2000s. The development finance community replicated the bank's resettlement policies with the OECD producing guidelines on resettlement planning in 1991. The European Bank for Reconstruction and Development produced its first environmental policy in 1991 and indigenous policy in 2008, the Asian Development Bank formulated a resettlement policy in 1996 and indigenous policy in 1998, the Inter-American Development Bank adopted resettlement policy in 1998 and an indigenous policy in 2006 and the African Development Bank produced a resettlement policy in 2002 (although it refuses to establish a stand-alone indigenous policy). The IFC as private arm of the World Bank, produced its own involuntary resettlement policy in 2002 and indigenous policy in 2006. The following year, the Equator Principles were approved by ninety financial institutions across thirty-seven countries covering over 70 per cent of project finance debt worldwide, to form a corpus of globally valid norms for commercial banks involved in project finance that were modelled on IFC standards. M Cernea, 'The "Ripple Effect" in Social Policy and Its Political Content: A Debate on Social Standards in Public and Private Development Projects', in M Likosky (ed.), *Privatising Development: Transnational Law, Infrastructure and Human Rights* (M. Nijhoff Publishers 2005), 65–104 for a history on involuntary resettlement policies within international financial institutions.

nature, values and prioritisation of different common law and international law sources of indigenous rights when they confront the hidden matrix of contracts, policies and behaviours that facilitate a formidable development paradigm of our time – the development project. Is the voice of international or domestic law cast into the shadows of these frameworks, visibility muted as a result of the mixture of private contracts, powerful actors, a recalcitrant state and its own inherent values? I discuss these issues as I map the legal framework around development projects in Chapter 3. I explore how concessionaires and financiers are able to rally powerlessness (in the vagueness of that legal framework) and power (in the many tools of contractual power illustrated in later chapters) to displace social risks such as a competing indigenous land claim to insulate the project from any risks that could jeopardise their return on investment.

In the chapters which follow, I seek to map the legal terrain around the understudied universe of transnational development projects as they increasingly interface with indigenous peoples' rights to land. I analyse how the transnational legal and policy architecture governing those projects recognises and in some cases, implements or alienates those rights. This is a bewildering task not least for the universe of transnational actors and fragmented array of norms that become visible once we peel back the layers of a project.

3   Linking Project Finance and Indigenous Peoples' Land Rights

Linkages between the contracts and policies used for asset-based project financing and indigenous land issues such as FPIC are an under-investigated field. Conversations with transactional lawyers working in project finance and natural resource governance demonstrate two contradictory characteristics. First, there is an understanding that the international finance market has entered a new stage. In the post 2008 financial climate, this stage is characterised by reduced debt liquidity, growing political uncertainty and greater demands for understanding the social consequences for companies of transnational operations. There is also a growing appreciation amongst business that failure to make provisions for the participation and consultation of indigenous peoples' can result in economic challenges such as reputational problems, crushing project delays, spiralling cost and social conflict in a project area. Policies for local financing, content and the increased recognition of the importance of conducting social risk due diligence for avoiding or mitigating human rights impacts through, for example, increased use of social impact assessments, are becoming the common sense thing to do. On paper at least.

Second, and this is the contradiction, when I delve deeper into what this actually means in practice (specific changes to existing loan covenants, borrower completion certificates and other loan terms to expressly incorporate FPIC issues being just a few examples) and ask who is doing this work, there is a tangible pushback and hesitancy to discuss these issues. This might come from a place of genuine uncertainty and lack of confidence in articulating the synergies between indigenous land rights, FPIC and financing and what the international legal framework looks like in this context, a point suggested in a study examining the advisory relationship between law firms and their clients on the human rights impacts of project operations.[15]

Yet, irrespective of governments, corporations and financial institutions have a responsibility to do no harm in the context of these projects, as understood in the UN Guiding Principles on Business and Human Rights and are expected to conduct due diligence to discharge this responsibility. Whilst these paper commitments are deeply persuasive, the devil has always been in implementation. Given the pushback around discussing the project finance synergies, lenders and borrowers maybe taking an easier road. This path blindly relies on environmental and social loan conditionality covenants. These are often included in project financing transactional documentation, and incorporate, for instance, IFC performance standards, as a way of demonstrating good citizenship, a commitment to doing business and human rights and even as a tool for showing private sector commitment to the Sustainable Development Goals. In some cases, performance standard covenants in a loan agreement could be helpful as they require a borrower to enter into a full blown due diligence exercise resulting in consultation and a negotiated access- and benefit-sharing agreement with indigenous communities, although aspects of these settlements can be criticised, as discussed in Chapter 7. In other cases, as illustrated in later case studies, safeguarding policies are simply never implemented or often, for reasons that have begun to emerge within community complaints filed with ombudsman mechanisms, policies and practices fail to hit the mark when

---

[15] 'Law Firms' Implementation of the Guiding Principles on Business & Human Rights: Discussion Paper', Advocates for International Development (2011) and the *IBA Practical Guide on Business and Human Rights for Business Lawyers* (2016).

it comes to land and FPIC issues and do not result in a meaningful due diligence exercise. This is because due diligence fails to interrogate crucial interfaces; specifically, between private mechanisms – the legal terms and structures that underpin the movement of enormous global capital required for these projects, and local or international legal norms on indigenous rights as well as the power dynamics and behaviours that drive decision-making at these hidden hotspots.

For these reasons, it is imperative to critically analyse how private entities, mechanisms and behaviours involved in constructing a trans-national development project recognise and implement rights to land for indigenous people or might be contributing to harm. Salient questions include how do concessionaires and financiers document, internalise and understand indigenous groups and implement their rights to land within the contractual framework, policy and governance architecture of the transnational development project? To what extent do company due diligence processes consider the ways in which a development project and its contractual matrix and the behaviours surrounding it contribute to poor recognition, implementation and vulnerability? Or are these matters just too difficult as they cut too close to a company's core business functions: shareholder return? Is the private sector compelled to step into the shoes of the state and if so, how is this facilitated, and what does this profusion mean for the implementation of indigenous peoples' land rights? Or does the lack of state regard for indigenous rights in these high-stakes projects create a vortex to the bottom where companies enjoy a legal- and regulation-free zone?

These are issues that call into question the content of community-corporate mediated outcomes and how safeguarding policies on land and indigenous peoples interplay with wider project contractual mechanisms and neoliberal behaviours and the result of those interplays for implementation (or lack thereof). They cannot be answered by a bland reference to a corporate policy or a referral to a set of DFI's safeguard policies. Ignoring the policy and contractual framework of development projects or casting it aside into a private law silo misses the larger point about the shared public and private nature of the problem. We need to know more about where the tension points lie in order to conduct better due diligence and make focused legal and policy recommendations for more effective implementation both before and throughout the project life cycle.

Undoubtedly, the challenges for rights implementation in this context are multiple. An overriding problem is a severe lack of transparency in the legal documentation governing development projects which include finance agreements, concessions, other project documents and community–corporate agreements. There is also secrecy around the behaviours through which contractual implementation is motivated. Consequently, there is little empirical clarity on how these mechanisms can displace indigenous rights recognition and implementation. Compounding this is, perhaps, the problematic terminology and jargon used by finance lawyers and a lack of knowledge on what constitutes the legal framework for development projects and how it impacts upon implementation of rights. These limitations make it difficult to ascertain how implementation occurs through private mechanisms and consequently, to understand how public and private lawyers could integrate solutions. Deficits also arise in the availability of uniform and transparent community–corporate agreement-making practices, illustrating what implementation looks like in different contexts. Companies point to the difficulty in finding a uniform practice as every project is so different. This argument diverts attention away from the point made in this book about how private contracts, policies, behaviours and power relations matter for implementation, and those practices are firmly within the control and leverage of a concessionaire and its financiers.

4   Chapter Outline

This chapter has provided some economic, social, legal and technical context to development projects and their interfaces with indigenous peoples' rights to land and the focus of this book. Chapter 2 then gives more clarity on indigenous peoples, the characteristics of the development projects I am concerned with and examines the legal nature of the contracts underpinning a project. Having defined the field, Chapter 3 critically analyses the surrounding contemporary formal legal framework for indigenous peoples' land rights that speak to the phenomenon of development and transnational development projects. I examine jurisprudential strands and general lacunas such as the lack of accountability of private actors and the complex and fragmented nature of a meaningful due diligence exercise in this field. Drawing on this, I identify salient themes within the formal legal framework that matter for rights recognition and implementation in development contexts. The point of this endeavour is multiple: to assess the existing coping strategies of formal law in this setting, to give some 'hard law' context to and commentary around the private mechanisms that I explore in later chapters and to appreciate judicial and non-judicial mechanisms as belonging to an ecosystem of potential remedies in the field of development projects. This legal interrogation picks up on the identified themes to consider why, despite the array of indigenous rights cases and international legal declarations, international and domestic norms rarely pierce the complex and highly regulated veil of private mechanisms that secure a transnational development project and fail to work as a legal threat. There are of course, other reasons that I discuss in later chapters, linked to power, the poor implementation of existing DFI policy tools and the behaviours that surround that implementation, that contribute to the overshadowing of the law in this field, keeping its visibility muted. My aim in Chapter 3 is to show the ways in which the legal framework endogenously contributes to an overall weakened rule of law for indigenous communities in that encounter.

Against this background, Chapter 4 analyses whether private mechanisms for recognising and implementing land rights in development projects can fill some of the gaps within the judicial mechanisms and legal structures. I set out the devices through which I analyse this question: project finance (PF) mechanisms involving DFIs and their borrower corporate clients and direct company agreement making with indigenous groups (analysed in Chapter 7). Might these mechanisms allow communities to leapfrog over the lacunas in the legal framework in Chapter 3 to mediate directly for fairer and more predictable legal outcomes with the concessionaires and financiers that hold the power in these circumstances, thus recalibrating community expectations towards private investors and away from the state? In this process, do aspects of these private mechanisms and the behaviours of implementing actors work to further marginalise indigenous peoples?

Answering these questions requires an understanding of the private legal rules that bring life and value to the project's assets. These often forgotten 'elephants in the room' are the technicalities within contractual and policy terms, the behaviours around which these mechanism are implemented and how those conditions impact upon indigenous communities and the recognition and implementation of their rights to land. This involves looking at the set-up and ordering of a PF transaction to see how it inherently treats issues of indigenous peoples' rights within a range of existing contractual mechanisms including loan covenants that operationalise DFI policy standards. I therefore provide an overview of specific points of interface between financial instruments and land rights issues that will be considered in greater contextual detail in Chapters 5 and 6.

Through reference to sample clause mechanisms from loan and project agreements, I look at how development projects structured through PF produce highly secured, standardised, almost algorithmic contractual interfaces with, and have unexplored ramifications for, the recognition and implementation of indigenous peoples' rights to land at points where vulnerability to dispossession is high. This specialised field of commercial contracting will interact with customary and domestic and international 'formal' indigenous rights regimes and still produce stable economic activities that promote neoliberal values. Analysis of these technical clauses does illustrate some positive features. However, the overall spirit of the contractual framework for conducting due diligence around the recognition and implementation of alternative claims to land is best described as recognition and implementation with a light, discretionary, delegated and fragmented touch and is, in any case, often conducted too late in the project life cycle to be effective. This suggests a serious governance failure for safeguarding policies addressing land and indigenous people. These clauses also showcase the high priority and universal quality given to the private property rights of concessionaires and financiers and the uninterrupted control they enjoy in recognising and implementing indigenous peoples' rights to land and resettlement practices in the context of large projects.

Chapters 5 and 6 then provide more context and illustrations of how PF mechanisms interface with indigenous land rights recognition and implementation and the effects of that convergence for communities. Chapter 5 analyses how concession contracts, finance contracts and lender policy standards on land and indigenous peoples deployed in PF loan mechanisms have contributed to deficient project due diligence, impacting upon the implementation of indigenous peoples' rights to land in projects in Mongolia and Panama. Related to this, I explore the behaviours of the financiers and concessionaires towards the implementation of those contractual and policy mechanisms. Analysing how lender safeguarding policy commitments are prioritised or de-prioritised through the ordinary, mechanical and predictable stream of PF decision-making and contractual networks that operationalise those policies shines light on the basic effectiveness[16] of those policies to deliver clear, fair, and predictable and rights compliant outcomes. For instance, I examine how private environmental and social experts that are hired by

---

[16] Drawing on aspects of the effectiveness criteria for non-state-based grievance mechanisms under principle 31 of the UNGPs which include accessibility, predictability and rights-compatibility.

the borrower and paid for by the financiers are given the serious role of delineating which social safeguard policies a borrower should comply with and how that compliance ought to be conducted. In this process a private expert will sort and prioritise the different local and international norms on indigenous rights with the rights of financiers. This provides further insights into the operation of law and power in this field: specifically, the fragmented, de-prioritised and powerless nature of different sources of indigenous rights norms as they sit against contractual and policy norms. The larger question is of an over-reliance on private experts in this field, the lack of transparency around their decision-making and the deficiency of independent regulatory oversight over this delegated process.

Chapter 6 examines the case of the Ugandan Bujagali Hydroelectric Power Project referred to in the preface. This case study is different from the others. It focuses on the interface of contractual and policy instruments with indigenous peoples' rights to land and then casts the net wider to examine how complex pricing terms and the inequitable negotiation of concessionary power purchase agreements (PPA) in which the government is the end buyer, will have implications for overall vulnerability; for example, by locking governments into an overall bad deal in which all the risk is passed onto the state which has little control over spiralling electricity costs. Thinking about these debt contract-community linkages and what might be done within the context of an important negotiated contract like the PPA is crucial for two reasons – that of the spread of supposedly cleaner hydroelectric projects worldwide to meet energy demand and the growth of the 'people first'[17] trend in public-private partnerships in the quest to mobilise the private sector to meet the Sustainable Development Goals.[18]

Chapter 7 extends examples of the second field of private mechanisms that I am concerned with and a burgeoning field of legal practice: direct mediated agreement-making between concessionaires and indigenous groups. Through transnational examples from plural contexts in Russia, Suriname, Australia and Mongolia, I illustrate how concessionaires plug lacunas in formal law through agreement-making, with mixed outcomes for indigenous communities. The findings suggest a link between the level

---

[17] UN Economic Commission for Europe, International PPP Centre for Excellence, www.uneceppp-icoe.org/people-first-ppps/.

[18] The IFC and the EBRD have given their express support to the goals, www.ebrd.com/news/2015/ifis-back-new-global-development-agenda-.html.

of recognition afforded to groups in an underlying formal legal regime and the quality of agreement-making. In some cases, private mechanisms when integrated with the domestic legal framework, might address some of the problems that exist within the contemporary legal framework for development projects mapped in Chapter 3, and provide clearer and fairer outcomes for communities. Other cases reveal negative practices around corporatised methods, behaviours and conditionalities through which integration is conducted. The praxis of confidential agreement-making hides the already disparate and largely opaque legal framework around development projects. Confidentiality around these mediated processes and the final arrangements has the potential to impede the development of a clear, fair and predictable legal framework for indigenous communities facing similar threats of vulnerability from projects across the globe. Confidentiality can also block the ability of communities to practically use agreements to hold concessionaires accountable for their promises or for communities in similar situations to demand similar agreements, although in cases of feared retribution, privacy is necessary.[19] This tension requires a nuanced approach when thinking about a one-size-fits-all rule-of-law based approach to transparency when considering and documenting a contractually mediated process.

Questions over the legal status of this field of contractual engagement are more difficult to answer given the lack of transparency around the terms of these mediated arrangements. Through specific contractual wording around the commercial arm's-length nature of the terms, the illustrations demonstrate a trend in identifying these mechanisms for addressing land-related grievances as belonging on the private plane even though they concern issues of public interest making. Consequently, these arrangements signal the growth of a new breed of highly specialised commercial and innovative contracts that merit consideration for their ability to speak to multiple dimensions. These include the formal legal regime, vulnerability, accountability and delivery of remedy in the absence of the state and the continued hegemony of development as an economic project.[20]

---

[19] For instance, a community might demand confidentiality in order to protect its identity as without it they could face abuse and retribution for entering into an agreement (referring to conversations with a DFI ombudsman panel member).

[20] K Bhatt, 'Innovative Contractual Remedies with Indigenous Peoples' in I Bantekas and MA Stein (eds.), *Cambridge Companion to Business and Human Rights* (Cambridge University Press, Forthcoming).

Chapter 8 draws the study together and provides concrete recommendations for the better integration of the judicial and private mechanisms discussed in this book so that they deliver fairer, clearer, more predictable and UNDRIP-compliant outcomes for indigenous communities in this field. The hard reality is that even with the most rights-compliant concessionaire, things can go wrong and so mechanisms are needed to intervene at much earlier points upstream in the project's governance arrangements than is currently the practice to prevent violations earlier on. For instance, national laws are needed that recognise the special vulnerability of land-connected people to large development projects (perhaps over an economic threshold of $50 million as is the benchmark for application of the Equator Principles) and impose a moratorium on any land disturbances until a developer has undertaken a preventative conflict-based assessment. That assessment must take no later than the point at which the state divests land and must necessitate a consultation and mediation process which interfaces with the many layers of issues around land that relate to race, class, ethnicity, legacy and postcolonial histories. I consider what this process looks like (which must include a legal ability of communities to say no at this point) and methods through which the cost and, crucially, the independence of such a process can be designed, such as a blind trust mechanism. Aspects of this assessment could, through the development of a code of practice, then feed into and tighten existing PF documentation at the specific points at which indigenous vulnerability to dispossession is high – as detailed in Chapter 8. This public/private integrated approach could strategically implement UNDRIP strategies of FPIC into more rights-compatible places within contractual structures, rather than keeping them endogenous to the contractual matrix existing as window-dressing policy statements on the websites of DFIs and sponsors. Other suggestions for integration and changes to the formal legal framework are made in that chapter. For those interested only in those recommendations and my response to the criticisms that might be levelled against this approach (which include an encouragement of private power or the diminishment of a human rights–based approach), please jump to that chapter.

5 Core Themes

This chapter overview introduces the following core themes that run through this book. These themes speak to heterodox thinking around law, development, economics and institutions in globalised contexts and whilst beyond the scope of this book, it would be fruitful to consider how they could add value to thinking about the role of law in development and development in law.[21]

5.1   Fragmentation and (In)Visibility

Fragmentation is a theme throughout. Chapter 3 maps the contemporary legal framework and judicial mechanisms currently available for addressing and implementing indigenous peoples' rights to land in the context of development projects. A core theme coming out of this analysis is that of a bias towards the scholarly examination of settler colonial jurisdictions for examining indigenous rights to land. This bias does not serve a universally fair approach to viewing the phenomenon of transnational development projects and creates a gap for thinking about rights recognition and implementation in non-settler colonial areas such as Mongolia and parts of Africa where these projects are commonplace. Another strand of this theme demonstrates how private mechanisms contribute to the fragmented legal setting that is characteristic of the field. The case studies demonstrate how rights implementation is frequently conducted through and influenced by hidden networks of private actors involving concessionaires, financiers and experts, with the state and its laws taking a less visible role. Together, this framework illustrates the constellations of local jurisdictional, regional, international and private norms at play.

5.2   Power(lessness), Delegation and Priority

Zooming further into the fragmented legal framework, we can discern various encounters between local jurisdictional, international and regulatory regimes on land rights with powerful neoliberal values of development and financing. These encounters have legal and social effects that can render communities powerless. For example, the case studies illustrate new insights into the paradigm of state delegation to private bodies

---

[21] C Tan, 'Beyond the "Moments" of Law and Development: Critical Reflections on Law and Development Scholarship in a Globalised Economy' (2019) 12(2) *Law and Development Review* 285–321 reviewing the contributions and limitations of law and development as a field of scholarship, and how it intersects with international law, socio-legal studies, international economic law and institutions. Also see K Pistor, *The Code of Capital: How the Law Creates Wealth and Inequality* (Princeton University Press 2019) on the role of private law in fostering concentrations of wealth and inequality.

and concurrently the day-to-day role of private bodies in the implementation of indigenous rights to land, which can mute the application of international and domestic norms. Regulating indigenous peoples' rights to land within development projects is further challenged through the practices and behaviours of delegation. As I illustrate through my analysis of contractual clauses, rights and responsibilities are blurred and hidden within confidential documents. These governance arrangements create the conditions for power, discretion, scheduling considerations and routine decision-making to determine outcomes for vulnerable people. As Jokubauskaite notes in the context of the categorisation of project 'affected communities', the World Bank and its borrowers have carved a space in which they alone have full discretion to 'tie' and 'untie', include or exclude, people from this category.[22] There is a lack of openness around just how large a hotspot for rights violations the pre-construction and construction phases are for indigenous communities, and how mechanisms within the contractual matrix can work against a do-no-harm approach during this period. Finally, analysing what happens to domestic and international law norms in this context and during the implementation of a project is helpful for discerning whether any normative priority exists within active development projects.

5.3 Fairness and Predictability in the Rule of Law

In the light of this fragmentation and hierarchy, development projects can be seen to represent a contemporary and living phenomenon that illustrates shifting sources of law that move towards a growing paradigm of idiosyncratic negotiated private norms in policy/contract. The level of hyper-plurality of norms and the interface of norms and behaviours discussed throughout this book, provide a window into the shifting sources of law and also the complete collapse of any distinction between public and private norms and an unhelpful profusion of the same. That implementation in this context can depend more on the power and economic incentives of private actors rather than formal legal norms, raises difficult questions about the role of the state and by extension,

---

[22] G Jokubauskaite, 'Tied Affectedness? Grassroots Resistence and the World Bank' (2018) 3 (5–6) Third World Thematics: A TWQ Journal 703–724. As I seek to demonstrate the key structural mechanisms through which her astute concept of tied-affectedness is fundamentally enabled are transnactional and technical: the contractual, policy and behavioural 'elephants in the room' analysed in Chapters 5, 6 and 7.

international law in facilitating this dynamic and creating the conditions for vulnerability in globalised contexts. There is therefore, a need for those interested in issues of vulnerability to think about how development projects and the legal regime underpinning them provide, or fails to provide, clear, fair and predictable outcomes for communities and thus deliver on the rule of law in today's globalised settings. As Lander[23] argues in her study of extractive development in Mongolia, the cumulative impact of multiple axes of transnational legal ordering involving international financial institutions, multinational companies, civil society and national actors, has created a new type of constitutionalism. This 'new constitutionalism' transforms and erodes national capacities and at the same time implants global alternatives into processes for state formation. As Lander observes, this evidences the constitutional contours of global capitalism more generally and has wider implications and unintended consequences for the development of the rule of law in Mongolia's mining regime. Adding to this – and for the reasons and through the illustrations in this book – I argue that large development projects as a rising global phenomenon raise complex and difficult constitutional questions; specifically, around the capacity of private actors through the contractual, policy and behavioural mechanisms examined, to heavily influence issues of democratic governance such as law-making and to impact upon the availability, clarity, predictability and fairness of citizens' basic services in energy, infrastructure and even legal remedy.

5.4   Integration as Part of Remedy

This level of legal fragmentation and the social urgency of the enquiry invites new thinking into how more and not less pluralism might improve outcomes for indigenous communities that sit in the shadows of these projects and what, if anything, can be done within and at earlier stages of the governance framework and throughout the project to redress power asymmetries. This hybrid approach differs from a purely human rights–based approach as it involves creative integration of the best aspects of public and private mechanisms that might together implement more predictable and fairer outcomes. It also differs from relying purely on a contract-based approach that depends on an after the

---

[23] J Lander, *Transnational Law and State Formation: The Case of Extractive Development in Mongolia* (Routledge 2019)

fact adversarial dispute resolution clause. I draw on aspects of McAuslan's[24] framework for building fair, successful and stable national land policies in developing countries that work with interventions and solutions from private actors to the extent they can offer practical and rights-compatible outcomes. This model is less about competition between public and private mechanisms and more about seeing the possibilities of integrated outcomes for less conflict and a more equitable, participatory and stable development project policy. In the field of development projects, the spirit of this hybrid and more contextualised approach is already witnessed through the trend of direct agreement-making and the mushrooming of independent accountability mechanisms within DFIs although, as I illustrate, there are severe deficits within these private mechanisms that require urgent attention. They do, however, move us towards a paradigm of increasing integration of public and private law mechanisms for rights implementation that could, with adjustments, be a tool for preventative remedy.

So, one measure could be to think about the contractual and policy interfaces as part of a mediated conflict-prevention assessment. The United Nations Environment Programme has conducted research on the growing number of land- and natural resource–based disputes and the significant consequences they have for international, regional and national peace and security. In a 2015 report, UNEP highlighted examples of successful multi-stakeholder mediations between indigenous communities and companies including the Great Bear Rainforest in Canada. It concluded that mediation offers a promising strategy that has, due to its highly technical nature, been underutilised by the international system in addressing disputes over natural resources.[25] Understanding how the private mechanisms and incentives underlying development projects will impact upon rights recognition is an overlooked technical factor that requires deeper consideration in community–company peace-building processes involving disputes over natural resources.

There are of course serious barriers and problems with this type of approach that I discuss through this book that question the viability and effectiveness of these mechanisms in terms of their predictability, clarity, rights compatibility and fairness. These include poor accountability, lack

---

[24] P McAuslan, *Bringing the Law Back in: Essays in Land, Law, and Development* (Ashgate 2003).

[25] *Natural Resources and Conflict: A Guide for Mediation Practitioners* (2015), United Nations Department of Political Affairs and United Nations Environment Programme.

of transparency, uneven results and an over-arching concern of vested interests determining outcomes. The level of contextualisation and detail required in an early mediated conflict-prevention assessment also comes at the cost of money, time and incentive structures. Without a sea change in short-term economic thinking, national laws requiring these changes or pressure from large institutional financiers that bank roll these projects, it is difficult to see how these preventative measures will penetrate the incentives that push a project forward. Despite these challenges, it is impracticable to entirely dismiss private mechanisms in a 'baby bathwater' mentality given, as I illustrate in Chapter 3, the poor track record of the state in these hard to regulate contexts.

An integrated approach may be a more fruitful way to proceed as neither the business community nor the international law community, can claim a monopoly on all solutions in the context of a development project that is characterised by hyper legal fragmentation and an enterprise-led state. Taking aspects of a human rights–based approach to the protection of indigenous peoples' land rights within targeted features of private mechanisms could prevent displacement, providing preventative approaches to remedy. A viewpoint that looks across the entire ecosystem of public and private mechanisms and behaviours for recognising and implementing indigenous land rights in development projects could distil policy tools for building comprehensive, fair and stable development policy in this field.

Characteristics of Indigenous Peoples and Development Projects

Having provided the backdrop to and focus of my enquiry, more definitional clarity is required on the concepts of indigenous people and development projects.

1 Indigenous Peoples

I use the term indigenous to refer to a state of vulnerability that coalesces on a struggle for recognition of a special way of life. That specificity is characterised by the traditional ownership of land, a cultural and often spiritual attachment to land and the natural resources thereon, and related to this, a unique type of discrimination and marginalisation experienced in ongoing processes of dispossession.[1] In the particular field of development projects, I contend that far greater emphasis must be placed on understanding the specific vulnerability of land-connected communities to the relentless global spread of projects that necessitate significant, and often irreparable, land disturbance and the transnational legal dynamics and behaviours that facilitate that disturbance.

As discussed in coming chapters, the overall legal conversation amongst scholars around the term indigenous is detrimental to enlarging the global movement of indigenous peoples beyond the narrow conceptualisation of research done in largely settler colonial contexts and focusing on the role of the state.[2] The proliferation of development projects in places that have no historical settler colonial history and the

---

[1] Drawing on B Kingsbury, 'Indigenous Peoples' in R Wolfrum (ed.), *Max Planck Encyclopaedia of Public International Law* (Oxford University Press 2012).

[2] K Gover, 'Settler–State Political Theory, CANZUS, and the UN Declaration on the Rights of Indigenous Peoples' (2015) 26 *European Journal of International Law* 345; U Secher, *Aboriginal Customary Law: A Source of Common Law Title to Land* (Hart Publishing 2014); PG McHugh, *Aboriginal Title: The Modern Jurisprudence of Tribal Land Rights* (Oxford University Press 2011); S Wiessner, 'The Cultural Rights of Indigenous Peoples: Achievements and Continuing Challenges' (2011) 22 *European Journal of International*

emphasis on settler colonial jurisdictions in examining indigenous rights and development projects to the neglect of other jurisdictions, such as Mongolia, necessitates a move away from the current prioritisation of legal thinking in those contexts. More effort is needed to think about the indigenous movement in a more pluralistic framework: as specifically vulnerable to development projects in a much broader geographical concern and one in which private concessionaires and financiers are, through contractual and policy mechanisms, shaping the global indigenous movement with significant impacts for rights recognition and implementation.[3] In addition to examples from Australia, I draw on cases in which private entities interface with land-connected groups in countries with differing levels of formal national and international legal recognition of indigenous peoples such as Mongolia, Uganda, Russia and Suriname, to show that those settings are worthy of attention. They permit insights to be drawn about the legal framework relating to development projects and natural resources that are not necessarily available to scholars and policy thinkers in jurisdictions such as Australia or Canada.

2   On Transnational Development Projects

You might have heard of development projects in other forms: a mineral development/concession agreement based on a first come, first served mining permit process or a negotiated open tender. Attached to this may be a separate infrastructure package permitting the concessionaire

---

Law 121; SJ Anaya, *Indigenous Peoples in International Law* (2nd edn, Oxford University Press 2004).

[3] Although notable exceptions exist that take a more pluralistic view. Borrows' work gives some attention to the Canadian experience in development project settings (J Borrows, *Recovering Canada: The Resurgence of Indigenous Law* (University of Toronto Press 2002)). Gilbert has examined litigation focusing on indigenous peoples' rights across the African continent (J Gilbert, 'Litigating Indigenous Peoples' Rights in Africa: Potential, Challenges, and Limitations' (2017) 66(3) *International and Comparative Law Quarterly* 657–686), Kingsbury has considered the challenges of indigenous (non) recognition in Asian states (B Kingsbury, 'Indigenous Peoples' in International Law: A Constructivist Approach to the Asian Controversy' (1998) 92 *American Journal of International Law* 414). Moving into other disciplines of anthropology and political science, Sarfaty analyses World Bank policies on indigenous people and their implementation in parts of North Africa (G Sarfaty, 'The World Bank and the Internalization of Indigenous Rights Norms' (2005) 114 *Yale Law Journal* 1791). Coulthard's work implicates not only the state and courts but also corporates and policy-makers in the limitation of modern indigenous recognition in Canada: G Coulthard, *Red Skin, White Masks* (University of Minnesota Press 2014).

(privately or through a public-private arrangement) to build connecting road or rail links to shift the product to market. Development projects could also include a hydroelectric power venture or a renewable energy project, under which a government entity will, through a power purchase arrangement, buy energy on a long-term basis and can also constitute an iron ore or coal project that sells ore to a Chinese market. Regardless of the type of development at stake, the transnational development projects I am interested in contain some common characteristics.

2.1 Algorithmic, Boilerplate, For-Profit Structures

These development projects are implemented through powerful con-tractual structures that assist in the financing, construction, develop-ment and operation of large greenfield projects (new projects without any prior track record or operating history). Development projects frequently take place in developing countries, although that is not a prerequisite. These ventures are entirely for profit and involve actions, persons or impacts in two or more national jurisdictions (a 'cross border' element). They comprise international financial transactions and flows involving multiple institutions from different countries that work col-lectively to alleviate investment risk and raise finance at a relatively low cost due to the 'club' nature of the structuring. They will involve one or multiple powerful sponsors or project concessionaires who contract with a host government on commercially favourable terms, to secure a con-cession in the case of a mine, or energy purchase agreement in the case of a power project.

A special characteristic of the financing documentation underpinning development projects lies in its high degree of boilerplate standardisation, which provides stakeholders with commercial predictability and comfort. Financing documentation is typically modelled on precedents produced by the London Loan Market Association.[4] The governing law of the debt

---

[4] Created in 1996, the key objective of the Loan Market Association (LMA) is to improve liquidity, efficiency and transparency in the syndicated loan markets in Europe, the Middle East and Africa. It does this by establishing widely accepted market practice and promot-ing the syndicated loan as one of the key debt products available to borrowers across the region. Thus, one of the most important activities of the LMA is the production of recommended documentation. Used as a model by large law firms, a variety of documen-tation is available on the LMA's website for different lending contexts. For example syndicated finance such as project finance, developing markets and export finance, to name a few. The documentation is very detailed and includes text, content and

instruments and commercial sale and purchase agreements that underpin a development project will be expressly written into the contracts and
are typically English– or New York–law governed. This is primarily for
the reasons discussed later in this chapter around the high degree of
contractual liberty and restricted number of public policy issues that
could injure and render a commercial transaction illegal under these
legal traditions. The result is the production of a highly mechanical,
standardised and specialised field of commercial contracting in which it
is difficult to ascertain (due to the confidential nature of the lending
documents), exactly how internal contractual mechanics might impact
upon issues of public interest.

The use of these standard form contracts, DFI policy mechanisms,
related resettlement management plans (discussed in this chapter and
Chapter 4) as well as the calculation of risk seen within the behaviours of
financiers,[5] raises issues around the routine and algorithmic nature of
these dynamics that support the commercial insulation and predictability
of the project and in parallel, routinely work to distance local specifics
from project technicalities. These algorithmic and standardised 'boilerplate' characteristics should be kept in mind when reading Chapters 4
and 5 which analyse the impacts of project finance (PF) mechanisms on
the recognition of indigenous peoples' rights to land.

2.2   The Special Role of Financial Actors: Delegating Safeguarding Policies and the Interface with Rights

Another feature of development projects is the abundance of actors,
contracts and financial instruments typically involved, insights into
which can be gleaned from the clause illustrations and diagrams in this
chapter. Along with the participation of the state in an albeit diminished
or economically conflicted role discussed in Section 2.3, comes a powerful project sponsor that will set up an arm's-length special-purpose
vehicle to enter into project contracts with key project counterparties.
These contracts will include the debt instruments, concession,

---

spreadsheets incorporating macros and electronic interfaces and their underlying assumptions, conversions, formulae, algorithms, calculations and other mathematical and financial techniques. This documentation is, of course, expensive and access to the products of
the LMA is limited to financial institutions and associate bodies such as law firms, rating
agencies, accountancy firms, smaller financial institutions and professionals with an
interest in the market.

[5] Analysed in Chapter 4 and the case studies.

construction, operation, sales, supply and any host government guarantees. Mechanisms within those contracts will repeatedly incentivise the quick and efficient construction and operation of the project and reduce the likelihood of any externalities from piercing the stability of the venture and the predictability of the investors' revenue stream. This section focuses on the special role of financial actors in this complex network of actors and instruments.

When a state has granted a licence to explore, exploit or construct on land, the investor to whom the right has been granted will usually seek to arrange financing to construct and operate the project as a special-purpose company to which a club or syndicate of other financiers (commercial banks, DFIs and export credit agencies,[6] for example) will contribute financing. This club financing structure is a typical method through which the risks of a capital intensive project are managed amongst the financiers. For instance, DFIs and export credit agencies are especially helpful in mobilising investment in markets where the political situation is more risky as they can provide government-backed loans, insurance and guarantees when commercial lenders are more unwilling to take political risks. In this respect they also create a domino multiplier effect which increases the overall debt capacity of the project.

Banks, corporations and DFIs often turn to PF's unique 'limited liability'[7] structure outlined in **Figure 1** and club mentality as a means to fund capital intensive and multi-risk development projects.

---

[6] Governments typically establish export credit agencies to assist in the export of goods or services which are sourced from that country. Usual categories of support involve direct lending to an importer or buyer, and the provision of insurance. A typical political risk insurance policy will provide that if as a result of a 'political event' the project company defaults on the payment of principal or interest on a project loan, the ECA will make good the default. It is customary that the events/risks covered include expropriation, war, and transfer of foreign exchange and restrictions on remittances. Additional insurance can be purchased such as cover against the risk of the host government breaking specific undertakings; for example, the breach of the government's undertaking to connect a power station to the national grid, thereby depriving a project company of any means to generate revenue. ECAs can also provide commercial risk such that the ECA 'guarantees' the whole or a portion of debt repayment. These mechanisms lower the risk for private lenders of operating overseas, especially in emerging markets, and thus place ECAs as major players in international trade and development finance.

[7] Chapter 4 discusses the impacts of project finance structures on the recognition and implementation of land rights.

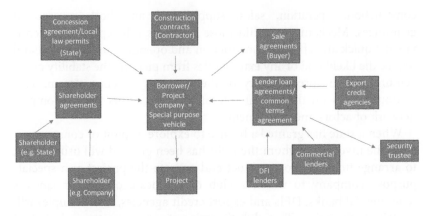

Figure 1:   This figure represents a simplified typical structure for a project using limited recourse finance in a special-purpose vehicle structure.

In 2017, Thomson Reuters[8] valued the global PF market at US$229.6 billion. The sectors in which project financing are used include power, oil and gas, mining and transportation projects and the geographical spread of these projects is truly transnational. The World Bank's (WB) private sector investment arm, the International Finance Corporation (IFC), typically provides debt and equity funding, or a combination of both, for these projects as part of a syndicate of other lenders who, through a PF structure, will share project risks and rewards. During 2014–2018, the IFC's long-term financing commitments stretched across projects in East, Central and South Asia, Europe, Sub-Saharan Africa, Latin America and the Caribbean with those commitments constituting a total value of between US$11 and US$17 billion for that period.[9]

The global PF market has, post the 2008 financial crisis, undeniably contracted as the international debt markets have shrunk. Nonetheless, as a result of its many attractive characteristics, PF has, over the last 40 years, consistently remained a leading method within the financial landscape for financing large-scale and long-term infrastructure projects involving high-risk investments in less developed countries.[10] The thirst

---

[8] Thomson Reuters, Global Project Finance Review, Managing Underwriters, Full Year 2017.

[9] International Finance Corporation website https://disclosures.ifc.org/#/landing.

[10] Some of the characteristics of PF that keep its attraction high include its ability to leverage large amounts of debt that can be blended from a variety of different public and private sources and an ability of participants to spread the risks of a project over all of those

for innovative financing sources to meet the Sustainable Development Agenda has gained huge popularity in developing countries with high political risk or weak creditor rights. Here, PF is seen to offer solutions through its bread-and-butter structural features, mechanisms and overall culture: government guarantees, political risk insurance, the participation of development banks to mobilise investment into 'difficult' countries and its reassuringly insulated and standardised nature. In addition to private operations for extractive projects, PF principles are used to finance the growing demand for infrastructure under public-private partnership schemes in which a public service is funded and operated through a partnership between the government and the private sector. This could involve electricity provision using a long-term power pur-chase concession agreement to meet growing energy demand or a tolling agreement to build a road or highway which will facilitate the mobility of goods and services – driving economic activity.[11]

Key players in a PF syndicate are international DFIs such as the IFC and regional or domestic DFIs such as the European Bank for Recon-struction and Development (EBRD), the African Development Bank (AFDB),[12] the Netherlands Development Finance company (FMO) and the German Investment Corporation (DEG). DFIs are curious creatures. Comprised of and funded by member states with a compulsory portfolio for lending into developing countries and varying commitments towards

stakeholders (including the government) under the umbrella of an initiative that osten-sibly contributes to development outcomes. For example, financial institutes like DFIs have an investment portfolio aimed at investing in projects with high risk and high developmental effect, thus requiring them to invest in projects in emerging markets which have the potential to deliver developmental returns. Commercial banks may not independently invest in projects in politically unstable countries or those with untested legal systems. Even a small DFI debt contribution to the financing plan will incentivise commercial banks to invest, thus creating a multiplier 'piggyback' effect that increases the overall debt capacity of the project. Another reason for project finance's attraction is the ability of the sponsors to spread risks over all of the project participants, including the lenders and the government, theoretically increasing the likelihood of success of the project.

[11] For instance the Government of Indonesia financed the construction of the Pandaan–Malang Toll Road under a PPP arrangement.

[12] Following the end of the colonial period, the AFDB was set up as a regional development bank to promote African unity and regional economic development. Owned by around 80 African countries, the AFDB can be seen as the economic development arm of the suite of international institutions such as the Organisation for African Unity (later replaced by the African Union) which seek to encourage political and economic integra-tion in Africa. The legal arm of this project promotes and protects international human rights in the African context through the African Charter on Human and Peoples' Rights.

poverty reduction, they function as private banking entities. The practices and behaviours of DFIs and their borrower clients can, as a result of
their safeguarding policies, rapidly become implicated in a larger political
and social history surrounding a development project, interfacing with
issues of vulnerability, race, ethnicity, class and postcolonial legacies.[13]
Conflicts are heightened through a mandate and legal framework that, as
I analyse in Chapter 3, creates legal limitations for the accountability of
these organisations to project-affected communities.

Not grant-making institutions, DFIs function as private organisations,
often using PF structures to lend money on commercial arm's-length
terms to their clients in order to develop, construct and operate
infrastructure, power, extractive and increasingly, renewable energy
projects, to name a few. In any given project, DFIs can lend for their
own account directly, up to a maximum specific sum per project. In
addition to direct lending on their own account, the IFC and other DFIs
such as the AFDB can, through what is called an A/B loan program, sell a
participation in a loan to commercial banks in order to mobilise investment into the project. Under those 'B' loans the commercial lenders will
pay the IFC full market rates of interest but it is the IFC that will hold the
loan formally as the lender of record and essentially on-lend those
amounts to the project. The commercial lenders have become 'covered'
lenders – lending under the cover of an 'IFC umbrella'. Although there is
no explicit political risk guarantee, lending under the IFC umbrella in
which the IFC remains the lender of record, is highly advantageous to
these commercial lenders. For instance, they will benefit from the IFC's
AAA credit rating and from the IFC's ability to secure preferential
payments through its preferred creditor status.[14] This financing privilege
means that commercial banks who lend to the IFC under the B Loan
structure are protected or 'covered' in the event of any state-enforced
debt moratorium, currency-inconvertibility event or debt rescheduling
taken by the state for public policy reasons. This was the case in
Argentina's[15] 2001 financial crisis when the government imposed a

---

[13] Referring to conversations with DFIs and illustrated within the case studies.
[14] For more information on preferred creditor status see the IFC's website www.ifc.org/wps/
    wcm/connect/Topics_Ext_Content/IFC_External_Corporate_Site/IFC+Syndications/
    Overview_Benefits_Structure/Syndications/Preferred+Creditor+Status/.
[15] In brief, the 2001 crisis involved the Argentinian government imposing a moratorium on
    government foreign debt payments. On 2 January 2002, Argentina abandoned the peso's
    peg to the US dollar. IFC requested the Argentine government to allow automatic
    convertibility and transfer of IFC US dollar loan payments, thus exempting IFC from

moratorium on external debt but continued and prioritised payments to IFC-backed projects, despite a crippling local economy. No IFC loan has ever been included in a sovereign debt rescheduling nor have payments to the IFC been permanently disrupted by a general debt freeze. This unique capacity for international institutions such as the IFC to move fluidly across public and private sectors, cherry-picking techniques that functionalise their economic mandate at all cost, in this case, allowing repayment to be 'preferred' to the IFC over any other domestic public policy payments, is what sets them apart from commercial lenders.[16] It is these types of transnational legal dynamics that impact on issues of public policy that expose international finance institutions to demands that they should be formal duty bearers.

Acknowledging the impacts that DFIs and their clients can have on issues of public policy, vulnerability and rights, most DFIs have developed safeguarding mechanisms that their clients are obliged to implement within an operational project. Law firms have advised clients in cross-border transactions on the use and implementation of these private environmental and social policies for many years. Safeguarding standards are important because through them many DFIs and commercial banks (that lend under the IFC umbrella or are members of the Equator Principles),[17] pledge their commitment to international law principles such as FPIC and agree to recognise and implement the rights of indigenous peoples affected by the projects they finance.

---

new regulations requiring prior Central Bank approval for foreign exchange transfers. See www.ifc.org/wps/wcm/connect/Topics_Ext_Content/IFC_External_Corporate_Site/IFC+ Syndications/Overview_Benefits_Structure/Syndications/Preferred+Creditor+Status/.

[16] Of course, secured creditors will also have their own carefully constructed inter-creditor rules for prioritising (between the lenders), competing claims over the project and its revenue streams, in the event of any payment default and foreclosure.

[17] The Equator Principles are a set of voluntary industry risk-management framework adopted by commercial financial institutions conducting project finance activities and bridge lending. They closely follow the IFC standards for determining, assessing and managing environmental and social risk in projects and provide a minimum standard for due diligence and monitoring to support responsible risk decision-making. Commercial banks that agree to follow these principles in their investment activities are called Equator Principle Financial Institutions. For a critical appraisal see R Shamir, 'Corporate Social Responsibility: Towards a New Market-Embedded Morality?' (2008) 9(2) *Theoretical Inquiries in Law* 371. In the context of project-financing transactions, commercial banks have, through the Equator Principles, harmonised their environmental and social standards with those of the IFC to require free, prior and informed consent. The presence of a DFI is not essential to the inclusion of environmental and social standards as the Equator Principles could apply to commercial banks that conduct project financing.

Central to the IFC's development mission is to carry out its investment activities with the intent to 'do no harm' to people and the environment. The safeguarding principles provide a crucial tool through which the bank achieves that commitment to avoid, minimise and where residual impacts remain, compensate or offset risks to communities and the environment caused by their projects.[18] Furthermore, the IFC and EBRD's operational policies explicitly recognise the responsibility of business to respect human rights and meet this responsibility within project operations. The EBRD goes further. It expressly connects the policy narratives on doing no harm and positive development outcomes with the universal respect for, and observance of, human rights and freedoms; specifically the right to adequate housing and the continuous improvement of living conditions contained in the Universal Declaration of Human Rights and the International Covenant on Economic, Social and Cultural Rights.[19]

The IFC principles state that regardless of the financing source, it will be the responsibility of the borrower to comply, or cause compliance, with those standards: to conduct due diligence assessment, identify the environmental and social risks and impacts of a project, engage local communities through the disclosure of project-related information, ensure consultation on matters directly affecting them and manage those risks throughout the project life cycle. Safeguarding policies also include specific standards on land acquisition and involuntary resettlement and indigenous peoples. The debt instruments signed with the project company will mechanise the company's responsibility to comply with performance standards through the unilateral decision-making practices discussed below, thus attaching an obligation on the company to conduct due diligence assessments. The details of those clauses and the behaviours through which they take shape and attach or fail to attach to the project is important for understanding the real nature and character of this social regulatory compliance. I analyse this black box of regulatory networks in Chapter 4. In addition to these requirements, the concessionaire must also comply with national law and those laws implementing host country obligations under international law.[20] Chapters 5 and 6 analyse whether this requirement for compliance with national and international laws pierces through the fragmented governance

---

[18] IFC Performance Standard 1, 3.
[19] EBRD Performance Requirements 5, 3.
[20] IFC Performance Standard 1, 5.

framework, in which the entity implementing these standards and oper-
ationalising a development project on the ground is not the DFI but the
borrower or a subcontracted private expert, and enters into the practice
of a development project. In the light of the lacunas in the international
legal framework that I will discuss in Chapter 3, there is a high likelihood
that the practices of lenders and concessionaires will overshadow any
formal legal framework.

Where land displacement is deemed necessary, an informal contracting out process occurs from state to project sponsor, starting a blurring of
rights and obligations. That delegation of authority is not typically
publicly documented. Instead, the state will tacitly agree, perhaps
through the terms of the confidential concession agreement, to let the
project company manage a resettlement process at its own discretion. In
parallel, the DFI will require its client, the project company (or more
likely, the sponsor(s) that own the project company), through the loan
documentation, to determine the level of environmental and social risk,
which standards will apply to the project, and to manage those risks. It
would then be up to the client, in accordance with the relevant involuntary resettlement or indigenous persons' policy, to make 'on the ground'
determinations, typically in conjunction with a privately hired environmental and social consulting company and, perhaps, an NGO, whether
indigenous groups exist in the project vicinity and whether and how
those communities are to be resettled, consulted and compensated. This
may or may not result in a formal agreement with an indigenous
community.

As illustrated in **Figure 2**, these actions illustrate a fragmented and
invisible double contracting out of legal responsibility in which the state
and DFIs actively enable and empower private entities to manage issues
of public interest such as land.

The IFC and other DFIs are not only acting as technocrats that draft
policy standards to empower their clients but also as economic stakeholders and mobilisers, as they provide substantial loans and other
preferred creditor benefits that will catalyse investment from commercial
lenders. DFIs will think like an investor and work with the project
company, behind closed doors, on issues around the implementation of
involuntary land standards and indigenous policies. Yet as I explore
below in relation to the governance deficits, the decision-making criteria
or governance framework for making those decisions is unknown.

For indigenous communities, these informal subcontracted processes
pose real accountability deficits when things go wrong. Space opens up in

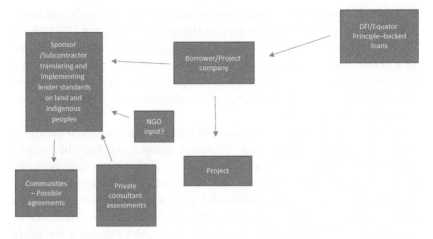

Figure 2: This figure illustrates a typical resettlement structure involving lender conditionality requirements.

which legal responsibility can be shuttled between the company conducting on-the-ground resettlement, the designer of the policy that the company is implementing and the state which stays on the sidelines. As I explore in Section 7 of Chapter 3 on the formal legal framework, DFIs typically have mandates that place them at an indeterminate intersection of being a private institution with varying degrees of public purpose. Given international law's inability to formally cope with private actors, these institutions, the implementation of their policies and the behaviours that guide that implementation operate within a legal grey zone. This structural deficit creates an accountability challenge for communities seeking justice when the implementation of these policies causes harm.

In addition, the borrower can easily sidestep those policies as a result of three major governance deficits that are illustrated in **Figure 3**'s timeline.

The first problem lies in the practical reality that land may have been fully or partially cleared as soon as the concession agreement is negotiated, which will usually happen a few years prior to DFI involvement. This is because as I discuss in Section 3.4 of Chapter 4, the sponsor having become increasingly sure of the viability of a project, will have started negotiating key project documents. In this process the sponsor (or a separate contractor) may have already conducted preliminary land clearance and construction works, perhaps using interim

Development stage (can be long – 5–6 years)   Financing and construction stage (can be long – 2–5 years)

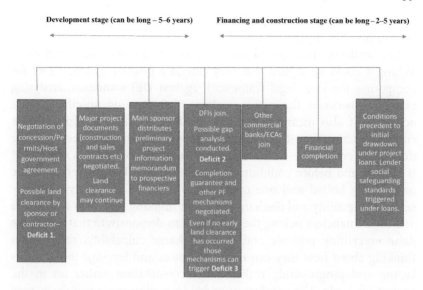

Figure 3:   This figure presents a simplified timeline illustrating the three governance deficits.

'bridge' funding committed from commercial lenders. This means that part of a resettlement process will have started whilst the sponsors wait to hear about the willingness of DFIs and other lenders to participate in the project. This occurred in the Oyu Tolgoi project analysed in Chapter 5.

A second scenario then presents itself: late DFI involvement often after resettlement has occurred.[21] Should DFIs decide to invest (after say, receiving information from the borrower in the preliminary information memorandum discussed in Chapter 4), they will, as discussed above, require their client to honour performance standards as a covenant in the loan agreement. Should a DFI, or multiple DFIs enter into the project later on, different safeguarding standards will apply. It will then be the job of the social standard advisors within the DFIs to jointly advise and empower their client with information on how to coordinate those standards on the ground. The remedy to this late DFI entry problem is a requirement for their client to conduct a retroactive gap analysis

---

[21] Informal conversations with members of international organisations discussed how projects often come to them late in the project cycle and after commencement of construction.

between local laws and the performance standards and pay compensation to communities if gaps are found.

Gap analyses are required for many environmental and social risks. Whilst it could be argued that they extend a positive practical tool for comparing the local legal framework against DFI standards, analysing any gaps between those two regimes and forming specific closure actions,[22] it also means that often, the DFI actually has no input or control function that it can use to empower the actions of the borrower during the crucial pre-construction and construction periods when land is cleared and before communities are disturbed. The proverbial horse has already bolted and one could argue that the gap analysis merely serves a culpability and discharge model of thinking. This sees companies and their financiers ticking the paper box to demonstrate that they have done everything possible and thus discharge culpability, rather than thinking about how they can use their power and leverage to close this lacuna and progressively realise better consultation earlier on in the project life cycle. The comfort provided by performance standards may not enter into the project life cycle until construction has started and then, only implemented through a retroactive process. In the context of resettlement, this gap analysis remedy is too late for uprooted communities, and for those who claim indigenous status, of little practical value, if any. This opens up the possibility of a large governance failure pertaining to the implementation of these private mechanisms in debt-syndicated arrangements.

Turning to the third governance deficit places a spotlight on the importance of incentives in development projects. Even if DFIs are included in the financing prior to any land disturbance, the period before and upto financial close, when the lenders are required to consider information from safeguarding standards as a condition to the first release of funds to the borrower to start construction, is a deeply conflicted one. At this stage economists and technocrats within DFIs (and of course the sponsor company) are heavily preoccupied with getting the deal done and getting the money out of the door. This is because construction happens shortly after financial close and, of course, construction necessitates land clearance. At this juncture, the consideration and implementation of indigenous performance standards will be pushed

---

[22] As was the case for the resettlement action plans produced for the Bugesera International Airport Expressway in Rwanda and the Lake Turkana Wind Power Project in Kenya, discussed in Section 2.3. A gap analysis was also conducted for the Oyu Tolgoi project.

to the lowest priority. As illustrated in the case studies, safeguarding standards will be rendered deficient in terms of content and timing, or disapplied entirely as not relevant to the project, too complicated and preventing the deal from completing.[23]

These economic anxieties are heightened in a PF setting which is based on long loan tenure and payment that needs to go out the door as repayment for the financiers and concessionaire is solely based on the project being constructed on time and on specification. Having to factor in tricky and time-consuming issues on FPIC-related processes at the stages leading up to financial close, disbursement of construction funds and the construction period is possibly the worst time in terms of economic pressures, tension and dilemma. Contributing to this is the reality that the construction period is one of the most risky and expensive stages for a lender and project company and is usually reflected in a higher interest rate attaching to the loan during this period.

These economic imperatives will over incentivise the key PF actors to clear the required land as soon as possible so construction can begin and complete on time and in schedule. The result is that issues around consultation will only pierce the project life cycle and debt instruments in an overly superficial manner as I analyse in Chapter 4, if they pierce them at all. Even if a DFI comes into a project later on (as discussed in the second scenario), PF incentives will, during the period leading up to financial close, weigh on the DFI as it would on any other commercial bank or the sponsor, potentially resulting in the suppression of consultation to fit project timelines and economic considerations.[24] In this governance context, the potential of safeguarding standards to take a

---

[23] For similar findings regarding the World Bank's implementation of indigenous peoples' performance standards see G Sarfaty, *Values in Translation: Human Rights and the Culture of the World Bank* (Stanford University Press 2012).

[24] I analyse the impact of these types of financial dynamics on the recognition and implementation of indigenous peoples' land rights in Chapter 4 and the subsequent case studies from Panama and Mongolia. In a 2015 report, the AFDB conceded that specific institutional, ideological and transaction-driven dynamics will compromise the implementation of indigenous policy standards. These dynamics include the lack of an effective framework for implementing FPIC in development projects, poor internal monitoring structures within the DFI, institutional fears over the time and expense required to comply with standards and a general discussion on how the project cycle itself will result in the compression of consultation processes. See Safeguards and Sustainability Series, Volume 1, Issue 3: Review of the implementation of the African Development Bank's 2003 Involuntary Resettlement Policy, 2015; https://esa.afdb.org/sites/default/files/SSS% 20-%20Involuntary%20Resettlement%20-%20En%20%5Bweb%5D.pdf.

human rights compliant approach[25] that requires FPIC prior to the approval of any project and before development commences, is limited.

Considering these gaps, it might seem plausible that the IFC as a designer of the performance standards on land and indigenous peoples provides its clients with a detailed governance framework or set of principles or standards considering some of these issues, which its clients can use for implementation. Yet, as of 2015, no such framework has been developed.[26] In sum, the above governance framework with its three problematic deficits does not deliver an FPIC-compliant project design as it structurally displaces the meaningful consideration of land and indigenous peoples' issues.

The above gap analysis remedy is one of many discussed throughout the book illustrating how project financing mechanisms are set up to encourage reactionary 'after the event' thinking. This reactionary ideology is practically manifested in many ways. These include the structuring of a project in which the project company has special project reserve accounts set aside and detailed within project budgets. These accounts are funded with sufficient money to service the lenders' loans upon the occurrence of specific events that have an adverse effect on the project company's liquidity. For example, an account can be used to alleviate expropriation risk and give the lenders time to work with the government over an expropriation event. This compensatory and reactionary mentality is seen as the most pragmatic remedy for concessionaires rather than one which could move towards a more preventative remedial approach to project design. Working with a community in a prevention mentality to build trust from the early stages of project exploration and throughout the project life cycle takes heavy contextual engagement, internal culture change, long-term financial commitment and planning and project presence all of which are expensive and time consuming and currently not part of project design.

In sum, the inclusion of DFIs within the legal framework on development projects brings large degrees of legal- and governance-related

---

[25] As contained in article 32 of the UNDRIP discussed in Chapter 3.

[26] Information requests were submitted to the IFC asking for a copy of an Implementation Paper which is referred to in the 2013 World Bank Group Strategy paper. The request was acknowledged and went onto state that for the 'Implementation Paper which is referred to in the World Bank Group Strategy paper 2013, the IFC has searched its records and databases but has not identified in its possession the document that you have requested, because the Implementation Paper has not yet been produced'. The response then referred to the involuntary resettlement standards.

uncertainty surrounding their implementation processes and ultimate accountability when the projects they invest in and the policies they purport to mobilise and monitor through their borrower client, have detrimental effects on communities. As contextualised in the case studies, questions can also be raised about the identity, role and accountability of social experts hired by the borrower to satisfy performance standards and advise on issues of indigenous recognition and rights implementation. These liability questions become more pertinent given the next characteristic of development projects: the reduced role of the state.

2.3   Diminished Role of the State

Crucial to these projects, is the understanding that the state's role and authority is to facilitate and administer the relevant project. Attracting foreign investment, acquiring foreign technology and skills, reducing public sector borrowing by relying on private funding of projects and the possibility of developing what might otherwise be non-priority projects are all factors that induce a state into a facilitator role. Whilst the role of the government will vary from project to project, at a minimum, it is likely to be involved in the grant of a long-term lease for the concessionaire to build the project and issuance of consents and permits both at the outset of the project and on a periodic basis throughout its duration. In some cases the government or a specific agency will be the purchaser of products produced by the project and in others, a minority shareholder in the project itself. Typically, governments in lesser developed countries will be expected to play a greater role in facilitating the project. This is primarily because of the political and legal risks involved in doing business and securing the investors' property rights in these contexts.

There are numerous mechanisms through which development projects achieve state rollback. First, through simple project structuring: many development projects financed through PF are shaped such that the state agrees to grant the concession to explore or exploit to a separate legal entity which is organised and registered solely to conduct specific commercial activities. DFIs and commercial banks will, after conducting their own risk or bankability assessments of the project contracts and drafting of debt instruments, piggyback into the project by lending money to that non-sovereign specially formed entity. Thus, the sponsors to the project are very much in control. There is no contract or conferring authority between the state and the project company through which the state empowers, controls or instructs the specially created legal entity to exercise elements of governmental authority in place of a state organ. These projects are in fact characterised by the antithesis of this: a state that is distanced from honouring its international human rights obligations through active participation in the project, an economic position which makes the state inherently conflicted when it comes to honouring its human rights obligations. This gap in conferring authority between the state and the concessionaire and the purely commercial nature of the project insulates the state against any attribution of international legal responsibility for the acts of private entities.

There is, of course, the possibility of attributing responsibility to the state should it fail to require a private entity to conduct due diligence[27] for a major project. However, many modern development projects will automatically satisfy this due diligence impact study requirement. This is because a concessionaire will – as a result of loan conditionality under IFC safeguarding standards, Equator Principles or good industry practice – conduct some sort of environmental and social risk assessment. Yet serious human rights– and land-related impacts continue even when those measures have been carried out and the legal due diligence requirement ostensibly satisfied. This signals that something is going wrong at the points in which social impacts interface with project design, financing and the behaviours through which safeguarding standards are implemented. The governance deficits outlined in Section 2.2 outline some major lacunas in the implementation of the safeguarding policy processes which are further elaborated and built upon in

---

[27] Based on the omission of the state to conduct due diligence, and to prevent, ensure or punish certain human rights abuses committed by private persons, resulting in a finding that the state has failed in its international human rights obligations. The principle was derived in *Velásquez-Rodríguez v Honduras*, Judgment of July 29, 1988 (Merits), Inter-American Court of Human Rights. The core of the negative obligation to act was applied to an important decision of the African Commission relating to the activities of Shell in its exploitation of oil reserves, *Social and Economic Rights Action Centre for Economic and Social Rights v Nigeria*, Comm no. 155/96 (2001). The African Commission found violations of the African Charter regarding the obligations of states with specific regards to private actors in the context of the people's rights to natural resources and the right to food. The commission found that the Nigerian government facilitated the destruction of the Ogoniland and that its practice fell short of the minimum conduct expected of governments in contexts involving private actors. In order to satisfy the state's duty to prevent human rights abuses by private persons, the African Commission laid down a minimum legal standard requiring the state to order, or at least permit, environmental and social impact studies prior to any major development. Those studies should provide meaningful opportunities for individuals to participate in development decisions affecting their communities.

Chapter 5. This, along with the legal lacuna in holding private actors legally accountable in international law and the dilemma in the positionality of the state, creates a substantial legal and regulatory gap. I argue that this gap forces greater attention to be thrown onto the hidden and understudied mechanisms deployed by concessionaires and financiers within the project ecosystem that sit within the shadow of international legal recognition and reach, yet have the power to impact upon indigenous peoples' rights to land.

In addition to the project structure, other methods for diminishing the role of the state include specific contractual arrangements and clauses within the contracts that underpin the project. Investors will expect the government to regulate and administer the relevant development project through the award of licences, favourable concession terms with tax incentives and stabilisation of law clauses, provision of host government support agreements or the delivery of a letter of comfort stating its support for the project.[28] The assumption is that the state will provide the enabling legal conditions, upon which the investors can explore, develop, produce and sell the asset being produced.

The following examples of clauses taken from concession agreements relating to the investor's property rights take stock of several points: the fragmentation of actors and norms involved in development projects, the subservience of the state to those actors and the blurring roles between the state and investor over issues of land access, which as I illustrate in Chapter 4 can become even more muddied.

> The State shall make available to Contractor for the needs of the Petroleum Operations the land it owns that is necessary for the performance of such operations. Contractor may build and maintain the necessary facilities there, above or below grade.[29]

And also the following clause from the same contract:

> **Relocation of Population**
> On the basis of the results of the environmental impact study, the State, with the financing of the Investor, shall proceed to the relocation of the population whose presence on the land shall be an impediment to the research, construction, operation and/or transformation works.

---

[28] The effect of some of these mechanisms on indigenous rights recognition and implementation are discussed in Chapters 4 and 5.

[29] Clause taken from a mining concession in the Republic of Guinea, on file with the author.

This stable and predictable legal framework constitutes part of the legal conditions that support the project's operation but does not provide the complete picture.

The state's facilitation and administration role is largely enabled through the distancing of international legal standards created by the position that international law acknowledges the general separateness or veil of corporate entities at the national level.[30] The purely commercial special-purpose nature of the project and the private legal structures through which a project is insulated from the scrutiny of international law is accepted. This fracturing creates a lacuna for any attempts to understand, monitor and regulate how these contractual mechanisms can impact upon the implementation of land rights for indigenous peoples' and thus matter for conducting effective and rights compatible due diligence.[31] Not only is the state a distanced bystander to these projects but it also frequently takes an active slice of the investment pie becoming a pure project stakeholder as illustrated by the following concession clauses:

> The Titleholder shall grant the Romanian Government, through the Agency, the pre-emptive right to the purchase of the mining production obtained under this License, at international market prices and under commercial terms.

---

[30] *Barcelona Traction Light and Power Company, Limited,* Judgment ICJ 1966, paras 56–59 except in those cases where the corporate veil is a mere device or a vehicle for fraud or evasion. Article 8 of the International Law Commission's Draft articles on Responsibility of States for Internationally Wrongful Acts, with commentaries 2001, reaffirms the default separateness for corporate entities unless they are exercising elements of governmental authority within the meaning of article 5. The later article specifically catches the phenomenon of parastatal entities, which exercise elements of governmental authority in place of state organs. There is justification for attributing legal responsibility to the state under international law for the conduct of parastatal entities, as it is the internal law of the state that has expressly conferred on the entity, the exercise of certain elements of governmental authority. In a purely commercial development project whilst there may be more generic changes to the legal framework that permit private ownership of land and recognise the scale of financial investment and security that is required, no internal law expressly confers onto a specific private entity, elements of governmental authority. Instead the project is structured and operates through a separate private limited liability legal entity as per the leading common law case of *Salomon v A Salomon and Co Ltd* [1897] AC 22.

[31] Whilst after the Ogoni case discussed earlier, the state has a duty of diligence, that duty is discharged by the state act of ordering an independent assessment which many investors now do as matter of course and good practice. The substance and conditions around that diligence assessment is not interrogated in the detailed ways analysed in this book.

And the following from a concession in Guinea:

> The State shall have the right to make an offer to [ ] to acquire, directly or indirectly, in the six months following the Effective Date of this Agreement, a shareholding in [ ] on market terms.

Moreover, it is made clear that such a stake will not be a controlling one stating

> This shareholding shall not in any way grant the State a power of direct or indirect control over [ ] or the Investor and shall be fully paid in US dollars and shall not imply any restriction or impact on the rights and guarantees granted by the State to the Investor.

The position of the state as a minority investor, intentionally or not, induces it towards disinterest in the manner in which a concessionaire implements the resettlement or indigenous safeguarding standard. The result is that the regulation of activities that result in involuntary resettlement and displacement could be shaped and blurred between state and non-state entities who are mutually interested in mobilising private property rights over a parcel of land to the exclusion of other traditional claims. Absent a clear domestic legal framework and within these opaque roles that pose systemic legal challenges, a vacuum is created through which the state will let a powerful developer plan issues relating to land acquisition and resettlement through governance processes that can be, as illustrated in Section 2.2 structurally deficient.

Indeed, this blurring legal and regulatory landscape is made tangible in the following clause taken from the IFC performance standard on involuntary resettlement policy which expressly gives the concessionaire a role to play in resettlement where there is no clear domestic legal framework:

> Where land acquisition and resettlement are the responsibility of the government, the client will collaborate with the responsible government agency, to the extent permitted by the agency, to achieve outcomes that are consistent with this Performance Standard. In addition, where government capacity is limited, the client will play an active role during resettlement planning, implementation, and monitoring.[32]

So, the IFC requires its clients to agree to play an active role in the planning, implementation and monitoring of resettlement issues especially in contexts in which government capacity is limited. The practical methods through which management and implementation are envisaged

---

[32] IFC Performance Standards 5 and 7, 30 and 21 respectively on private-sector responsibilities.

include production of a gap analysis and a resettlement plan that brings government resettlement measures up to the requirements contained in the policies. If no government measures exist, the concessionaire is required to conduct land acquisition and resettlement in accordance with the policy standards. It should at a minimum, identify affected people and impacts. Negotiated settlements are also envisaged as well as the concessionaire's financial responsibilities relating to resettlement.[33] The overall point is that the policy wording foresees a situation in which a private entity is conducting governmental responsibilities with no independent oversight or control.

We therefore observe a trend towards a lack of governmental authority or control over the development-related activities undertaken by the concessionaires and financiers. Simultaneously, we have legal accountability gaps in which the IFC and its client have carved out a space for both implementing and policing issues of public law concern through these types of insulated commercial activities. Examples of this structure in practice can be seen in a number of resettlement action plans; for instance, in the Oyu Tolgoi project analysed in Chapter 5 in which Rio Tinto conducts resettlement in accordance with IFC performance standards. Other examples include resettlement conducted to make way for the Bugesera International Airport Expressway in Rwanda[34] and the Lake Turkana Wind Power Project in Kenya.[35]

For the Rwandan project, given IFC involvement, a gap analysis between Rwandan law on expropriation in the public interest[36] and IFC standards was conducted. Pursuant to this, IFC performance standards on land and involuntary resettlement were found to have more favourable treatment of project-affected persons in comparison to Rwandan law, and thus the IFC standards took precedence and were implemented. The government initially conducted a valuation of assets affected by the project but in 2018 the project company, BAL Limited,

---

[33] IFC Performance Standard 5, 31.
[34] Developed by Bugesera Airport Limited which is a joint venture between a subsidiary of the Mota-Engil Group and the Government of Rwanda and financed by a consortium of international lenders including the IFC.
[35] Lake Turkana Wind Power Limited is a consortium of private equity partners including the Norwegian state–owned private equity company Norfund. The project enjoys financing from international commercial lenders and development banks such as the European Investment Bank, which has its own set of performance standards modelled on IFC requirements.
[36] Specifically, Law N° 32/2015 of 11/06/2015.

commissioned a local private consulting firm Newplan Limited, to redo that valuation. BAL or its contractors[37] then negotiated land and compensation agreements with land owners.

According to the resettlement plan for the Kenyan wind power project, the project developer, Lake Turkana Wind Power Limited, assumed responsibility for implementation and delivery of resettlement procedures. According to the plan, a key reason for this assumption of responsibility was because no single agency in Kenya has the mandate for the planning and provision of resettlement and compensation in cases where people are involuntarily relocated for development projects. In this context, it was therefore deemed to be 'common practice'[38] that the project proponent assumes responsibility for resettlement implementation and oversight, although there may be the involvement of local authorities. A comparative analysis this time between Kenyan laws and the performance standards of the European Investment Bank was conducted with the bank standards deemed more favourable and thus implemented in many resettlement-related aspects.[39]

This profusion and the glimpses within the contractual clauses of the power dynamics at play raise genuine queries over the ability of development project structures and the policies within them to deliver on the recognition and implementation of indigenous peoples' rights to land in clear, predictable and fair ways. It would be reasonable to wonder whether the IFC performance standards, and their various avatars within the development finance and PF landscape, are merely iterations of a new public management[40] approach to the governance of public policy issues. This type of approach operationalises indigenous rights to land within

---

[37] Ramboll Limited, Resettlement Action Plan: Final Version with Budget, New Bugesera International Airport Expressway, 2018 www.miga.org/sites/default/files/archive/Documents/SPGDisclosures/UK11-24483_4_NBIA_Expressway_RAP.pdf.

[38] Lartech Africa, Resettlement Action Plan, Lake Turkana Wind Power, Kenya, Sirima Nomadic Pastoralist Relocation of the Community Encampment, 2014, 70 https://old.danwatch.dk/wp-content/uploads/2016/05/Ressetlement-Action-Plan-2014.pdf.

[39] For instance, the bank standards were deemed more favourable than Kenyan law with respect to the identification of project-affected persons, the preference for 'land for land' compensation and compensation for loss of usage rights for customary and historical interests in property. The latter includes use-rights (grazing) or rights of access to natural resources, all of which are protected under the safeguarding standard on land and involuntary resettlement.

[40] C Hood, 'The "New Public Management" in the 1980s: Variations on a Theme' (1995) 20 Accounting, Organisations and Society 93; M Ugur and D Sunderland, Does Economic Governance Matter? Governance Institutions and Outcomes (Edward Elgar 2011).

these projects with a technocratic, box-ticking and arm's-length ration-ality that adjusts implementation of policies to idiosyncratic concerns over the financial value and dynamics of the project.

Overall, the transnational development projects I am concerned with are characterised by certain defining features. They possess a historical lineage in privatisation processes aimed at opening up the market to business through policies advocating decreased state intervention. The complex and fragmented array of project-financing debt instruments and related project documentation designed to mobilise these projects show-case a profusion of actors and interests at play in these projects, and they neatly demonstrate the legal distancing of the state and, importantly, the priority the state has itself extended to norms of contract and financing over public interest.

Section 3 discusses a question that may have sprung to mind when reading the above analysis: is this legal? If so, what is the legal status of the complex contractual framework that I have outlined above and will explore in more detail in later chapters? The question of legality is a final important characteristic of transnational development projects to which I now turn.

3   Is This Legal?

A quick answer to this question is yes. Understanding the legal status of the complex contractual framework regulating a transnational develop-ment project involves a brief look across both public and private law. For the types of contractual arrangements dealt with in this book, it is useful to examine the status of concession contracts and the finance and commercial documents separately for what it tells us about the mixed legal framework governing these projects.

Questions around the legal status of international concession contracts made between a host state and a private party have been controversial.[41] This is primarily because of the public-private nature of these arrange-ments in which a state entity contracts with the private sector for a

---

[41] Fluctuating between whether concessions could be classified as a quasi-treaty thus elevating a private company to a sovereign status on the international place or character-ising concessions as a contract between two private parties. The latter would transform the state into a private actor that cannot rely on any sovereign powers to amend the terms of the contract, whatever the demands of public welfare. See M Sornarajah, *The Inter-national Law on Foreign Investment* (Cambridge University Press 2009).

specific project. Whilst debates around the formal legal classification of concessions are interesting, they are semantics given that practice illustrates that the functions and mechanisms within those contracts are more aligned with fundamental private law principles around freedom to contract. This gives them a more commercial quality that mobilises the investors' desire for stability and priority. Let us consider a few illustrations of this point.

LIAMCO[42] recognised that governments and investors can freely negotiate and enter into agreements that depart from the laws of the host country, bringing a private law quality to concession contracts. In this regard, when negotiating choice of law with a host government[43] the investor normally wants to stabilise the applicable law, so that changes in the national law of the host country do not apply to the investment contract. At the same time the host government, as sovereign, naturally wants its domestic laws to apply. So whilst many concession contracts will concede to a government's demands that domestic law govern the contract, an investor will, in tandem, negotiate to limit or reduce the application of that law through negotiated clauses. The investor's commercial position will then necessitate a number of contractual features which the host state will, in its desire to attract foreign investment but keep its own governing law, agree to. These terms will limit its ability to make commitments about its future actions as a sovereign and erode its decision-making power. For instance, it is customary for concessions to require that the government waive its sovereign immunity.[44] The contract might also include mechanisms that make it practically challenging

---

[42] Governments and investors can negotiate and enter into agreements that depart from the law of the host countries. '[I]t is an accepted universal principle of both domestic and international laws that the parties to a mixed public and private contract are free to select in their contract the law to govern their contractual relationship', *LIAMCO* v *Libya*, Award (April 12, 1977), VI Year Book Com. Arb. 89, 92 (1981).

[43] Expressly choosing the law (even host state law), is common practice as an express choice will bring legal certainty to the contract and mean that in the event of a dispute between the parties, any tribunal or court will have little difficulty in ascertaining and applying the choice of law written into the contract.

[44] For example, Mineral Development Agreement between the Government of Liberia, Putu Iron Ore Mining and Mano River Iron Ore Ltd, 2 September 2010 Art. 31 (The Government hereby irrevocably waives, in relation to any dispute arising out of, in relation to, or in connection with, this Agreement, whether relating to acts of a sovereign or governmental nature or otherwise, all claims of immunity from the jurisdiction of, and from the enforcement of any arbitral award rendered by, an arbitral tribunal constituted pursuant to this Agreement as well as all claims of immunity from the service of process or the jurisdiction of any court situated in any state, country or nation in aid of the

for the government to alter the terms of the concession in accordance with public interest issues; for example, through terms that require the host government's law to be consistent with the terms of the investment contract,[45] require mutual written agreement to amend the contract[46] or require enactment of the contract into law.[47]

I discuss other contractual mechanisms within concession contracts that work to insulate the economic viability of the project from external factors and thus displace the consideration of factors such as the recognition of indigenous land rights in Chapter 4. On land issues specifically, those mechanisms include clauses that require the government to extend a myriad of contractual assurances over the investor's land- and water-access rights and clauses with investor-friendly detailed procedures for resettlement. Other structural mechanisms discussed in later chapters include the issuance of a host government support agreement or requirements for an expensive completion guarantee from the government sponsor. Further mechanisms include the negotiation of political risk insurance from an agency such as the World Bank's insurance agency MIGA, which will prepay the financiers their outstanding debt obligations in the event of a state taking.[48] The investor will then seek to

jurisdiction of such arbitral tribunal or in connection with the enforcement of any such award). Other examples on file with author.

[45] NIOC-ERAP Agreement, Art. 44, reprinted in OPEC, Selected Documents of the International Petroleum Industry 1966 (1970). (The provisions of the Mining Act of 1957 shall not be applicable to this Agreement, and any other laws and regulations which may be wholly or partly inconsistent with the provisions of this Agreement shall to the extent of any such inconsistency be of no effect in respect of the provisions of this Agreement).

[46] Mineral Development Agreement between the Government of Liberia, Putu Iron Ore Mining and Mano River Iron Ore Ltd, 2 September 2010 Art. 32.3 (Any modification or amendment of this Agreement shall be by the mutual written agreement of the parties (with the Minister, the Minister of Finance, Minister of Justice and the Chairperson of the National Investment Commission, or such other persons as may be notified by the Government to the Company, acting for the Government) and shall not become effective until (i) approved by the President of the Republic and (ii) (except for nonmaterial modifications and amendments), approved by the Legislature).

[47] Petroleum Concession Agreement between the Arab Republic of Egypt and the Egyptian Petroleum Company and Dovers Investment Limited in the East Wadi Araba Area Gulf of Suez (A.R.E), Art. XXIX. (This Agreement shall not be binding upon any parties hereto unless and until a law is issued by the competent authorities of the A.R.E authorising the Minister of Petroleum to sign this agreement and giving this agreement full force and effect of law and the agreement is signed by the Government, EGPC and Contractor).

[48] Of course, MIGA will have the right under the insurance policy to take legal action against the government to recover the money paid out through the working of a standard insurance subrogation clause. Through this clause the insurer will be subrogated or

secure all of their contractual arrangements with the government through the issuance of a legal opinion from a reputable local law firm. That opinion will confirm that the legal obligations of the government constitute legally valid and binding obligations and do not contravene public order.

Questions around the legal status of the financial and commercial documentation underpinning a transnational development project are less controversial as these contracts are entered into between private parties[49] on an entirely commercial arm's-length basis. The underlying legal principle running throughout these contracts is that of freedom of contract, and in this context, achieving security of contract and protection of the creditors' contractual assets receives primary credit. This is because of the ability of these principles to establish a functional market-based economy in which predictability is paramount.[50]

It has been suggested that one best practice method through which human rights or ethical standards might be incorporated into commercial contracts is through the provisions of the United Nations Convention on Contracts for the International Sale of Goods (CISG), especially article 7(2).[51] That article provides that 'questions concerning matters governed by this Convention which are not expressly settled in it are to be settled in conformity with the general principles on which it is based'. The optimism is that those general principles may be interpreted with reference to international human rights law thus offering a potential contractual mechanism to safeguard human rights in the context of, say, an oil and gas supply chain where the end buyer is a sophisticated company.

Whilst the spirit of this best practice suggestion is commendable, the problem with including these types of clauses into development finance practices is challenging and perhaps best highlighted by reference to the

---

'stepping into the shoes' of the insured party in order to sue the third party for the loss incurred by the insured.

[49] For instance, the project company, lenders (including DFIs who are treated as private parties for the reasons analysed in Chapter 3) and facility/security agents on behalf of the syndicate of lenders.

[50] D Weber 'Restricting the Freedom of Contract: A Fundamental Prohibition' (2013) 16(1) *Yale Human Rights and Development Journal* article 2 and GHL Fridman, 'Freedom of Contract' (1967) 2(1) *Ottawa Law Review* 1–22.

[51] S Brabant, Setting Human Rights Standards through International Contracts, Herbert Smith Global Legal Briefings, 2016 www.herbertsmithfreehills.com/latest-thinking/setting-human-rights-standards-through-international-contracts.

governing law clause from an alumina sale and purchase agreement taken from a project-financed African mining project:

> This Agreement shall be governed by and construed in accordance with the substantive Law for the time being of England but without regard to its Laws concerning conflicts of Law. The United Nations Convention on Contracts for the International Sale of Goods is hereby expressly excluded from application to the terms and conditions of this Agreement.

This small contractual example provides an illustration of the highly regulated contractual field that communities and their legal advisors will struggle to pierce. The purpose of this express clause is to bring legal certainty into the transaction by excluding any conflict of law and preventing any future argument that any governing law other than the parties' express choice will apply to the contract. The result: exclusion of the CISG provisions to prevent the seepage of legal uncertainty into a highly structured contractual network that is reliant on the prompt sale and purchase of alumina to repay loan commitments.

This type of clause would not be considered illegal or contrary to public policy, even though by expressly excluding its terms the parties have successfully excluded general provisions of international law. Private law scholars argue that this is due to the liberal form–orientated bias[52] that is built into English choice of law rules which is, in turn, derived from the basic contractarian principle. As long as no illegality or public policy violation is involved, freedom of contract prevails.[53] Questions over what constitutes illegality in contexts of English law–governed commercial transactions will typically investigate key areas of contract law on restraint of trade and undue harshness, for example, involving a penalty clause or the validity of an exclusion of liability clause. Lawyers for the financiers will be required to deliver a legal opinion to their clients confirming that all of the documents drafted for the project constitute legal, valid and binding obligations on the borrower. Given the restrictive

---

[52] By this I mean the English law rule that the proper law of the contract is what the parties have indicated it should be. So in a situation where the parties have done more than reveal a connection between the contract and a specific system of law, and have gone to the lengths of stating that they wish the contract to be governed by a named legal system, would be an even clearer exclusive choice of law. Fridman, supra n. 50, 18.

[53] *Esso Petroleum Co v Harper's Garage (Stourport) Ltd.*, [1967] 1 All ER 699, 712. Public policy clauses constitute a reserved power to reflect the application of laws perceived to be injurious or harmful and are used infrequently and restrictively relied on in English law. See K Murphy, 'The Traditional View of Public Policy and Order Public in Private International Law', (1981) 11 *Georgia Journal of International and Comparative Law* 591.

and vague notion of public policy in the Anglo-American tradition,[54] it is difficult to see how issues pertaining to public interest or human rights could be raised under a public policy exception in an English law–governed debt instrument or major project document for a defined commercial project.[55]

Chapter 7 extends illustrations of contracts entered into between concessionaires and indigenous communities that concern issues of public interest such as land access, consultation and compensation. Questions over the legal status of this new field of contractual engagement are more difficult to answer given the lack of transparency around the terms of these arrangements. The illustrations do, however, demonstrate a trend for classifying these types of contract as belonging to the private plane. This is achieved through wording that distinguishes the commercial arm's-length nature of the contract.[56] Whether this is the correct legal classification for these types of contract is moot. However, for those contracts drafted within legal traditions that share strong contractarian principles, there is a likelihood that they will be treated as private instruments if the governing law is written into the contract, and of course no company would enter into a contract without certainty over governing law.

The question of whether the contracts underpinning a transnational development project are legal can be answered in the affirmative. More specifically, they enjoy a private law nature, are highly effective for shielding private gains and thus set a stage on which public interest issues will find it challenging to make an appearance. Having defined and characterised my field of research, Chapter 3 analyses one part of the legal framework pertaining to transnational development projects involving indigenous peoples – the formal legal framework, and thus provides some hard law context to the private mechanisms explored later.

---

[54] Murphy, supra n. 53.

[55] There have been some efforts in Europe to expand the use of public policy vertically to sources external to the state such as through EU law and human rights law. However the practice in this area remains uncertain and has pointed to a restrictive practice when this challenges the internal market. See Jan Oster, 'Public Policy and Human Rights' (2015) 11 (3) *Journal of Private International Law* 542–567.

[56] For example, wording stating that 'nothing in this document will be construed as creating the relationship of partnership, principal and agent, trust or any fiduciary relationship between the parties' (Art. 42.16, Contract between Rio Tinto and an indigenous group analysed in Chapter 7).

3

In the Shadows of the Operational Development Project

Coping Strategies, Lacunas and Fragmentation in the Formal Legal Framework

This chapter maps and assesses the formal legal standards and jurispru-dential strands on indigenous peoples' rights to land that most directly apply to the phenomenon of large development projects to see how they cope with this high level of power and fragmentation. The framework mapped here constitutes one part of the overall network of norms and legal strategies that have bearing on a transnational development project. As I have outlined in Chapters 1 and 2 and detail in Chapter 4 and further case studies, applicable norms also include those from the private sphere.

1 Summarising the Implementation Gap and Values in the Formal Legal Framework

The main formal legal strategies that speak to development projects affecting indigenous peoples' rights to land are findings of violations of rights to property and culture, rights to free, prior and informed consent (FPIC) and rights to fair compensation. I will deal with each in turn, critically discussing how these strategies have been operationalised within legal instruments and judicial mechanisms. Aspects of that legal framework display salient characteristics; these include neoliberal values and where rights to property, culture and to FPIC have been legally recognised in priority of developers' property rights, those rights are frequently vitiated through a poor enforcement record. Legal practice on compensation quantum for the extinguishment of non-economic rights also demonstrates a striking lack of development. These legal shortfalls, as well as the other lacunas analysed in this chapter, contribute to an implementation gap through which developers' rights end up on top.

As I demonstrate, the overall legal framework is characterised by patchy legal sources: non-binding international law declarations, regional court judgments, domestic statutory[1] and constitutional norms[2] and, as I have outlined in Chapter 2 but will discuss in more detail, a structural accountability gap for holding private concessionaires and financiers to account. Moreover, regardless of the legal source of indigenous rights, reverberating through the cases is the theme that the recognition and implementation of rights will, as a result of judicial interpretation analysed in this chapter, dilute the implementation of those rights when they contest with the neoliberal developmental demands of the state. Features that broadly reflect the state's prioritisation of economic development over the rights of communities emerge within the jurisprudential strands analysed in this chapter. These values also assert themselves within rights that derive from higher legal sources. Consequently, claims to indigenous recognition and land rights implementation largely fail to stand up to the forward motion of a transnational development project. These diluted rights then face a larger structural lacuna of an international law system that does not speak directly to concessionaires and financiers in these complex circumstances. These structures block the visibility of commercial entities and the mechanisms they use from detailed legal interrogation and in parallel, limit the visibility and relevance of formal legal instruments to commercial parties engaged in 'doing development'.

Resulting biases, lacunas and power imbalances are, therefore, already embedded within a formal legal framework that makes it inherently difficult for indigenous communities to have their rights implemented in circumstances of transnational development projects. Aspects and illustrations of these deficits are provided in case laws throughout this chapter. In this context, it becomes easy for concessionaires and financiers to operate in the shadows of the legal framework, cognisant that the

---

[1] For instance, under the Australian Native Title Act 1993 (amended in 1988) and in South Africa, the use of, occupation of and access to land relating to any tribal, customary and indigenous practices is protected under the Interim Protection of Informal Rights to Land Act 1996.

[2] In Canada, indigenous groups are legally recognised under Section 35 of the Canadian Constitution Act 1982. In India, the rights of indigenous people are guaranteed within the Fifth and Sixth Schedules of the Constitution. These offer special laws on indigenous peoples' land rights and are applicable to designated parts of the country with high tribal population including central India and the North-East state. Moreover, the Forest Rights Act 2009 incorporates FPIC principles by recognising the village councils (gram sabhas) as an enabling decision-making mechanism and through provisions requiring the free informed consent of the gram sabha to any proposed resettlement.

law holds little threat to their operations. They can hide behind some or all of the lacunas of a highly fragmented regime, and can rely on distinctions around the type of soft legal norms that tend to regulate this field and poor enforcement practices. Consequently, private actors are able to ignore issues of indigenous recognition and implementation or develop their own self-regulated private mechanisms and behavioural practices around implementation discussed in later chapters.

2   Legal Strategies for Implementing Free, Prior and Informed Consent

There has been considerable international legal attention to indigenous peoples' rights to land over the last few decades. It is not my intention to give a detailed account of this body of law, which has been done by excellent indigenous rights scholars before, but only to analyse aspects of these modern strategies for legal recognition and implementation as they relate to development projects.

The 1989 ILO Convention[3] constitutes a clear and legally binding elaboration that indigenous and tribal peoples enjoy the full measure of universal human rights. It protects their traditional activities, recognising them as important factors for economic self-reliance and development.[4] Whilst its efficacy is questionable given the low number of ratifications,[5] the convention was a crucial springboard for the augmentation of these rights into what has been referred to as 'a milestone of indigenous empowerment',[6] the UN Declaration on the Rights of Indigenous Peoples (UNDRIP). The declaration gives communities collective or group entitlements to land, property and culture that are entrenched within the field of human rights.[7] For the first time, a legal instrument has categorically stated that indigenous communities have the right to self-determination. Because of this, communities can freely determine their

---

[3] ILO Convention No. 169 – Convention concerning Indigenous and Tribal Peoples in Independent Countries (ILO Convention).
[4] Article 23 of the ILO Convention.
[5] Twenty-two countries have ratified the convention.
[6] J Anaya and S Wiessner, 'The UN Declaration on the Rights of Indigenous Peoples: Towards Re-empowerment', JURIST Forum (2007) www.jurist.org/forum/2007/10/un-declaration-on-rights-of-indigenous.php.
[7] S Weissner, 'The Cultural Rights of Indigenous Peoples: Achievements and Continuing Challenges' (2011) 22(1) European Journal of International Law 121–140 – noting how the effective protection of indigenous culture is key to its understanding.

economic, social and cultural development using democratic processes[8] for indigenous participation and consultation; for instance, in the formulation, implementation and evaluation of national and regional plans and programmes that affect them and their self-development.

Specifically, in the context of a large development project, one specific right stands out: that of free, prior and informed consent. This entitlement is an acknowledgement of the special cultural attachment that indigenous peoples have to land and, flowing from this, it permits communities to have a say and to actively participate in decisions affecting them and their land. Article 32 states

1. Indigenous peoples have the right to determine and develop priorities and strategies for the development or use of their lands or territories and other resources.
2. States shall consult and cooperate in good faith with the indigenous peoples concerned through their own representative institutions in order to obtain their free and informed consent prior to the approval of any project affecting their lands or territories and other resources, particularly in connection with the development, utilisation or exploitation of their mineral, water or other resources.

As can be seen, a crucial aspect of FPIC is consultation. Indigenous peoples must be consulted on all matters that may affect them – that consultation must be voluntarily given, be aimed at reaching agreement, be conducted in good faith, through their own representative institutions and in a manner that is understandable to the communities. The consultation must be sought prior to approval of any project and certainly before construction commences.

The standard also states that the 'consent' of groups is required meaning that they *should* have the right to withhold consent, veto development or offer it with conditions. FPIC's participatory underpinning is, therefore, a practical tool for guaranteeing the economic, social and cultural development of indigenous communities and their individual and collective survival in the face of encroaching development. It becomes especially relevant for the conduct of development projects and for the grant and implementation of concessions in ancestral territories. This is because the design of projects, the contracts

---

[8] J Gilbert, 'Indigenous Rights in the Making: The United Nations Declaration on the Rights of Indigenous Peoples' (2007) 14 *International Journal on Minority and Group Rights* 207–230 – referring to the declaration as a democratic project.

underpinning them and the behaviours surrounding them can cut through formal legal strategies designed to protect indigenous culture and by extension, ancestral rights to land. Consultation can be ignored by powerful companies and a conflicted state, or undertaken without proper authorisation. Furthermore, in light of the three governance deficits identified in Chapter 2, consultation can occur far too late in the project life cycle and under highly conflicted conditions, if at all. It can rapidly deteriorate into a highly formalistic, tick-the-box, paperwork-based, reactionary process that is characterised by a high degree of discretion. Yet, in the face of state-granted concessions for logging, mining and dams, courts have elaborated clear legal strategies for recognising and implementing indigenous peoples' right to land. Legal cases are of course highly varied in their facts, context and geography. However, cases involving development projects and indigenous groups do illuminate some positive guidelines and core strategies for protecting the special land-connected culture.

The genesis of FPIC within the UNDRIP is derived from numerous cases which collectively form a substantial body of legal opinion and strategies of direct relevance to responsible concessionaires and financiers. Jurisprudence confirms that infringements on the cultural rights of indigenous communities may simply not be proportionate to the public interest in a given development initiative. In the *Ominayak* case[9] concerning the exploitation of timber, oil and gas within Canadian indigenous territory, the Human Rights Council held that development can threaten the way of life and culture of the Lubicon Lake Band under article 27 of the International Covenant on Civil and Political Rights. Following from this, in the *Kdsivarsi*[10] and *Selbu*[11] cases, the Supreme Courts of Finland and Norway held that indigenous Sami rights to graze reindeer on private land can place brakes on government economic development policies. One way of democratising state economic development policies is through the requirement for consultation regarding all proposed development on indigenous territory. The *Länsman*[12] case

---

[9] *Chief Bernard Ominayak and Lubicon Lake Band* v *Canada*, CCPR/C/38/D/167/1984, UN Human Rights Committee, 26 March 1990.

[10] *Kdsivarsi Reindeer Herders' Coop* v *Ministry of Trade and Industry*, File No. 1447, Supreme Administrative Court of Finland, 15 May 1996.

[11] *Jon Inge Sirum and others* v *Essand Reindeer District and another*, 21 June 2001, serial number 4B/2001.

[12] *Jouni E. Länsman et al.* v *Finland*, Communication No. 671/1995, UN Doc. CCPR/C/58/D/671/1995 (1996).

from Finland involving private logging concessions over indigenous Sami territory requires the state to take positive procedural measures to ensure effective participation through consultation and negotiation processes.[13] Legal consensus has now matured into the expectation that states have a minimum duty to consult[14] in good faith with groups regarding developments on their ancestral land, making consultation a fundamental component of the canon of indigenous land rights.

3   Challenges around Implementing Consultation Strategies

Although numerous legal systems have specific statutory or constitutional provisions[15] recognising so-called informal and indigenous rights to land and the duty of the state to consult with rights holders, there remain significant blocks to the implementation of those legal strategies.

3.1   Lack of Indigenous Veto and Legal Priority to Development

First, consultation does not constitute a veto right.[16] Second, in countries where a right to consult or negotiate is enshrined in statutory or constitutional norms, that right is time-limited. In Australia, the domestic legal framework gives communities a right to negotiate for a statutorily prescribed period of six months.[17] During this period, there will be a moratorium on any economic activities and parties are required to negotiate in good faith. However, at the end of that period if no agreement is reached, indigenous groups are not permitted to withhold consent and the state can expropriate. As set out in the Native Title Act, commercial activities can continue after the expiry of the minimum

---

[13] Ibid, 7.8.

[14] *Delgamuukw v British Colombia* [1997] 3 SCR, *Brownley v State of Western Australia* [1999] FCA 1139, *Saramaka People v Suriname* [2007], Judgment of 28 November 2007 (Inter-Am. Ct. H. R. (Ser. C) no. 172) (2007). The ILA Committee on the Rights of Indigenous Peoples, Interim Report (2010), 51, identifies customary international law norms concerning indigenous peoples which includes the right to be consulted about any project that may affect them.

[15] Supra n. 1 and 2.

[16] Commission on Human Rights, Sub-Commission on the Promotion and Protection of Human Rights; Working Group on Indigenous Populations, 'Standard Setting: Legal Commentary on the Concept of Free, Prior and Informed Consent' (2005) UN Doc E/ CN.4/Sub.2/AC.4/2005/WP.1 (14 July 2005) 47.

[17] Section 35 of the Native Title Act.

consultation period through a ministerial determination based on national interest and payment of compensation.

A similar statutory arrangement exists in South Africa. Whilst courts have recognised that communities with informal land rights cannot be evicted by a private concessionaire without a process of prior consultation and compensation,[18] it is important to keep in mind that a power imbalance still remains within the legal framework between the interests of a mining right holder and the land occupier. Provisions of the South African mining regime[19] contemplate that if negotiations between the affected parties and the mining right holder are deadlocked, the regional manager can recommend to the Minister of Minerals and Energy that the land be expropriated.[20] The practical result is that a community can be lawfully evicted through the payment of compensation and the act of going through a consultation process that has complied with procedural rules. A solution would be for domestic legislation to state that no permit or concessions can be granted by the relevant government agency without the full and informed consent of communities – a standard that would reflect the position of the UNDRIP – although such a position is likely to be subject to intense political and corporate lobbying. The High Court of South Africa has moved towards this position in the *Xolobeni* mineral sands project case.[21] However, one must be careful about transposing this as a general rule applicable to transnational development projects given that access to land in South Africa is deeply linked to its special history.

This short analysis raises the obvious question of what the current legal consultation standard achieves when a community cannot say no to a project. This signals an inherent legal failure and bias. If a community cannot veto a project and the legal system itself does nothing to address the underlying power imbalance between a community and developer, it has shifted the burden of development onto a community that is least able to shoulder it.

---

[18] *Maledu and Others* v *Itereleng Bakgatla Mineral Resources (Pty) Limited and Another* (2018) ZACC 41.

[19] Section 54(5) of the Mineral and Petroleum Resources Development Act 2002 (MPRDA).

[20] Section 55 of the MPRDA provides for 'expropriation and the payment of compensation in respect thereof'.

[21] *Baleni and Others* v *Minister of Mineral Resources and Others* [2018] ZAGPPHC 829. This is a landmark high court judgment stating that a minister must obtain the full and formal consent of indigenous communities prior to granting a mining application.

3.2   Powerful Interests Fragmenting Legal Rights

Even if a legal regime requires consultation with customary rights holders, power dynamics and procedural issues can make its practice unsatisfactory. The six-month consultation period detailed above in relation to the native title framework might seem long, but securing meaningful consultation in a community–company relationship that is characterised by substantial power asymmetries and, perhaps historical mistrust, could require far more time and energy to build local resources. Other practical issues that will jeopardise the efficacy of a formal legal or policy framework include identifying exactly who the affected community is. As I discuss in Chapter 4 and the case studies, challenges also lie in contractual mechanics that give concessionaires and financiers the power to make these types of determination.

Another issue, particularly in many African countries, is that large parts of undeveloped greenfield land are held under customary tenure through powerful chieftaincies. In Sierra Leone, the cultural and political leaders of a chiefdom – Paramount Chiefs – act as key gatekeepers to and holders of political, cultural and economic power. They enjoy representation in parliament and direct links to the president,[22] and may have participated in preliminary meetings with the investor to promote the project.[23] Whilst Paramount Chiefs in Sierra Leone are only the custodians of land and cannot lease land to companies without consent from the household heads of the land-owning families, the decision-making power over land lies de facto with them.[24] A corrupt Paramount Chief along with the political elites' desire for a development project can offer almost ideal conditions for a company.[25] These types of power dynamics will frequently result in the poor participation of customary land users and the inability of communities to advocate for their own interests and accept or reject deals.

Unsurprisingly, threats to the implementation of a legal regime that recognises indigenous groups and their consultation rights can also

---

[22] A Hennings, 'Plantation Assemblages and Spaces of Contested Development in Sierra Leone and Cambodia' (2018) 18(6) *Conflict, Security & Development* 521–546.

[23] S Vermeulen and L Cotula, 'Over the Heads of Local People: Consultation, Consent, and Recompense in Large-Scale Land Deals for Biofuels Projects in Africa' (2010) 37(4) *The Journal of Peasant Studies* 899–916.

[24] Ibid.

[25] During a post in Sierra Leone, I heard from local NGOs about specific development projects agreed to by paramount chiefs without the consent of the customary land owners.

arise from companies. In the Indian context, the *Common Cause*[26] case reminds us that private interests have routinely hijacked the implementation of Supreme Court verdicts requiring the free, prior and informed consent of indigenous peoples. In that case, writs filed with the court demonstrated a mining scandal where companies had rapaciously illegally mined iron and manganese ore destroying the lives of indigenous people in the project vicinity. *Common Cause* sent a clear message to Indian policy makers to give serious consideration to mining policy and private governance structures that permit powerful companies to routinely subvert principles of sustainable development including land use. Specifically the Supreme Court directed the government to take a fresh look at national mineral development policy with regard to sustainable development and to produce an effective and implementable policy.[27]

Whilst much attention is, deservingly, placed on the activities of the private sector, frequently forgotten is the role of the state in facilitating these projects. *Common Cause* shines a light on the adverse social effects for indigenous communities resulting from the state's economic participation in these types of development project, its interaction with companies and the judicial support for public–private development activities. Cases such as *Common Cause* and *Reliance*[28] shine a positive light on the work of the Indian judiciary to protect customary land rights in the face of development projects, but this practice is not consistent and has at times, aligned with the neoliberal priorities of the state. So, in the earlier case of *Narmada Bachao Andolan* v *Union of India*[29] the Supreme Court justified the relocation of tribal people to allow for the Sardar Sarovar private dam project in Gujarat. The court stated that that 'populations shall not be removed without their free consent from their habitual territories ... except in accordance with national laws ... or in the interest of national economic development'. Even if they were removed,

---

[26] *Common Cause* v *Union of India & Ors* (2017) SCC Writ Petition (Civ) No. 114 of 2014.

[27] K Bhatt, 'Does India's Draft Mineral Policy Recognise and Implement Public Trust over Mineral Resources and Intergenerational Equity?' (2019) 4(1) *Business and Human Rights Journal* 171–176.

[28] In *Reliance Natural Res Ltd.*, v *Reliance Indus., Ltd.*, (2010) I.N.S.C 374, 95 the court ordered renegotiation of private natural gas contracts. It unequivocally stated that private parties must be held accountable to the constitutional set-up which recognises public trust and intergenerational equity.

[29] (Unreported), 18 October 2000 (Sup Ct (Ind)).

the judges concluded that 'their gradual assimilation into the mainstream of society will lead to betterment and progress ... and would not result in the violation of their fundamental or other rights'.[30] More recently, the Odisha state government has approved a long-term linkage policy permitting state-owned companies such as Odisha Mining, to enter into private concessions with companies with potentially exploitative consequences.[31]

The dire impacts on the recognition and implementation of indigenous land rights that can be partially facilitated through the state's economic participation in these projects is felt not only in India, but transnationally. Illustrations include the Oyu Tolgoi Mining Project in Mongolia and the Bujagali Power Project in Uganda analysed in Chapters 5 and 6. Other examples are seen in the Nam Theun 2 dam in Laos in which the government enjoys a minority shareholding through Lao Holding State Enterprise. Approximately 6,200 indigenous people living on the Nakai plateau were resettled to make way for the reservoir. Two further illustrations can be seen from projects in Ethiopia and Mozambique. The Gibe III Project in Ethiopia is a hydropower project in which the government-owned Ethiopian Electric Power Corporation is a minority shareholder. The project threatens the livelihoods and food security of indigenous peoples' in the Lower Omo Valley. The Mozambique liquefied natural gas project is a joint venture of seven international companies in which the state-owned oil and gas company owns a 15 per cent share. The project company Mozambique LNG has openly admitted that once the project commences its construction phase, it will mark the beginning of industrial-scale land clearance, excavations and earth-moving activities, and the nature and scale of construction activities will not allow for communities to remain and continue their subsistence livelihoods in close proximity to the LNG processing plant.[32] Many other examples can be found on the websites of Banktrack and the IFC's Compliance Advisor Ombudsman. Even in development project cases that have successfully prioritised indigenous peoples' rights to land such

---

[30] *Narmada Bachao Andolan* v *Union of India* (Unreported), 18 October 2000 (Sup Ct (Ind)) 26.

[31] M Mohanty, 'Odisha New Bauxite Linkage Policy to Benefit Vedanta', *The Economic Times* (21 February 2018) https://economictimes.indiatimes.com/industry/indl-goods/svs/metals-mining/odisha-new-bauxite-linkage-policy-to-benefit-vedanta/articleshow/63018502.cms.

[32] Mozambique LNG, www.mzlng.com/News/FAQs/.

as *Endorois*,[33] *Sawhoyamaxa*[34] and *Yakye Axa*[35] analysed in Section 6, state enforcement of those judgments have not trickled down into the domestic sphere. As I discuss in Section 4, that implementation gap also results from a broader legal context of prioritising economic outcomes over alternative land claims in development circumstances.

Analysing the consent strategy under UNDRIP and the practical implementation of that principle when it encounters large development projects reveals a sizeable implementation gap resulting largely from the state–investor marriage of economic interests that keep a project in motion. The result is that in the context of development projects at least, requirements within the UNDRIP for the consent and by implication, protection of indigenous peoples and their *sui generis* culture becomes more of an aspirational principle than a concrete reality. These legal requirements can be overshadowed through economic interest and by implication, related contractual practices that mobilise those interests. This dilution and fragmentation of rights continue as I analyse patterns around the judicial interpretation of rights to property and indigenous self-development in Section 4.

4   Unveiling Legal Values on Implementing Rights to Property through Jurisprudential Strands

4.1   *A Disingenuous Approach to Aboriginal Rights and Title*

Other than consultation, legal strategies around indigenous peoples' rights to land also recognise that development projects on indigenous land can constitute a breach of property rights under international human rights law, should a state fail to protect the communal rights to land of indigenous communities.[36] There is, of course, a strong cultural

---

[33] *276/03 Centre for Minority Rights Development (Kenya) and Minority Rights Group International on behalf of Endorois Welfare Council* v *Kenya*, African Commission on Humans and Peoples' Rights, 46th Ordinary Session, 25 November [2009].

[34] *Sawhoyamaxa Indigenous Community* v *Paraguay* [2006] Judgment of 29 March 2006 (Inter-Am. Ct. H. R. (Ser. C) no. 146).

[35] *Yakye Axa Indigenous Community* v *Paraguay* [2005] Judgment of 17 June 2005 (Inter-Am. Ct. H. R. (Ser. C) no. 124).

[36] *Sawhoyamaxa* case supra n. 34. *Mayanga (Sumo) Awas Tingni Community* v *Nicaragua [2001]*, Judgment of 31 August 2001 (Inter-Am. Ct. H. R. (Ser. C) no. 79), *Yakye Axa Indigenous Community* supra n. 35, *Maya Indigenous Community of the Toledo District* v *Belize* [2004] Case 12.053, Report No. 40/04, Inter-Am. C.H.R., OEA/Ser.L/V/II.122 Doc. 5 rev. 1, 727, and in an African context, the *Endorois* case supra n. 33.

foundation to this right given the cultural importance of land to indigenous communities.

Much scholarship on indigenous rights has gravitated around countries with a settler colonial context such as Canada and Australia. Seminal cases of *Calder et al v Attorney-General of British Colombia*[37] and *Mabo v Queensland (No. 2)*[38] recognised aboriginal rights as a form of property right. These cases marked a watershed in legal practice which sought to distance the law on indigenous rights from the discovery period's discriminatory *terra nullius* doctrine – which gave legal currency to the colonial practice that land was not owned prior to European colonial encounter. In Canada, the modern law of aboriginal rights was codified in Section 35 of the 1982 Constitution Act which recognises and affirms the existing rights of the aboriginal peoples of Canada. In Australia, rights are legalised under section 223 of the Australian Native Title Act 1993 (NTA). The precise scope of those rights and, crucially, how they might compete against development or a development project scenario has been elaborated within judicial decisions.

Close reading of the jurisprudence around development projects and indigenous property rights presents an unfortunate reductive, pro-development tendency. When courts have recognised rights, they have been fragmented and comprised of non-exclusive[39] and site-specific rights to use and access a specific site of land to perform a particular activity. Canadian courts have recognised community and site-specific usufructuary fishing rights in *R v Sparrow*[40] and discreet hunting rights in *R v Powley*.[41] In Australia, section 223 of the NTA also frames traditional rights in terms of specific 'rights and interests' with sub-section 223(2) stating that rights and interests include hunting, gathering or fishing rights and interests, ceremonial rights and access rights.

The key takeaway here is that these free-standing rights are different from a claim to title. The former amounts to rights to pursue activities on the land, whereas aboriginal title amounts to a right to the land itself. As I analyse in Section 5, a claim to aboriginal title involves a claim that the land belonged to the aboriginal claimants, in accordance with their practices, customs and traditions. Considering such a claim in terms

[37] [1973] SCR 313.
[38] [1992] 175 CLR 1 (HCA).
[39] *Delgamuukw*, supra n. 14.
[40] [1990] 1 SCR 1075.
[41] [2003] 2 SCR 207.

cognisable to the common law legal system, it would be akin to a claim to ownership. If established, it should entitle the claimants to conduct any activities permitted by law on the land for as long as their title endures.[42] However, as I discuss, the legal conditions for securing such a title claim are cumbersome with courts taking the lesser route of extending rights to access land to conduct a specified activity, rather than a right to the land itself.

In *Delgamuukw*, Lamer CJ states that the critical concern regarding the source and proof of aboriginal title is one single variable: the legal burden on aboriginal people to establish continuous occupation of lands in question at the time when the Crown asserted sovereignty over those lands. Typically, proof needed for establishing occupation requires both common law and aboriginal perspectives of occupancy.[43] At common law, this amounts to physically occupying and controlling land which is proof of possession at law, and will grant title to the land. In an aboriginal rights context this was interpreted to require proof of exclusive occupation or a 'sufficiently significant connection'[44] between present and pre-sovereignty occupation. As the court noted, 'physical occupation may be established in various ways, including the construction of dwellings through cultivation and enclosure of fields to regular use of definite tracts of land for hunting, fishing or otherwise exploiting its resources with less intensive uses giving rise to different rights'.[45] This was even though, as the court acknowledged, occupancy of this nature itself maybe practically impossible for transient aboriginal and nomadic groups.[46]

So, the 2005 case of *R v Marshall*, involving native fishing and selling rights, asserted that notwithstanding the semi-nomadic culture and lifestyle of the Mi'kmaq community, occasional visits to an area did not establish title; there must be 'evidence of capacity to retain exclusive control'[47] over the land claimed. This was despite strong dissenting opinions that those occupation tests are unsuitable and too strict to be consistent with the semi-nomadic culture of the community.[48] This legal

---

[42] K McNeil, 'Aboriginal Title and Aboriginal Rights: What's the Connection?' (1997) 36(1) *Alberta Law Review* 117–148, 125.

[43] U Secher, *Aboriginal Customary Law*, Chapter 2, supra n. 2.

[44] *Delgamuukw*, supra n. 14.

[45] Ibid, 149.

[46] Ibid, 155.

[47] *R. v Marshall; R. v Bernard* [2005] 2 SCR 74.

[48] Ibid.

position remains. In the 2014 decision of *Tsilhqot'in Nation v British Columbia*,[49] a semi-nomadic group of six bands were granted aboriginal title but were still required to demonstrate occupation in the sense of regular and exclusive land use.[50] In *Tsilhqot'in*, the band were able to meet the legal threshold of regularity, exclusivity and control, however the continued legal application of Western ideas around occupation and possession within the landscape of indigenous rights is damaging for other claims in which groups may struggle to meet these challenging legal tests. This legal desire to break open and unbundle indigenous land into specific rights rather than title to the land empowers conditions through which the commercial exploitation of land and its resources becomes easy and efficient for the state and project developers.

4.2 A Neoliberal Approach to the Development of Aboriginal Rights

Modern jurisprudential strands have also grappled (often with unhappy outcomes for communities) with the situation of aboriginal groups wanting to develop and modernise their traditional rights. The problem for groups wishing to develop existing aboriginal rights is that, in the common law context at least, they need to overcome debilitating tests. Broadly speaking, these tests echo those for proving title, as they require practices and customs to be integral to the distinctive culture of a group[51] and for those practices to be substantially uninterrupted by each generation since sovereignty,[52] thus bringing a fixed quality to them. Burdensome common law requirements like these not only prevent and deter communities from using the formal aboriginal rights regime in those countries to protect their cultures but also stifle the ability of groups to adapt and re-animate those cultures to meet their modern social, cultural and economic needs. In other words, they work to prevent communities from elaborating their traditional rights to land on an equal basis to private developers or the state.

So, when a vibrant, dynamic community that embraces its history seeks to re-animate its customs for the modern day using formal legal methods, claims have been dismissed on the grounds of substantial

---

[49] [2014] 2 SCR 257
[50] Ibid, 2.
[51] *R v Sparrow* [1990] 1 SCR 1075.
[52] *Risk v Northern Territory of Australia* [2006] FCA 404, 97(c); supported on appeal in *Risk v Northern Territory* [2007] 240 ALR 75, 78–79.

interruption of traditional practices.[53] Courts have fixed the acceptable amount of evolution such that a pre-sovereignty aboriginal practice cannot be transformed into a different modern right.[54] In *R v Gladstone*,[55] the courts only recognised a commercial right to fish for the first time, as, 'for the Heiltsuk band trading in herring spawn on kelp was in itself, a central and significant feature of Heiltsuk society and an integral part of their distinctive culture prior to contact'. In *R v NTC Smokehouse*,[56] the courts rejected an application for the recognition of an aboriginal right to exchange fish for commercial purposes as the appellant failed to demonstrate that the tribe had a historic and distinctive cultural right to exchange fish for money.

Lax Kw`alaams Indian Band v Canada[57] also involved the unsuccessful claim to the commercial harvesting and sale of fish within traditional waters which would enable the indigenous community to develop and maintain a prosperous economy and achieve food security. Similar to *NTC Smokehouse*, the court rejected the claim on the grounds that transformation of the pre-contact eulachon fish oil trade into a modern commercial fishery would not be evolution, but the creation of an entirely 'different right'.[58] The courts accepted that aboriginal rights can evolve but that when it comes to evolving the subject matter of the aboriginal right, the situation is more complex. The judicial discussion in the case is highly insightful for illustrating how judges will settle conflicts in property rights. So, a 'gathering right' to berries based on pre-contact times could not, for example, evolve into a right to gather natural gas within the traditional territory. The surface gathering of copper from the Coppermine River in the Northwest Territories in pre-contact times would not support an aboriginal right to exploit deep shaft diamond mining in the same territory.[59]

The judicial discussion in *Lax Kw`alaams* on turning aboriginal practices into natural gas and mining rights betrays an internal judicial conflict – that of developing aboriginal rights so far that they might compete with the rights of the state to develop or sell land for commercial exploitation at a later date. A choice is made to relegate aboriginal rights

[53] *Risk v Northern Territory* [2006] FCA 404.
[54] *Lax Kw`alaams Indian Band v Canada* [2011] 3 SCR 535 51.
[55] [1996] 2 SCR 723.
[56] [1996] 2 SCR 672.
[57] [2011] 3 SCR 535.
[58] Supra n. 54, 59.
[59] Supra n. 54, 51.

so that they can never compete with modern development paradigms and practices. Therefore, commercial rights are afforded legal currency only if there is evidence of those rights existing upon colonial encounter. This process freezes aboriginal rights by reference to pre-contact practices. It denies communities the right to adapt, as all peoples must, to the changes in the society in which they live,[60] and stifles the elaboration of indigenous rights to land and their related socio-economic needs in development contexts.[61] The judicial discussion runs entirely contrary to provisions in article 32 of the UNDRIP on the rights of indigenous peoples to determine and develop priorities and strategies for the development or use of their lands, illustrating a disharmonised and fragmented legal approach to indigenous rights within the law.

One appreciates a few points from these decisions. First, a disingenuous legal structure upon which aboriginal property rights are constructed such that they might never equally compete with the state or a private developer, leaving the future path for developing traditional rights through legal means, unclear. In the context of a state that favours the taxes brought in by a development venture, it is clearly more commercially efficient to package traditional land claims into thinner, limited fishing or hunting rights that are alienable only to the state,[62] rendering them much easier to expropriate. Second, a judicial predisposition towards framing rights in a traditional or overly authentic manner; this points to a parochial view around the development of indigenous land rights and related socio-economic needs in cases that pit development against indigenous peoples' land rights.

Put together, in the context of development, significant strands of common law judicial discourse display themes of fragmentation, unfair outcomes and a bias towards power dynamics that favour commercial interests and economic development over the continuous socio-economic and cultural development of indigenous peoples. Finally, when these judicial practices and the economic realities surrounding development projects are placed against strategies in the UNDRIP for the

---

[60] The dissenting opinion of McLachlin J in *R v Van der Peet* [1996] 2 SCR 507, 632.

[61] For more on this approach see J Borrows, *Recovering Canada*, Chapter 2, n. 3.

[62] This general inalienability gives common law aboriginal rights their unique or *sui generis* status, in contrast to Western property rights in which alienability is a key attribute. PG McHugh, *Aboriginal Title, The Modern Jurisprudence of Tribal Land Rights* (OUP 2011), 334. In *Delgamuukw* supra n. 14, 'this sui generis interest is not equated with fee simple ownership; nor can it be described with reference to traditional property law concepts. It is personal in that it is generally inalienable except to the Crown.'

development of indigenous peoples' rights in development contexts, one appreciates another mismatch between how the law aspires to protect indigenous peoples and the reality of formal law. This again raises the larger question over formal law's ability to regulate this field that I continue to interrogate in the following sections.

5   Underdeveloped Compensation Strategies

Until recently, courts have had difficulty with awarding damages to indigenous groups for extinguishment of rights and interests that are essentially inalienable rights to land with no market value. Interpreting constitutional requirements of just terms and fairness in this context was finally discussed in the recent Australian *Timber Creek* case.[63] There the High Court upheld an award of $1.3 million for non-economic loss that reflects the special significance of the land to an aboriginal community, and the injury caused to that community as a result of land loss. Noting the lack of assistance from previously decided cases outside Australia on the same point of compensation in the context of development projects, the judge located only three cases from the Inter-American Court of Human Rights, *Saramaka*,[64] *Sawhoyamaxa*[65] and *Yakye Axa*[66] that shared aspects with *Timber Creek*. According to the court, those shared aspects included the nature of the people as hunter/gatherers, the central importance of their land and the history of dispossession although there were notable factual differences between *Timber Creek* and those cases.[67] Drawing on those cases the judge upheld the amount of $1.3 million, stating further non-economic loss claims could result from extinguishment if, as in the cases before the Inter-American Court, communities could show ensuing suffering and social disadvantage.

---

[63] *Northern Territory v Mr A. Griffiths (deceased) and Lorraine Jones on behalf of the Ngaliwurru and Nungali Peoples* [2019] HCA 7 on appeal from *Northern Territory of Australia v Griffiths* [2017] FCAFC 106.

[64] *Saramaka People v Suriname* [2007], supra n. 14.

[65] *Sawhoyamaxa Indigenous Community v Paraguay*, supra n. 34.

[66] *Yakye Axa Indigenous Community v Paraguay*, supra n. 35.

[67] For example the size of the land, the fact that the Inter-American Court ordered the return of the land in *Yakye Axa* and that the award in that case included an element for the grave living conditions of the community. In *Yakye Axa*, the state was ordered to pay US $950,000.00 to a community development program. In *Sawhoyamaxa*, a case with almost identical circumstances to *Yakye Axa*, the community was awarded US $1,000,000,000 for non-pecuniary damages in addition to the return of their traditional land. In *Saramaka* an award of $600,000 was made for loss of traditional land.

Whilst these cases show a growing body of jurisprudence examining the quantum for non-economic compensation in circumstances of indigenous land dispossession for development, the legal framework here is strikingly underdeveloped, leaving a large degree of legal uncertainty for similar communities that are vulnerable to development projects worldwide. More efforts in scholarship and litigation beyond these contexts and in the circumstances of development projects would be welcome for developing the legal framework in this area.

6 Poor Enforcement

Whilst the award of a favourable legal judgment is an important part of recognition and implementation, for communities those awards only have meaning if they can be practically enforced. Looking through the cases in which indigenous rights to land have been successfully upheld brings me to my final point on the slow and poor track record of legal enforcement in contexts of powerful development projects.

There are numerous examples of state failure and delays in implementing judgments largely due to the economics and politics of land in these contexts. Examples include the Kenyan government's continued failure to implement the recommendations in the *Endorois* case which include the restitution of traditional land, the payment of compensation and the development of agreements for the sharing of benefits derived from existing tourism and mining activities.[68] Furthermore, the claims of both the *Sawhoyamaxa* and *Yakye Axa* communities, although initiated in the early 1990s, remain largely unsettled. In Suriname, the government still refuses to recognise the indigenous status of some indigenous Maroon communities despite the number of cases from the Inter-American Court recognising the indigenous status of communities in Suriname and requiring the state to implement positive measures such as land demarcation and compensation.[69]

Studies on the adjudication and implementation of indigenous land rights judgments in Paraguay highlight the crucial role that political will

---

[68] The government has followed through on one recommendation – to register a body to represent the Endorois community. This is clearly the least onerous and politically charged of the African Commission's recommendations.

[69] These tensions form the backdrop to agreement-making between Newmont Mining Corporation and indigenous communities in Suriname. The content of the agreement and how it interfaces in positive and negative ways with legal strategies around FPIC are discussed in Chapter 7.

and economic incentives play in the timely and effective implementation of rights.[70] Whilst the Paraguayan state has the technical capacity and professional expertise to demarcate the land and execute the recommended reparations, a favourable policy framework in place to support such efforts, and legally recognises indigenous rights, adjudication and implementation politics show that the state lacks the will to guarantee those rights in a timely or effective manner.[71] The result is a slow and uneven process of state implementation that is reflexive of a deeper power dynamic in which accessing land and natural resources is intimately bound up with the exercise of power and authority.

Lack of state will and aspects of the legal framework discussed above that fail to censure the state in this context also links to a larger issue on legal recognition as 'indigenous' in the context of transnational development projects. Much thinking has already gone into the potential problems and gaps within the definition of who is indigenous. Those include historic remarks from the UN pointing at a bias towards a settler colonial understanding of the term,[72] and related to this, the problematic application of the definition in Africa or Asia.[73] At the same time, arguments also exist against stretching the definition too thinly so that it covers self-identification (which is currently the standard elaborated in the

---

[70] J Correia, 'Adjudication and its Aftereffects in Three Inter-American Court Cases Brought Against Paraguay: Indigenous Land Rights' (2018) 1 *Erasmus Law Review*, 43–56.

[71] Supra n. 70, 55.

[72] UN Sub-Commission on the Promotion and Protection of Human Rights, Prevention of Discrimination Against and the Protection of Minorities: Working paper on the relationship and distinction between the rights of persons belonging to minorities and those of Indigenous peoples, 19 July 2000, E/CN.4/Sub.2/2000/10. The report notes how the approach to the drafting of indigenous rights has been influenced mainly by developments in the Americas, Europe and in the Pacific region making indigenous identity profoundly America- and Europe-centric. The argument is that the legal definition only gives recognition to one type of transnational historical context in which indigenous people are those people beyond Europe who lived in the territory before European colonisation and settlement and to which European settlors crossed 'salt' or 'blue' water to reach.

[73] Report of the African Commission's Working Group of Experts on Indigenous Populations/Communities (2005) 92 noting how the Western understanding of indigenous people as people living in a place requiring the crossing of 'salt water' and an encounter with European colonisation is less useful for recognition and standard setting in Africa or Asia where dominant as well as non-dominant groups within the state can claim indigenous status. B Kingsbury, 'Indigenous Peoples in International Law: A Constructivist Approach to the Asian Controversy' (1998) 92 *American Journal of International Law* 414.

UNDRIP), as well as input from practitioners signalling a policy view that all communities regardless of whether they are indigenous should benefit from special consultation rights.[74] Notwithstanding all of these fragmented understandings around the term, dry academic arguments and differing viewpoints on formal legal status and protection, the most pressing issue for land-connected people is that regardless of nomenclature, they are still denied their rights to land, territories and resources. This is partially a result of the inherent biases within the formal legal framework on indigenous rights in contexts of development (aspects of which I have analysed in this chapter) and the state's economic participation in a project. The result is a legal framework that lacks the capacity to regulate the state in this context.

Ensuring legal definitions are broad enough to capture development projects that occur within and beyond settler colonial jurisdictions is a crucial first step and more policy thinking, scholarship and litigation should go into this. What is more pressing is that processes around development projects are recognised as contributing to vulnerability, sensitive to the vulnerability they pose to land-connected peoples and engage all parties into processes of recognition and implementation at the earliest stages of project design.[75]

7 Deficits in Legal Accountability for Private Actors in Transnational Development Projects

I started this chapter with a discussion on how the UNDRIP has provided some laudable legal strategies for recognising and implementing indigenous peoples' land rights in contexts of development. That said, a major stumbling block in the declaration's efficacy lies in its non-binding quality with some asking whether after more than twenty years of time and effort spent on the development of a non-binding declaration has been time well spent.[76] Frustrations over the non-binding nature of the legal regime may be expressing concern over what these standards practically offer in real-world contexts. Transnational development projects shine a light on one such context in

---

[74] Interview with senior land policy advisor at a government department responsible for delivering aid, promoting sustainable development and eliminating poverty, on file with author.
[75] Recommendations around this are discussed in Chapter 8.
[76] Supra n. 8, 230

which irresponsible concessionaires or financiers are, despite the best international legal efforts to regulate, able to stand behind persuasive declarations that are addressed to states. Concessionaires and financiers can therefore point to structural deficits in which international law has failed to regulate the dilemmas in large development projects. It is too easy to state that these standards simply do not apply to their projects. Or, if a voluntary policy commitment is made to comply with international standards, to unilaterally control and police the strategies through which that commitment is implemented. The result can be the de-rooting of legal standards away from the way in which it was intended when drafted.[77]

In addition to the jurisprudential legal dynamics analysed in previous sections, numerous structural legal issues make the formal legal framework to all intents, largely out of sight and out of mind for the private entities that control and manage large development projects. In this section I analyse some of those structural legal gaps, all of which are fundamentally embedded in international law's allegiance to the binary distinctions between public and private law. When seen through the operation of large development projects, these binary structures of public and private norms and actors fall apart and have, as I discuss here, created some legal structures that have been unhelpful for the development of clear and fair legal outcomes for communities.

As identified in Chapter 2, DFIs are constituted of states, bring crucial policy safeguarding standards to the table and enjoy a high degree of independence in their daily functions as a result of their economically orientated mandates and hands-off agreement with the UN, discussed later in this section. For example, the IFC, as a member of the World Bank Group, shares its mission to reduce global poverty and specifically, to use the private sector as a means to contribute to the Sustainable Development Goals.[78] Yet, its formal mandate conflicts with this goal. Article 1 of the IFC's articles sets out its unique economic motivation to further economic development by encouraging the growth of productive private enterprise in member countries, particularly in less-developed

---

[77] Illustrations of this practice are contained in Chapter 7 on direct agreement-making.
[78] IFC's Contribution to the Sustainable Development Goals (2018). http://documents .worldbank.org/curated/en/209181525334626293/pdf/125915-WP-IFCs-contribution-to-the-SDGs-PUBLIC.pdf.

areas and later refers to its non-political mandate.[79] In practice, it interprets this feature as prohibiting the bank from formally engaging with issues of human rights when carrying out its economic development functions.[80] The EBRD on the other hand expressly includes consideration of human rights (within the preamble of its constitutive documents[81]) but in its mandate, focuses entirely on the development of market-orientated economies with no mention of a poverty reduction mandate.[82] The FMO has an ambiguous social development and entrepreneurial focus.

One point of commonality amongst these institutions is that they subscribe to the IFC Environmental and Social Performance Standards on land and indigenous peoples (or their own derivation thereof), which are also mirrored in wider environmental and social management risk requirements for commercial banks under the Equator Principles.[83] The IFC performance standards are now the gold standard upon which other regional and national DFIs will base their own indigenous peoples' standards within their projects, causing a 'ripple effect'[84] within the private development finance community. For the IFC and other DFIs, the IFC performance standards are a functional tool for managing

[79] Article III, Section 9 of IFC's 2012 Articles of Agreement states that the Corporation and its officers shall not interfere in the political affairs of any member; nor shall they be influenced in their decisions by the political character of the member or members concerned. Only economic considerations shall be relevant to their decisions.

[80] IF Shihata, F Tschofen and AR Parra, *The World Bank in a Changing World: Selected Essays* (M Nijhoff Publishers 1991), 99 in which the bank's ex-general council advises that the articles of agreement explicitly prohibit the World Bank Group from taking non-economic considerations into account in their decisions; referring also to conversation with senior bank staff via webinar, discussed in Chapter 5 within the Oyu Tolgoi study.

[81] Stating that 'the contracting parties, committed to the fundamental principles of multi-party democracy, the rule of law, respect for human rights and market economics'. It welcomes 'the intent of Central and Eastern European countries to further the practical implementation of multiparty democracy, strengthening democratic institutions, the rule of law and respect for human rights and their willingness to implement reforms in order to evolve towards market-oriented economies'.

[82] Article 1 states that the purpose of the bank shall be to foster the transition towards open market-oriented economies and to promote private and entrepreneurial initiative in the Central and Eastern European countries committed to and applying the principles of multiparty democracy, pluralism and market economics. The fact that the EBRD does not have a poverty alleviation goal was expressly referred to in informal conversations.

[83] Chapter 2 explains the Equator Principles.

[84] Cernea, 'The "Ripple Effect"', Chapter 1, supra n. 14.

human rights risks[85] and promoting the SDGs.[86] Yet, in light of the bank's non-political mandate, and as I discuss in later chapters when analysing the practical implementation of these standards into the financing arrangements, priority is always given to the commercial functioning of the bank.

In the context of a remote state or one with a weak or poorly enforced legal framework on land and indigenous peoples, these standards will quickly become the primary legal standards through which public law issues of land, involuntary resettlement and indigenous peoples' rights to land are implemented. Clear evidence of the role that investors seek to play in implementing public law issues on land acquisition and resettlement can be seen in the policy clauses on private-sector responsibilities analysed in Chapter 2. This is an undesirable situation given the structural legal vacuum in which these policies and the behaviours that guide them are implemented and their potential impact on human rights- and land-related issues. For example, policy choices to finance projects defined as 'Category A'[87] for their significant and potentially irreversible social risks and often large-scale evictions go unquestioned. Furthermore, due diligence is not conducted to ensure that a project and its underlying contracts do not displace or incentivise project stakeholders (which can include the state), away from compliance with government's obligations under international and national human rights law.

Yet whilst DFIs and their clients have afforded themselves the right to implement resettlement plans and call them private-sector responsibilities, there is no corresponding international legal liability on DFIs as international organisations comprised of states if their policies result in poor on-the-ground implementation practices or a company decision not to implement a policy in local contexts where it would be prudent to do so. There is also no international legal oversight around how DFIs develop these safeguarding policies and how their corporate clients implement them throughout the project life cycle. This is a worrying regulatory deficit and should concern international lawyers as DFIs are

---

[85] The IFC and the EBRD's performance standards explicitly refer to the protection of human rights, water and climate change within project operations, adding further ambiguity and contradiction to the legal framework.

[86] EBRD website: www.ebrd.com/news/2015/ifis-back-new-global-development-agenda-.html.

[87] The case studies in Chapters 5 and 6 were all Category A projects.

comprised of and funded by member states that have widely ratified the UDHR.[88]

International economic law has limited the legal liability of multilateral DFIs such that they can operate as an independent legal entity pursuing the functions of their articles of agreement. In this regard, the IFC for instance, enjoys a hands-off clause[89] within its relationship agreement with the UN pursuant to which the UN recognises that loan-related matters are to be solely determined by the bank. To this end, the UN regards that making any recommendations to the bank regarding its loan and financing functions would not be sound policy. That laissez-faire relationship gives the IFC sole discretion to determine financing matters and ultimately, power to shape and shift its scope of responsibility in accordance with its mandate and articles of agreement. As discussed above, for the IFC this specifically means no interference in the political affairs of its members and ensuring that all decisions are made on purely economic considerations unless the bank voluntarily permits otherwise through, for instance, the implementation of its safeguarding policies.

One can appreciate how those goalposts can be unilaterally moved according to the policy and internal behaviour and incentives of an institution. The UN-sanctioned mandate creates the conditions under which the IFC can argue that its lending practices will qualify as being immune from suit regardless of how rights incompatible they are. Naturally, this legal insulation undermines the position that international finance institutions such as the IFC have international legal personality, as a result of which they are subjects of international law, and are capable of possessing international rights and duties.[90]

---

[88] D Kinley, *Civilising Globalisation: Human Rights and the Global Economy* (Cambridge University Press 2009); and P Sands and P Klein, *Bowett's Law of International Institutions* (6th edn, Sweet & Maxwell 2009) for discussions on the legal and moral international legal responsibilities of ambiguous international financial organisations.

[89] Whilst the General Assembly is permitted under article 62 of the UN Charter to make non-binding recommendations to its specialised agencies, for the IFC this power is much weaker. Article 2 of the 1947 UN-IFC relationship agreement states that the General Assembly can only make recommendations after prior consultation with the agency, and article 4 further erodes this position through its conclusion that UN recommendations on all loan-related matters are not appropriate and thus, hands off.

[90] *Interpretation of the Agreement of 25 March 1951 between the WHO and Egypt*, Advisory Opinion, Judgment, ICJ Reports 1980 73.

Inroads into injuring the IFC's veneer of immunity have been made in the *Jam*[91] case, at least in respect to the potential for business and human rights litigation in US courts. Originally brought before the IFC ombudsman mechanism, which found a number of counts of non-compliance with the IFC's own performance standards, the case concerned the construction and operation of a coal-fired power plant in Gujarat, India that had destroyed the natural resources relied upon by generations of local families for customary fishing and animal rearing. Rejecting the IFC's defence that it enjoys absolute immunity through the United States' International Organizations Immunities Act (IOIA) of 1945, the Supreme Court decision opens the door for US courts to determine the nature of the IFC's legal responsibilities to communities affected by the projects it finances. There are, however, significant practical limitations to such a route that remain to be tested in lower courts,[92] and the restrictive backdrop of *Kiobel*[93] should not be forgotten in this context. The *Jam* case does however shine a much needed spotlight that requires critical reflection; specifically, on how international law has, through a binary approach to public and private legal disciplines, not kept up with the now-normal blurred operational schemas of law in transnational contexts, enabling a potentially irreconcilable accountability gap for communities affected by transnational development projects.[94]

---

[91] *Jam et al* v *International Finance Corporation* [2019] 586 U. S. is the first case in which project-affected communities have taken legal action to hold an international financial institution accountable for funding a harmful project.

[92] D Desierto, 'SCOTUS Decision in Jam et al v. International Finance Corporation (IFC) Denies Absolute Immunity to IFC…With Caveats', EJIL Talk, 28 February 2019. The decision exposes international organisations to potential liability if their actions fall within one of the exceptions to the Foreign Sovereign Immunity's Act 1976 (FSIA), which includes the exception for 'commercial activities'. However, the court had doubts over whether the IFC's lending activities would constitute purely commercial activities thus furnishing the IFC with a potential defence. In addition, other stringent legal requirements would have to be met including that the commercial activity has a significant connection to the United States and that the lawsuit must be based on the commercial activity itself. The court also opined that if the essence of the lawsuit is based on tortious activity abroad, the suit is not based on commercial activity within the meaning of the FSIA's commercial exception rule.

[93] *Kiobel* v *Royal Dutch Petroleum Company* [2013] 569 US 108.

[94] Acknowledging that international law, and international economic law, is making efforts to amend international treaties to include human rights issues and thus consider issues of precarity. The point is that treaties may have limited impact on the many communities affected by development projects financed and regulated through bespoke public-private

8   Lost in the Space of International Law: The UN Guiding Principles, Transnational Development Projects and Fragmented Private Due Diligence

To recap, the structuring and development of transnational development projects through arrangements in which the project company is a separate private legal entity and the state actively facilitates the project makes it challenging to regulate these projects through through formal 'hard' law for the multiple reasons discussed in this chapter.[95] Concerns around the lacuna in the international legal framework that prevent corporations and private organisations from being held legally accountable for human rights abuses in settings of rapid globalisations are not new, and significant advances have been made towards articulating the human rights responsibility of companies. Yet, there still remains few binding legal obligations on private actors to conduct human rights–related due diligence in these circumstances.[96]

The most prominent initiative is the 2011 UN Guiding Principles on Business and Human Rights (UNGPs), although it is worth noting that the UNGPs did not come out of a black box but are part of a lengthy process to formulate the human rights responsibilities of companies at the international level which started with the Global Compact Initiative.[97] Structured around three pillars: the duty of the states to protect human rights, the responsibility of businesses to respect human rights and access to remedy, the UNGPs go much further than the Compact in their clear articulation of a soft law responsibility on

---

financing methods and the heavily negotiated contractual arrangements that underpin them which do not rely on general treaty arrangements for their legal status.

[95] Referring to the analysis in Chapter 2 on the diminished role of the state in these projects.

[96] There are ongoing discussions regarding the creation of a binding treaty on business and human rights. Some good advances have been made at the state level. In 2017, France took an ambitious step of passing the Loi n° 2017-399 du 27 mars 2017 relative au devoir de vigilance. The new 'duty of vigilance' law imposes civil liability for a parent or subcontracting company's failure to act with vigilance or conduct due diligence. Companies are now legally required to identify risks and prevent infringements on human rights, fundamental freedoms, health and safety, and the environment. Following a national campaign, in 2019 the Finnish government committed to human rights due diligence legislation at the national and EU level. It is still unclear whether this will apply to Finnish companies operating globally.

[97] Launched in 2000 by the UN General Secretary Kofi Annan, the Compact is comprised of ten principles in areas of human rights, labour and the environment. The Compact has more than 13,000 corporate participants and other stakeholders in more than 170 countries.

companies to respect human rights, not to infringe on the rights of others and to do no harm through their operations. Its wording as a responsibility and therefore voluntary initiative, is perhaps an indication that a binding legal obligation on companies was, by 2011 at least, an unrealistic stance and might also lead to opposition from international lawyers concerned over the fragmentation of the international legal framework.

A key success of the UNGPs is the business community's acceptance of the due diligence principle. A corporation is now expected to discharge its responsibility to do no harm through a process of due diligence.[98] Principle 17 sums up what companies should do:

> In order to identify, prevent, mitigate and account for how they address their adverse human rights impacts, business enterprises should carry out human rights due diligence. The process should include assessing actual and potential human rights impacts, integrating and acting upon the findings, tracking responses, and communicating how impacts are addressed.

It is not my intention here to discuss the UNGPs at great length; there is abundant excellent literature on the topic,[99] except to say that in the context of transnational development projects, significant gaps appear that will impact upon an effective due diligence exercise. This is because current due diligence practices unfortunately do not give enough attention to the impact of governance mechanisms (in contract and policy) and the behaviours that implement them as a factor for conducting good human rights due diligence.

This requires a little context as despite developments in the law of state responsibility based on omission of the state to conduct due diligence to prevent human rights abuses committed by private persons, an implementation gap occurs that matters for due diligence. Since the 2001 *Ogoni* case discussed in Chapter 2, a state can satisfy its duty to ensure due diligence by requiring a concessionaire to conduct an environmental or social impact assessment. These assessments are now widely practised internationally as a predictive study that is part of the regulatory

---

[98] S Deva, 'Guiding Principles on Business and Human Rights: Implications for Companies' (2012) *European Company Law* 9(2) 101–109; J Bonnitcha and R McCorquodale, 'The Concept of 'Due Diligence' in the UN Guiding Principles on Business and Human Rights' (2017) *European Journal of International Law* 28(3) 899–919.

[99] N Bernaz, *Business and Human Rights History, Law and Policy - Bridging the Accountability Gap*, (Routledge 2017). Deva, Bonnitcha and McCorquodale, supra n. 98.

approval process for infrastructure and resource extraction projects.[100] Whilst, historically, it can be said that social impact processes which incorporate issues of land and indigenous peoples, were once the orphan of the diligence process,[101] concessionaires are commissioning more social impact assessments or combined environmental and social impact assessments[102] as part of their project financing due diligence loan conditionality, as illustrated in the Oyu Tolgoi project[103] analysed in Chapter 5. The concessionaire, as a result of an IFC loan conditionality covenant, will take control of the assessment process. At this point of interface the state is essentially off the hook and will not look into any of the intricacies in scheduling or substance of the assessment.

Although arguably an overall positive development, the question remains whether development project due diligence on important matters of land, displacement and indigenous peoples are best placed in a document that is controlled by the project sponsors and is characterised by fragmented responsibility, potentially delegated actions to an unknown entity hired by a sponsor, power asymmetries and legal accountability gaps for communities. Substantive issues over the content, timing and overall monitoring and effectiveness of the social assessment shift entirely to the private sphere. As assessed in Chapter 5, concessionaires and financiers will have complete control and discretion of that process through taking decisions under the debt agreements around whether to trigger and implement involuntary resettlement or indigenous peoples' policies in any given project. The turn to 'governance' over 'government', has gone too far.

For example, the IFC has through the revised 2012 performance standards, accepted that FPIC principles will apply to the indigenous peoples' policy standards in the projects they finance, thus providing groups with the right to be involved and consulted within project design and outcomes that might adversely affect them. The standards are clear on the general responsibility of companies to work with affected

---

[100] AM Esteves, D Franks and F Vanclay, 'Social Impact Assessment: The State of the Art' (2012) 30(1) *Impact Assessment and Project Appraisal* 34–42, 25.

[101] R Burdge, 'Why Is Social Impact Assessment the Orphan of the Assessment Process?' (2012) 20(1) *Impact Assessment and Project Appraisal* 3–9.

[102] Esteves, Franks and Vanclay, supra n 100 and conversations with senior lawyers at law firms.

[103] The Oyu Tolgoi Environmental and Social Impact Assessment, August 2012, http://ot.mn/environmental-social-impact-assessment. The IFC website contains numerous examples of social impact assessments for funded projects.

communities of indigenous peoples to ensure a meaningful engagement process, including on achieving FPIC where appropriate.[104]

In terms of defining FPIC for the purposes of the standards, IFC notes that no universally accepted definition exists but that the principle builds on and expands the process of informed consultation and participation. Furthermore, FPIC will be established through good faith negotiation between the client and the affected communities of indigenous peoples. In concrete terms the company is required to find a mutually accepted process, ensure the meaningful participation of the community in decision-making and consultation as early as possible, and evidence agreement between the parties on the outcome of the negotiations.[105] For the IFC, the FPIC process does not necessarily require unanimity and may be achieved even when individuals or groups within the community explicitly disagree. Guidance notes are also clear that FPIC does not confer a veto right. This overall policy position broadly mirrors the jurisprudence on this topic which sees the FPIC process as a method of good faith consultation with communities but ultimately, one that does not prevent projects from taking place. Performance standard 7 also places a reciprocal responsibility on indigenous people to work with the company to establish an agreement process. Requirements exist for parties to agree, on reasonable terms, avenues of recourse such as mediation from mutually acceptable third parties, for when differences of opinion arise and delays occur.[106] There are therefore, some positive aspects to the elaboration of FPIC within the performance standards in their ability to add some flesh to the jurisprudence analysed earlier in this chapter. For instance, clear requirements for early participation and consultation, mutually agreed consultation processes and evidence of agreement-making.

However, some aspects are deeply troubling in their ability to entrench power asymmetries, such as those that place a new responsibility on

---

[104] Guidance note 23 to IFC Performance Standard 7 on Indigenous Peoples.

[105] The guidance notes state that agreement making should be commensurate with the scale of impact and vulnerability and be done through a framework document or plan that identifies representatives of affected communities of indigenous peoples', the agreed consultation process and protocols, the reciprocal responsibilities of parties to the engagement process and agreed avenues of recourse in the event of impasses. Where appropriate, it should also define what would constitute consent from affected communities of indigenous peoples' and that the client should document support for the agreed process from the affected population.

[106] Supra n. 105.

communities to work with the company to establish an agreement process. At the same time, these requirements highlight that no veto right exists, and so unlike commercial stakeholders, communities have no control over project governance and development strategies that will adversely affect them. Examining the details of how the IFC functionalises the FPIC norm also reveals negative aspects. Under the IFC's performance standards, it is clear that project-level FPIC requirements are entirely distinct[107] from any state-level obligations or commitments to ensure that indigenous peoples provide their free, prior and informed consent to matters pertaining to the overall development of indigenous territories in the host country. For diligence purposes, this is an illuminating position. On one hand, the IFC has acknowledged that it can owe direct obligations to indigenous peoples to obtain their FPIC. On the other hand, gaps and uncertainties appear due to the ambiguous policy wording around the different nature of that obligation to the state obligation and how FPIC will be practically implemented through financing instruments, project contracts and thus, the project life cycle.[108] It is these types of uncertain practices that sit, largely free from legal scrutiny, in the shadows of the international legal framework discussed in this chapter. Currently the UNGPs do not grapple with how the practices around the implementation of private policy mechanisms through the project governance framework matter for building a due diligence framework for transnational development projects and indigenous peoples rights to land. Neither do they link the importance of these synergies with land-grabbing debates.

Of course, understanding exactly what the implementation of performance standards looks like in a development-project setting is an opaque business for due diligence purposes given the level of secrecy around private mechanisms. First, it is not fully transparent exactly who the entity conducting resettlement is and the legal relationship that entity has with the project company (is it one of the project sponsors, an entity connected to one of the sponsors or an independent company hired by the project company to conduct an ad hoc process?). This fragmented informal delegation practice makes it challenging for a community or its legal representative to locate and target the right

---

[107] IFC Performance Standard, Guidance note 26 to Performance Standard 7.
[108] Chapters 4 and 5 analyse the effect of some of these private mechanisms in financing contexts and Chapter 7 discusses some positive and negative issues around concessionaires translating and implementing FPIC in direct agreement making with groups.

business entity. Second, resettlement is then conducted under the condition of deficient governance and heightened commercial incentives outlined in Section 2.2. of Chapter 2.

Having taken an overall view of the formal legal framework surrounding transnational development projects, some positive and negative characteristics emerge. The UNDRIP contains a valuable set of legal standards and strategies. Some of the challenges within the current legal framework lie in its aspirational and persuasive legal status that only speaks to states. Whilst helpful, this architecture does not adequately address the legal regulation of transnational development projects involving a consortium of private and public actors. Moreover, when we peel back some of the jurisprudential strands that speak most directly to the circumstances of development projects and upon which the declaration has been developed, the judicial treatment of indigenous rights to land itself looks compromised by a number of factors. Those discussed in this chapter include neoliberal tendencies, fragmentation and underdevelopment of some important aspects like compensation, the easy subversion of rights to executive vested interests and a weak enforcement regime that is arguably hijacked by the powerful political economy of land and its revenue value to the state.

A major issue for rights implementation is that this (albeit limited) legal framework sits on an interface in which the actions of those with power in these projects, e.g. financiers and concessionaires, are left largely unscrutinised. This has been partially enabled by a number of legal features that have allowed governance to go too far. These include a legal framework that is addressed to states, has afforded immunity to actors that could be targeted as they are comprised of member states, does not catch commercial endeavours, and at best, contains a soft law due diligence framework that does not reach far enough to question the fragmented and unclear implementation mechanisms of performance standards that regulate issues of indigenous rights within the universe of transnational development projects. Consequently, the legal framework mapped in this chapter cannot pierce the veil of the operational development project, remaining largely invisible to those with power in these settings.

4

Bridging the Gap through the Elephant in the Room?

Private Mechanisms and Behaviours for Implementing Indigenous Peoples' Rights to Land

1 An Introduction to Private Mechanisms in Development Projects

When placed in conversation with the lacunas in the legal framework discussed in Chapter 3, the ability of state-based remedial mechanisms to address the legal recognition and implementation of land rights for indigenous peoples in situations of development looks constrained. Against this background, the following chapters analyse whether private mechanisms can fill the lacunas in international legal structures and judicial mechanisms. This requires an understanding of, what I term, the elephant in the room: contracts. Concretely, they are the technical contractual ecosystem and behaviours around which those contracts are implemented, and an understanding of how those conditions impact upon indigenous communities. They provide insightful illustrations of the hidden devices or 'codes of legal capital'[1] that are entrenched within legal structures and produce law's values. I consider whether private mechanisms allow communities affected by development projects, to leapfrog over the lacunas in the legal framework analysed in Chapter 3[2] and mediate directly for fairer and more predictable legal outcomes with the concessionaires and financiers that hold much power in these circumstances. Or, do specific aspects of these private mechanisms and the behaviours of implementing actors work to further marginalise indigenous peoples?

---

[1] K Pistor, *The Code of Capital, How Law Creates Wealth and Inequality* (Princeton University Press 2019).

[2] Although not discussed in Chapter 2, indigenous communities will also have problems in gaining access to local courts for example as a result of geography and political and economic conditions. Y Ghai and J Cottrell (eds.), *Marginalized Communities and Access to Justice* (Routledge 2010).

I examine these questions in relation to the following private mechanisms: asset-based lending (so called project finance (PF) mechanisms) involving DFIs and their borrower corporate clients and direct company agreement-making with indigenous groups. My analysis of these mechanisms in this and the following chapters and my recommendations on the integration of indigenous peoples' rights to land into the ecosystem of debt instruments, policy instruments and contractual agreements, contribute to growing thinking around the effectiveness, rights compatibility and social impacts of finance and private remedial mechanisms more generally. As part of the UN's ongoing efforts to implement the UNGPs and, in particular, access to remedy in contexts of business infringements, the Office of the High Commission of Human Rights has, since 2016, been working on an Accountability and Remedy Project[3] aimed at strengthening implementation of access to remedy. The third phase[4] of that project focuses on non-state-based grievance mechanisms – private mechanisms with a mandate to identify and analyse challenges, opportunities and best practices with regard to non-state-based grievance mechanisms that are used by business enterprises to demonstrate global accountability.

1.1   The Effectiveness of Private Mechanisms in Two Fields

Perhaps the most directly relevant discussion and analysis around the effectiveness of non-state-based remedy mechanisms in development projects has come about as a consequence of the establishment of private grievance mechanisms associated with DFIs.[5] Independent Accountability Mechanisms (IAMs) were created to hold DFIs and their borrower clients accountable to the DFIs own policies (for example on involuntary

---

[3] UNGA 'Business and human rights: improving accountability and access to remedy' Human Rights Council 38th Session A/HRC/38/L.18 (2018).

[4] The first phase focused on accountability and remedy-examined judicial mechanisms. The second phase focused on practical steps that could be used to improve the effectiveness of state-based non-judicial grievance mechanisms (for example, OECD national contact point mechanisms), in achieving access to remedy in business and human rights–related abuses.

[5] Created in 1993, the inspection panel of the World Bank was the first such mechanism. Since then there has been a rapid transnational proliferation of mechanisms with more than a dozen created by multilateral development banks such as the IFC, regional development banks like the EBRD and the Asian and African Development Banks. More recently, domestic banks such as the Dutch and German development banks have grouped together to form an independent accountability mechanism.

displacement and indigenous peoples), and to provide access to remedies for individuals and communities that are adversely affected by the projects they finance. IAMs vary in their functions, structures and procedures but they all provide a private mechanism through which those whose human rights have been adversely affected by an institution-financed project, can bring their concerns to the IAM through a complaint. Indeed, DFIs frequently hold IAMs out as a practical tool through which people can obtain justice in countries with weak rule of law and poor domestic judicial mechanisms.

If the IAM determines the complaint eligible it can help the parties find a mutually satisfactory solution through a mediation or problem-solving function or it can conduct an investigation into the DFIs compliance with its own policies (a compliance review), or a combination of the two. These mechanisms constitute a rapidly growing part of an ecosystem of non-state-based remedy mechanisms for achieving access to remedy in contexts of transnational business and human rights–related abuses. Another part of this ecosystem is the trend of direct agreement-making assessed in Chapter 7.

Attempts to evaluate the effectiveness of these mechanisms observe how the legitimacy of many IAMs is questionable as they do not operate in a truly independent world from the DFIs that administer them. Establishing the independence of mechanism staff is critical for building legitimacy and trust in these mechanisms, with some doing better than others.[6] Another important factor for evaluating the legitimacy and effectiveness of IAMs is the heavy environmental and operational constraints imposed on the IAM by the administering DFI. According to a 2016 report from the Dutch NGO SOMO,[7] these constraints impede the effectiveness of IAMs from the very beginning by hindering accessibility; for example, by failing to compel their clients to disclose the existence of these private mechanisms to project-affected people and by limiting the window of time during which an IAM can accept a complaint. The ability of IAMs to offer clear and predictable solutions has also been questioned by findings of an overall failure within DFIs to consistently respond to

---

[6] For instance, the IFC CAO has a more independent process compared to the FMO/DEG complaints mechanism as IFC ombudsman staff are appointed through a nomination process consisting of civil society, academia, and the private sector, whilst the FMO/DEG mechanism contains no selection process involving civil society or other external stakeholders.

[7] C Daniel, K Genovese, M van Huijstee and S Singh (eds.), *Glass Half Full? The State of Accountability in Development Finance* (SOMO 2016).

findings of non-compliance by their IAMs, and when DFIs do develop an action plan to address the findings, adequate consultation is rare.[8] The SOMO report examines the negative aspects of these mechanisms but does not go far enough in considering how the internal contractual mechanisms, incentives and behaviours that mobilise a development project can frequently result in rights-incompatible outcomes that will render the job of IAMs ineffective from the outset.

Finding that the environment surrounding the administering DFI can constrain the effectiveness and accessibility of an IAM does not go far enough to discuss the much larger governance gap of relevance to the effectiveness of IAMs. This gap relates to the first field of private mechanisms considered in this book: the contractual documents that underpin the financing of a development project and the behaviours that surround the implementation of those contracts as they interface with the DFI's own policy standards and issues around the recognition and implementation of alternative land claims rights generally.

There has been little work done to highlight and analyse these governance interfaces[9] and think about how changes to technical documentary structures can assist in creating best practices that could be adopted by all DFIs. Of course, exposing gaps, power dynamics and incentives as well as identifying best practices will not automatically mean that no harm will occur. Yet identification of those hotspots can, alongside advocacy and research around redressing the legal lacunas explored in Chapter 3, motivate DFIs to change their development models and leverage pressure on their clients, knowing, for instance, that contracts and the implementation of policy mechanisms are under scrutiny. In light of the *Jam* case, these linkages could contribute to future legal action. Identifying these interfaces could help IAMs become more effective by bringing these issues to light and allowing them to provide clear recommendations to bank operation teams that can assist in preventing such issues from

---

[8] Supra n. 7.

[9] Although aspects of these linkages between financing, rights and sustainable development have been broadly considered in the context of environmental impacts caused by the Chad–Cameroon Oil Pipeline Project and the Sakhalin-II Liquefied Natural Gas Project in Russia. See D Ong, 'The Implications of the Chad Cameroon and Sakhalin Transnational Investment Agreements for the Application of International Environmental Principles' in S Leader and D Ong (eds.), *Global Project Finance, Human Rights and Sustainable Development* (CUP 2011) and generally M Salomon, A Tostensen and W Vandenhole, *Casting the Net Wider: Human Rights, Development and New Duty-Bearers* (Intersentia 2007).

arriving at an IAM's door. Open discussion around these issues could also bolster IAM legitimacy. In this chapter and the case studies in Chapters 5 and 6, I consider salient aspects of these financial interfaces with debt instruments and project contracts that specifically relate to indigenous peoples' rights to land. These contracts are the elephant in the room.

The second field to which the integrated remedy approach speaks to is that of contractual mediation.[10] Companies might, as a preventative measure, choose to directly enter into negotiations and draft contracts or heads of terms with communities that self-identify as indigenous. Any discussion around the effectiveness of those negotiations and good and bad practices around them must, as a starting point, take into account the power dynamics underpinning those agreements and whether companies have taken measures to address those asymmetries and build early trust. For example, by providing communities with information (before any construction activity has taken place) on the proposed project early on in project design, which must contain details of project ownership and exactly who will be conducting any planned resettlement. Other measures could include the provision of independent legal advice to communities in negotiating a contract through the mechanisms suggested in Chapter 8. Through an examination of different practices of agreement-making, I am interested in analysing whether mediated outcomes might address some of the problems within the contemporary legal framework for development projects analysed in Chapter 3, to provide clearer and fairer outcomes for communities.

1.2   Can Integration of Public and Private Mechanisms Help or Hinder Effectiveness?

Chapter 1 identified one of the core themes in this book as being integration of public and private law mechanisms as part of remedy, with the rationale for that approach stemming from the hyper-plurality and fragmentation of the norms bearing on development projects. Strategies for specific interventions into debt instruments and other project documents which directly embed core UNDRIP strategies around FPIC, for instance, into strategic places within debt instruments and project contracts, are part of a larger dialogue around the incorporation of human rights or ethical standards into contracts. As I map in this

---

[10] C Faircheallaigh, 'Negotiating Cultural Heritage? Aboriginal– Mining Company Agreements in Australia' (2008) 39 *Development and Change* 25.

chapter, debt instruments already contain some points of interface with DFI safeguarding policies on land, indigenous peoples as well as any national laws on those issues. However the effectiveness of these mechanisms is severely constrained through hidden implementation practices discussed in this chapter and the following two, which have not been questioned enough for how they displace indigenous rights recognition and implementation within the contracts that seek to uphold policy safeguards.

For instance, lender decision-making practices written or 'coded' into contracts frequently permits financiers to waive social-impact assessments required under a lender policy at key moments in the debt financing. There is therefore, no obligation on financiers to withdraw funding when the borrower fails to comply with safeguarding covenants in the loan. The practice of financiers is to threaten loan default, negotiate with the borrower[11] and waive the breach. In cases of serious and persistent borrower non-compliance, lenders can trigger a prepayment mechanism within the loan contract requiring the borrower to make a mandatory loan prepayment, thus giving financiers an efficient exit route.[12] An approach which shines light on and addresses these governance deficits and looks to integrate public and private mechanisms could be one way for financiers and concessionaires to walk the talk and set a high standard of compliance with the UNGPs that moves beyond policy dialogue towards more meaningful implementation practices. Making specific interventions into debt instruments and other project documents which redress the current deficits in existing instruments, work to implement human rights–compliant FPIC strategies at key moments in a development project life cycle, and make those strategies public, would be a practical method for demonstrating substantive private-sector commitment to due diligence within development finance practices.

2   Opening the Black Box of Asset-Based Lending

Entering into the universe of project finance (PF) debt instruments might seem a step too far for someone interested in indigenous peoples' rights.

---

[11] P Simons and A Macklin, *The Governance Gap: Extractive Industries, Human Rights and the Home State Advantage* (Routledge, 2014), 149.

[12] Discussions with an interlocutor at an international financial institution.

However, for the reasons discussed[13] and for those that follow, thinking that the private mechanisms at play in finance transactions have little to do with the recognition and implementation of indigenous peoples' land rights, would be an oversight. More broadly, PF itself is a pool of assets which when meticulously organised and negotiated by lawyers is rendered real and productive: giving the asset holder long-term stability, priority and wealth. In doing so, these dynamics can set the stage for long-term expulsions, inequality, human rights and environmental concerns.[14]

Project finance is a large topic to deal with and so I approach my discussion in the following way. In the following sections, I give a brief explanation of project financing and its characteristics. Concretely, I consider how general aspects of PF will interface with and create tension points for the recognition and implementation of alternative land rights claims. I then break down three key moments of a development project in which PF mechanisms and characteristics will interface with indigenous peoples' rights to land. Those moments are the development, financing and construction phases. Each of these stages will provoke varying degrees of contractual and policy interface with land rights issues, and as we move through the stages the tensions between the financing contracts and the borrower's policy commitments on indigenous rights, heightens.

It is, therefore, more informative to discuss those moments by reference to specific PF features (contracts and concrete clauses) that dominate the minds of the sponsors and financiers during those periods and to open up exactly how their features can displace rights recognition and implementation. For instance, aspects of the concession arrangement, construction contract and host government guarantee in the development stage, and in the financing and construction stages, specific features of the debt instruments relating to the implementation of performance standard policies and the completion certificate. Along with this technical analysis, I analyse behavioural aspects of financiers and

---

[13] Including a state that is more enterprise driven than rights driven, the structural and jurisprudential deficits in the legal framework and the proliferation of DFI policies on land and indigenous peoples' that have plugged gaps in domestic and international law and swept issues of indigenous rights and resettlement into the sphere of 'private sector responsibilities'.

[14] Leader and Ong (eds), *Global Project Finance*, supra n. 9, 3 noting how PF mechanisms do affect, both positively and negatively, key social and environmental concerns and is an 'important force at work when human rights and environmental values are at stake'.

concessionaires that can contribute to the recognition and implementation or de-prioritisation of rights within transnational development
projects in unexpected ways. Chapters 5 and 6 then add context to this
technical analysis, looking at specific cases in which the implementation
of contractual and policy mechanisms have interacted with domestic and
international legal norms with tangible consequences for rights recognition and implementation. As I consider in the Panamanian study, these
tensions can become so heightened as to spill over into circumstances
where financiers will completely sideline domestic laws for the protection
of indigenous peoples' rights. Drawing on these findings, in the final
chapter I explore what interventions within the documentation might be
possible to redress adverse impacts.

3   Contractual Interfaces and Behaviours: Tensions between Project Finance Mechanisms, Policy Implementation and Indigenous Rights to Land

It is worth pointing out some general observations on the contractual
documentation upfront that will help to frame my discussions on rights
recognition and implementation. Overall, the legal framework around
project financing operates as a highly insulated private market. As
necessary details for monitoring their investment, lenders are in a
unique position to periodically receive on a confidential basis, non-
public information regarding the project company, its assets and all
potential risks (including social risks) that can impact upon project
development.

These policy requirements translate into the debt instruments at
various documentary locations. Throughout PF documentation are references to resettlement, environmental and social policy standards and
thus, rights to land that would compete with the sponsors' right of way.
Positively, that means that there are contractual spaces that pre-empt and
provide for the inclusion of rights to land other than those of the
concessionaire and financiers. Obviously, the larger governance failure,
discussed in Chapter 2, is that for indigenous land rights issues safeguarding standards can enter into the project life cycle after the sponsor
or its subcontractor has conducted full or partial resettlement. Even if no
resettlement has taken place prior to DFI involvement, and reliance is
placed on policy standards, the mechanisms through which those policy
standards are implemented is unclear as all of this information stays
within the private domain covered by the confidential relationship

between lender and borrower.[15] The lenders and concessionaire will, through the mechanisms discussed in this chapter, clothe themselves through financial terms, with considerable discretion at important points to determine among themselves, how much weight to give to a specific piece of information at a particular time in the financing. As I illustrate, this discretion can entirely erode a human rights–based approach that requires FPIC prior to project approval and construction.

The regimes explored in this chapter constitute a family of contractual and policy instruments that, as shown in the case studies, at times interact with local and international norms and frequently result in the prioritisation of the project's property rights over the rights of indigenous peoples. This is because the PF schema establishes significant dynamics for guiding corporate decision-making, lenders' incentives and subsequently, the recognition and implementation of involuntary resettlement through indigenous peoples' performance standards. As discussed in Chapter 2, lenders in PF settings will take great comfort that the market demands a standardised and thus predictable, precedent-based approach to loan-making that follows uniform, predictable and portable documentation, governed by English law and produced through the London Loan Market Association. Given the global ripple effect of environmental and social safeguarding policies as discussed in Section 2 of Chapter 1 and Section 2.2 of Chapter 2, it is now market practice for loan agreements to contain a covenant requiring the borrower to comply, or cause compliance, with a set of performance standards which will include the FPIC principle. The exact set of standards will depend on the project financiers involved.

Thus, those policies do not sit inside a black box but are implemented within a powerful governance network of debt agreements, project contracts and incentivised behavioural practices. These contracts and behaviours will constrict the applicability and effectiveness of safeguarding policies and ultimately shape whether IAMs can ever be truly effective for policing a DFI's commitment to do no harm. Thus understanding the

---

[15] The lenders are entitled to share information about the borrower and its project-related activities with other financiers in the syndicate on a confidential basis. The loan agreements will contain an express provision for banker–client confidentiality stating that the terms of the loan and other information cannot be disclosed to third parties unless the borrower and lenders have consented to do so. This means that the loan agreements may require amendment so that IAM ombudsman panel members can have sight of the documentation when conducting an investigation. Of course, lenders and borrowers are not legally obliged to agree to any such amendment.

interfaces between the debt instruments and project contracts and policies; where, how and under what conditions those policy commitments currently appear inside the major debt instruments; and project documents regulating a project financing, should be a part of any human rights due diligence assessment for the financial sector. Unfortunately, they are not.

Discerning these interfaces to inform a thorough due diligence of a PF transaction is no easy job and there are many barriers to doing this type of work. They include the confidentiality of the documents themselves, pushback from law firms, concessionaires and financiers to open up these documents for critical analysis and a lack of clarity on who within the project life cycle is conducting the social-impact analysis relating to issues of land rights. An unregulated black box is created. Whilst it is a positive step that environmental and social scientists are conducting assessments, the unknown circumstances around those assessments, how the findings of assessments guide the contractual and policy framework and the overarching fact that these consultants are hired by the borrower and paid by the lenders, have the potential to undermine current safeguarding efforts.

3.1 What Is Project Finance? Secure Investment and Insecure Rights

Project finance refers to a non-recourse- or limited recourse-secured[16] financing structure in which debt, equity and credit enhancement are combined for the construction and operation, or the refinancing, of a particular facility or capital-intensive industry. Under such arrangements, lenders base credit approvals on the projected revenues from the operation of the facility, rather than on the general assets or the credit of the sponsors of the facility, and rely on the assets of the facility, including the revenue-producing contracts and other cash flow generated

---

[16] The financiers will, through an appointed security agent, take various security interests over all of the project's proprietary assets which would include revenue streams. Should the project run into financial difficulty, laws governing secured interests will enable the security agent (on behalf of the creditors) to take control of the project, and if need be, force a sale of the project's assets to recover their losses. To enable this, the security deed will give the secured creditors long-lasting rights to exercise those secured proprietary interests over all other claimants. In some jurisdictions, shielding the creditors' interests might require changes to domestic law that give priority to public auction for property which constitutes rights in rem.

by the facility, as collateral security for the debt.[17] The lenders' reliance on repayment from the constructed and operational assets of the project rather than the sponsors' assets makes PF a long-term and high-risk endeavour, but nevertheless, one which carries high return in terms of fees and interests rates. In this context, lenders and sponsors will look to structure the documentation in ways that incentivise completion, minimise the risk that the project will not come to fruition and maximise financial return for the sizeable risks they undertake.

PF is different from other types of financing due to this limited recourse nature. This means that a lender will have no or as is more usual, limited recourse[18] to the general assets of a sponsoring company (which often owns several projects), in the event of its failure to repay the loan. It is, however, rare that the sponsors will be able to enjoy no recourse. During the high-risk construction period, lenders will usually require some form of limited financial guarantee (called a completion guarantee or debt-service undertaking), obliging the sponsors to guarantee repayment of the lenders' debt payments, should construction not occur by a key date specified in the guarantee. I return to this limited recourse notion in Section 4.3 as it becomes a crucial feature of the documentation in the construction phase with real implications for the recognition and implementation of indigenous peoples' land rights.

So, in a PF transaction, one observes a corporate model where a company, group of companies and in some cases, the state in a minority participatory shareholding, sets up a private limited liability special purpose vehicle (SPV) to develop, construct and operate the project. A legal 'blank slate', the SPV, has no pre-existing assets or liabilities on its balance sheet and is ring-fenced away from the general assets of the sponsor. This structure extends a protective shield to the sponsors from threats to its assets that would otherwise be posed by the project's failure.[19] Moreover, as an entirely commercial endeavour enabled

---

[17] S Hoffman, *The Law and Practice of International Project Finance* (Cambridge University Press 2009).

[18] One way in which this limited recourse is achieved is by ring fencing the specific development project away from the general assets of the sponsor. The project is structured through the incorporation of a shell-limited liability project company that has no existing liabilities and is set up only to own, construct and implement the project.

[19] Leader and Ong, *Global Project Finance*, supra n. 9, 6. The sponsor stands to lose the money it has already invested in the special purpose vehicle, but its explicit understanding with the lender is that the latter will not have recourse against its other assets, a contractual position that is supported by the limited liability of the project company.

through the creation of a private company (with, at most, a state taking a minority shareholding), the company enjoys general protection against international legal principles from piercing its corporate veil.[20] Should the company follow legal principles on FPIC as part of a lender policy programme, for example, as I explore throughout the case studies, the translation of those principles can be sidelined in the routine decision-making, structures and incentives for mobilising a project financing and in some cases de-rooted from their grounding in human rights.

Rather than thinking about the blank sheet SPV structure as an ideal opportunity for the early entrenchment of creative changes for ongoing community engagement into the existing governance arrangements, the shielded, SPV structure results in a heightened project emphasis on fast and predictable revenue flow. Consequently this motivates a 'trickle out' mentality towards any risks, rights or actions that could injure or delay project fruition. This needs a little explaining. In the context of asset-based project financing the process of bankability, as the name suggests, refers to the acceptability to the lenders of a project's overall structure. It is comprised of an analysis assessing the financial and legal status of the borrowing entity[21] and, by inference, a careful analysis of the borrower's rights and obligations under all project documents, including the credit-worthiness of the borrower's contractual counterparties and the legal regimes and contracts applicable to the project. Given that banks will have recourse only to the assets of the project for repayment (or only limited recourse to the sponsor assets during construction), lenders will place much store on a careful analysis of the project company's contractual rights and obligations under key project documents such as the concession, power purchase and construction contract and may require changes to them to meet their financiers' needs. The policy is to ensure that as much risk as possible is passed away from the project company and to the party with the greatest ability to manage that specific risk. This is not trickle-down or trickle-up, but trickle away, often to an entity that is least financially able to deal with that risk.

This pass-through of risks is the ideal outcome for the shareholders as the project company is essentially just a blank vehicle established to develop and operate the project. Subsequently, any risks left with the project company that are not supported by another project party such as

---

[20] Discussed in Chapter 3.
[21] G Vinter, *Project Finance* (Sweet & Maxwell 2005), chapter 6.

the government through a guarantee for example, could become an increased project cost and thus sponsor liability. Through this bankability analysis, shareholders and other parties, including the contractor, operator, suppliers and buyers, will all assume crucial roles for the successful development of a project, making this analysis a crucial process through which banks decide to invest. At present, that analysis does not cover human rights impacts of the project and depending on when the lenders have entered into the project, may include issues relating to land and indigenous communities.

One result of this amplified focus on knowing the key bankability risks is that the initial stages of PF mobilisation will see the sponsor negotiating a raft of complex project agreements in which the project company will be a contractual counterparty. These include agreements securing land ownership (through a concession agreement) and various contracts for the construction, operation and maintenance of the specific asset such as an oil pipeline, mine, dam or road. Contracts will also be required to secure access to any commodities required to operate the asset – for example, water, and sales agreements for the purchase of the relevant end product produced at the project site. Those project agreements will then be secured in favour of the syndicate of commercial banks, DFIs and export credit agencies who will, through a global facility agent, advance funds for the construction of the project in accordance with the terms of the loan agreements. Given the sheer number of lenders involved in disbursing funds, the financing terms that are common to the lenders, many of which will relate to environmental and social issues, will be harmonised into an agreement of common financial terms called a 'common terms agreement'.

The terms of all these project contracts and debt instruments will, in a bankability analysis, be finely tuned to the reality that in a PF transaction the loan is repaid from one source only: a single project. This results in a single-minded emphasis on securing a clear, predictable and stable contractual framework that will mobilise the project on time so that revenue can be generated. The lenders' analysis manifests into various tensions and pressures on the contracting parties which will conflict with indigenous peoples' rights as I illustrate in this chapter. Moreover, as I show later in this chapter and in the context of the Bujagali project, these contractual dynamics can also have enormous ramifications for a country's development agenda through the financial burdens imposed by the project and its financiers in order to create that clear, stable and risk-free investment framework.

Broader research has been undertaken on the human rights impacts of long-term stabilisation of law contractual clauses used in foreign direct investment practices. These clauses provide continued business certainty to corporates investing in long-term development projects through clauses that freeze laws applicable to the project to those in place at the date of signing the investment agreement.[22] They are effectively the lenders' red lines that afford them adequate protection from government actions. Used in concession contracts entered into between states and private investors, studies illustrate how they can trigger normative tensions between different host government obligations to honour contractual commitments on the one hand, and the obligation to comply with evolving international (human rights, environmental) law, on the other. The result is a state that is demotivated from taking action to protect human rights or apply new laws that may affect profits – in other words those clauses can motivate the wholesale trickle out of rights considerations. Tensions such as these emerge through the sponsors' and lenders' economic need to secure protection of their property rights within the state–investor concession. Overlooked is the fact that stabilisation of law clauses can also apply to land and property issues as seen in the following clause from a mining concession in the Democratic Republic of Congo:

> For as long as this present Convention remains in force, the State guarantees to [ ], to its shareholders, to its consultant(s), to its company representatives, to its salaried expatriate officials and to its sleeping partners, stability in the legislation and regulations which were in force on the Date of this present Convention, and in particular in spheres of legal, land/property, fiscal and customs, commercial, monetary, social and labour issues, and with respect to work and residence conditions for foreigners, health and mining regulations.

Positively, as a result of the research and activism[23] around the effects of stabilisation of law clauses, the guidance notes to the IFC Performance Standards now acknowledge that the agreements companies negotiate

---

[22] L Cotula, 'Regulatory Takings, Stabilisation Clauses and Sustainable Development', *OECD Investment Policy Perspectives* (OECD Publishing 2009) 10. A Shemberg, 'Stabilization Clauses and Human Rights – A Research Project conducted for the IFC and the UN Special Representative to the Secretary General on Business and Human Rights', IFC/ SRSG Research Paper, 11 May 2008. In *Global Project Finance,* Leader and Ong discuss the adverse human rights effects of these clauses in the Baku–Tbilisi–Ceyhan Oil Pipeline Project.

[23] Amnesty International, *Contracting out of Human Rights – The Chad-Cameroon Pipeline Project* (Amnesty International UK 2005).

with host governments should not be drafted in a way that could interfere with the human rights of parties potentially affected by the project and the state's bona fide efforts to meet its human rights obligations.[24] However, the notes do not go far enough in recognising the potentially negative impact of PF mechanisms, including the debt instruments, project agreements and the surrounding behaviours, all discussed in this book, that prioritise the consistent advancement of the project over all other considerations. Instead of addressing this governance gap and acknowledging the role of DFIs in creating this gap as they are signatories to the common terms agreement,[25] the guidance notes take a mechanical approach, simply noting that contractual complexities are 'not directly addressed in the performance standards'[26] and fragmenting out all responsibility for those issues to the company that it has financially empowered.

As I illustrate throughout the following chapters, the unique drive in PF for predictable revenue flow and a bankable project creates other tension points. Another common red line for lenders investing in countries seen as posing a high level of political risk will be to seek through the borrower, in addition to the signing of favourable concession terms, additional undertakings from the government in the form of separate guarantees or indemnities, discussed later in this chapter. These types of commercial red line can significantly increase liabilities for the government resulting in anti-developmental outcomes.[27] Aspects of this paradigm are seen in the case study of the Bujagali project in Chapter 6. Since the financial crises these commercial requirements have become stricter, pushing governments towards a paradigm in which bankability is only about mobilising private finance at all costs through the mechanical and algorithmic contractual structures assessed here. Tighter commercial red lines around public-private financing for development projects reduces value for money and leads to increased liabilities or costs on governments or end users. This economic context creates tensions between governments, DFIs and companies by constricting the policy space for them to

---

[24] IFC Guidance Notes: Performance Standards on Environmental and Social Sustainability, 46 specifically referring to stabilisation of law clauses but they could go further to examine the types of interfaces discussed here.

[25] When lending to the project, the DFIs, through the facility agent and security agent, are a signatory to the debt instruments and a beneficiary to all rights under the key project agreements that are secured in favour of the lenders by the security trustee.

[26] Supra n. 24.

[27] As discussed in Sections 3.4.1.2 and 3.4.1.3 and in Chapter 6 on the Bujagali project.

think about bankability in terms of social and developmental outcomes for the country.

In the remainder of this chapter I unpack the three key moments in which PF mechanisms will directly impact upon rights and through sample clauses, illustrate how these global/local tensions practically arise.

3.2   Three Phases of Project Finance Interface with Indigenous Peoples' Land Rights

The following three sections break down the development, financing and construction stages in a project financing to show how specific private mechanisms in those phases will impact upon indigenous peoples' rights to land. Those interface points will be primarily interested in securing the developer's property rights as evidenced through sample illustrative clauses. Seeing where these interfaces take place signals a point where, as I discuss in Chapter 8, advocates, NGOs and others can pursue concrete strategies for better, more predictable and clear inclusion of indigenous peoples' land rights into PF mechanisms.

3.3   Private Documentation and Behaviours Relating to the Three Phases of Indigenous Interfaces

In the development phase I am concerned with how concession contracts (including power purchase agreements which are a form of concession) and host governments support agreements, interface and incentivise or de-incentivise the implementation of land rights. I then deal with the financing and construction phases together for two reasons. First, in a project financing, financing is inherently linked to construction as the loan proceeds will largely be used to pay construction costs. Given PF's limited recourse nature, the concessionaire, financiers and even host government are married through a common incentive of ensuring that the project is built on time, on specification and on price. Through the contractual mechanisms analysed in this chapter they will action that outcome. The result of these mechanisms is to put immense pressure on all stakeholders to construct a project, to the exclusion of other factors.

Second, these powerful contractual incentives to construct can contest with the clearance of land to make way for construction, if clearance has not already taken place. In terms of rights, this means that construction and the forward economic movement and viability of the project is persistently at odds with rights-related issues. These would include recognising that a community is indigenous and is therefore entitled to free, prior and informed consent rights or, pursuant to performance standards, to benefit-sharing agreements that will include continued access to land and natural resources,[28] the negotiation of which will require much time and cost. An obvious choice is created for the concessionaires to ignore the very policies they are meant to uphold. Of course, the financiers at this stage have a conflict of interest as an economic participant and in any event, are not on the ground conducting resettlement. The extent to which the contractual mechanisms steer negative choices are considered here and illustrated in the case studies.

3.4   The Development Stage

The development stage will include a lengthy exploration or prospecting stage and the start of a period in which the sponsor considers how the project will be financed, resulting in the financing stage which sees the negotiation of multiple finance and security documentation. It would be reasonable to assume that the sponsors will, during the initial exploration stages, have encountered local communities within the project area. In principle, this means that they would have had an opportunity to determine the identity of and existing grievances within that community and could have started an early fact-finding and mediation process. There is also the possibility that in this process, the sponsors will have begun to remove local communities, perhaps with the assistance of the state and incentivised by the terms of the concession agreement analysed in Chapter 5. Given that DFIs may not have entered into the project at this early stage, there is no impetus for sponsors to routinely document facts and think about strategies for any indigenous rights claims encountered at this stage even though it would be good practice to do so.

During the development stage sponsors will, however, if the commercial viability of the project is positive, become serious about exploring its economic and technical feasibility. They will look to negotiate as many of the core project documents so that they can approach the financiers with details of the contracts they have secured. At a minimum those will include what are termed as major project documents. These include the concession contract with the relevant state entity, the construction contracts, operating and maintenance contracts, sales agreements and

---

[28] Required pursuant to IFC Performance Standard 7.

contracts for any raw materials required for the project. Those agreements may take the form of initial heads of terms or full-blown negotiated contracts. The sponsors will, later into this stage, make the project documents available to prospective lenders in the form of a preliminary information memorandum (PIM), discussed in Section 3.4.1.1. Should lenders agree to finance, their international legal counsel will perform a thorough bankability assessment of those major project documents including the concession, some of which might require amendment to meet lender requirements.

For any transnational development project, the negotiation of the concession agreement with the government is a critical document in the development stage. A key issue during this period is securing all relevant governmental permits. Depending on the local legal framework this could include environmental law permits; authorisations to explore, exploit and access land (and possibly water); permits for ongoing land access to the site to repair and maintain the project assets for the entire duration of the project which can stretch up to thirty years or more; as well as permission to construct the project facilities and hire international employees. This is, therefore, a critical early stage during which important decisions over land divestment are being made that can irreparably affect communities. The pre-construction development stage would be the optimal point for the concessionaire and the government to start building trust with communities through consultative and mediation processes. Of course systemic changes in national laws are also required that recognise alternative land claims prior to any land disturbance, as suggested in Chapter 8. The Australian case study in Chapter 7 shares some aspects with this type of arrangement; however, the conditions for facilitating this model are challenging, especially in the context of poor domestic law and in rural areas.

Unsurprisingly, regular practice in this field does not reflect this pre-emptive and progressive model. Evidence of this is seen in the following sample contractual clauses which make little clear reference for accommodating land rights that can compete with the rights of the concessionaire. In the context of the weak legal framework outlined in Chapter 3 and the reduced post-financial-crisis policy space within which governments can negotiate bankability requirements, the temptation for the state to ignore, relocate or sacrifice, for business interests, the rights of indigenous people living in the project vicinity is, at this important contractual interface, high.

3.4.1 Existing Practices on Land and Resettlement in the Development Stage

As the following sections analyse, existing contractual practices surrounding the recognition and implementation of competing land rights within concession agreements are patchy and unclear, with the potential to contribute to land grabbing.

3.4.1.1 The Preliminary Information Memorandum A potential early entry point for issues of indigenous rights to enter into the project life cycle is the Preliminary Information Memorandum (PIM). Drafted by the sponsors, this document starts to put together a memorandum setting out key project details, which is then delivered to prospective financiers as a basis upon which they will decide to invest. The aim of the PIM is to sell the project to all the financiers. It will include details of contracts or agreed heads of terms for key project contracts, details of key licensing and permitting provisions that the sponsor has negotiated, along with salient contractual terms. In relation to a concession contract, the PIM will contain information about the host government's grant of rights such as the right to construct the facility, occupy and use land, stabilisation of law clauses and fiscal provisions for the development project.

An analysis of a PIM for a Middle Eastern gas project illustrates the provision of government assurances to assist the sponsor in obtaining the necessary government approvals relating to unoccupied land so that it is available for the project.[29] The PIM therefore provides a tangible document in an early part of the project life cycle in which sponsors could include specific statements to the financiers regarding processes they have commenced for identifying land-related communities on the ground and entering into the participatory dialogue and potential mediation efforts. Sponsors could use the PIM as a concrete vehicle for documenting and mobilising FPIC strategies prior to construction. Unfortunately, PIMs do not contain this type of social information. as illustrated through the PIM referred to for a Middle Eastern gas project.

Given that DFIs will be a recipient of this information and will use the information in the PIM as a legal basis for investment, it would be reasonable for DFIs (that, not forgetting, are comprised of states that have signed the UDHR), to use their leverage to compel their clients at this stage to pursue governance strategies that better recognise and

---

[29] Reference to a PIM relating to a Middle Eastern gas project.

incorporate indigenous rights. Suggestions could be simply for their clients (the sponsor) to include information about social impacts in the PIM mechanism and to demand that the company produce, as an attachment to the PIM, a copy of a local legal opinion and independent NGO report outlining strategies that the client is considering for consultation with indigenous communities before financiers make a decision to invest.

3.4.1.2 Concession Contracts

More and more modern mining laws such as those in India, Australia and Sierra Leone[30] have taken steps to recognise the rights of indigenous peoples or places of religious or cultural significance, placing legal restrictions around mining in those areas by requiring the project company to consult with groups. I have discussed state limitations for implementing consultation strategies in Chapter 3 and now, concerned with whether private mechanisms can fill those legal lacunas, turn to the role of concession contracts in filling or exacerbating these gaps.

In terms of taking the initial step to acquire land for project operations, concessions can oblige the relevant government body to expropriate or divest land from communities. One method of securing the investors' property rights is to place that expropriation obligation on the private plane by incorporating it into the concession, even in cases where occupation has been long term.[31] Long-term usage of land due to its social, spiritual and cultural importance is a defining characteristic of indigenous land usage[32] and this type of clause will empower the state and the company towards the extinguishment of long-term usage regardless of the underlying legal framework.

As the following clause from a concession agreement demonstrates,[33] it is not unusual to see blanket requirements that the state agree to

---

[30] The Forest Rights Act 2009 (India) and provisions in the Mines and Minerals Act 2009 (Sierra Leone) restrict the holder of a mineral right from exercising rights without the written consent of the owner or lawful occupier in respect of land of religious or cultural significance, and of course, the Native Title Act 1993 (Australia).

[31] Reference to oil production sharing contracts in Gabon.

[32] Report of the African Commission Working Group of Experts on Indigenous Populations/Communities (2005) giving numerous examples of long-term generational use of land due to its special cultural and spiritual ties by reference to the San in Botswana and the Masai in Kenya.

[33] Reference to a concession agreement between a private developer and an African state relating to a port development attached to a mine.

prioritise the developer's rights to land and any water resource required to construct a facility:

> The state hereby grants the Investor, without restriction, an exclusive concession over the Industrial Zone and the Port Areas, conferring upon the Investor the exclusive right to develop, design, construct, finance, own, operate and maintain the Port Installations and the Industrial Installations and Equipment...., including, without limitation, the exclusive right to use, without restriction, the lands, waterways and seaways for the purposes of the Port Installations

This remarkable scope can be supported through laws that entitle a licence holder to utilise water and other resources like timber, as necessary for mining operations and erect all machinery, plant and buildings required for operations.[34]

Concession contracts also have the ability to alter domestic law. For instance, mining laws in Sierra Leone require a mining licence holder to pay fair and reasonable compensation for land disturbances, on demand of any owner or lawful occupier of land.[35] Yet, a negotiated agreement can obfuscate this provision with the terms removing the direct legal obligation of the concessionaire to compensate land owners on demand. This means that a confidential agreement can blur what is a clear legal position requiring the *company* to pay compensation and pass that compensation liability onto the state, requiring it to indemnify a concessionaire against any claims by owners and occupiers of land arising during the terms of the agreement.[36] This language imposes a contingent financial liability on the government. It also creates legal uncertainty for those owners and occupiers who no longer enjoy a direct legal right to demand payment from a deep-pocketed concessionaire that by this stage is in de facto and de jure control of the project area. This leaves communities in an unenviable position of having to shuttle their compensation claims between two powerful entities: the state and the concessionaire.

This type of contractual indemnity would result from bankability incentives required for financing a large development project. Those incentives work to drive risks away from the project company and onto

---

[34] Mines and Minerals Act 2009 (Sierra Leone), section 114.

[35] Section 35 of the Mines and Minerals Act (Sierra Leone) states that the company must pay for land disturbances in this context.

[36] Reference is made to a confidential cost-benefit review of concession contracts in Sierra Leone. This provision essentially ousts section 35 of the 2009 mines and minerals law.

the shoulders of the state. In the eyes of the financiers and concessionaire, the state is seen as the best party to control and manage the risk of any competing land claim. Thus having the state indemnify the company for any costs relating to that issue is the optimal way to manage that risk and in so doing, create financial predictability within the contracts. One can appreciate how the financial liability placed on the state through this clause can generate a policy situation in which the state will ideologically align itself with the concessionaire's desire to advance the project. The state's desire to avoid having to indemnify the concessionaire, in conjunction with the concessionaire's sole purpose of advancing the project financing process creates perfect conditions for ignoring the presence and rights of occupiers on the project site, potentially resulting in forced evictions.

In contrast to the negative features of the above concession contracts, others have a slightly more positive approach to competing land claims in the sense that those claims are acknowledged but only through provisions that assume resettlement outcomes and thus still work to prioritise the project's right of way. A relevant clause of a concession referring to resettlement reads as follows:

> The State guarantees to the Investor that:
>
> (i) It is unaware of any fact likely to undermine the implementation of the Project or the Project Activities or the effective completion of the Project;
>
> (ii) If the Investor is not in a position to carry out the resettlement of populations affected by the Project in compliance with applicable World Bank (IFC) Guidelines, the State shall carry out such resettlement in compliance with all applicable World Bank (IFC) Guidelines upon the request of the Investor.[37]

This is an interesting provision for the snapshot it extends into resettlement practices in development project circumstances. The clause tells us that competing land claims are recognised but that they are subordinated to investors' rights with the primary solution being one of resettlement rather than consultation, compromise or agreement-making. The contract then firmly attributes the legal risk and anxieties of making the project site available until effective completion of the project at the door of the state entity, and in so doing gives the concessionaire a priority right of way. It also signals a high degree of fragmentation of rights and

---

[37] Reference is made to a concession contract in an African state.

obligations that blur and move between state and developer, the dynamics of which can prove challenging for accountability efforts. In the above clause, we see that in the first instance, the investor will handle resettlement in accordance with IFC policy. What we see is a negotiated contractual distinction of duties and obligations that harmonises and concretises IFC policy on 'private sector responsibilities'[38] under which the IFC requires its clients to play a defined role in managing resettlement issues.

In this way, the concessionaire has strategically negotiated many benefits that will support the clarity and predictable forward motion of the project. It has apportioned the legal risk of making the land available to the state but has taken over de facto control of a resettlement programme. In conducting resettlement itself the company has contractually navigated itself into a private legal space in which it is challenging to attribute legal accountability on the concessionaire, should those activities be conducted in suboptimal ways. It has secured all of the benefits and incurred no burdens. The provision also foresees the situation in which the investor is not able to conduct resettlement. In that case the investor can compel the state to conduct resettlement. Responsibility then retreats back to the most suitable project participant, the state. It is contractually obliged to conduct resettlement in accordance with IFC standards and could in principle, be held legally accountable should resettlement processes result in forced evictions and other human rights violations. The overall result is a clear legal framework in which the state is an active party for guaranteeing effective completion of the project, but a far more fragmented and uncertain result for resettlement strategies that silently move between the state and developer (at the developer's behest) and with consultation strategies entirely absent.

Analysis of another concession, specifically for the early exploration phase of a coal project in Africa, requires the government and the developer to jointly appoint an independent private resettlement expert or NGO to conduct a resettlement survey during the exploration phase.[39] This survey along with who is conducting it is important as the contract envisages that it will form the basis for any negotiation of a resettlement action plan. Failing to have community participation which is legitimate in the eyes of the community at this initial stage can potentially sow the seeds for conflict throughout the project life. It is therefore problematic

---

[38] Discussed in Chapter 2.
[39] Reference is made to a concession contract in Mozambique.

that the clause envisages the appointment of that expert by two highly enterprise motivated protagonists: the state and developer. A fairer approach should have seen that expert appointed on a tripartite basis to include input and legitimacy from the local community.

The contract sees the costs of this survey passed onto the government. The fact that the survey is done during the exploration phase and thus prior to construction, is a positive aspect. Another positive aspect is that the concessionaire agrees to carry out its resettlement obligations in accordance with 'applicable law'. In the concession 'applicable law' is specifically defined to expressly include common, customary, constitutional and regulatory, including self-regulatory practices or requirements, which would incorporate IFC standards. This type of contractual provision is wider than the previous example that limits resettlement compliance to IFC policy standards. It therefore mirrors the IFC's own policy, requiring its clients to comply not only with the performance standards but also with national law and those laws implementing host country obligations under international law. However, in Section 3.5.4.1 on compliance through lender performance standards, I show how these references to constitutional or customary norms are then rolled back and displaced within the implementation of the financing documents so that the financing documentation only refers to voluntary performance standards, a practice that contradicts the IFC's own policy. The case studies then go on to demonstrate how this rollback is further exacerbated in the practical implementation of policy standards.

3.4.1.3 Host Government Support Agreements and Non-discrimination Clauses
Another noteworthy feature of concession contracts are associated host government support agreements,[40] which provide the concessionaire and financiers with further legal assurances of government support for the project. These commitments are especially sought after in developing countries where financiers will seek an additional layer of comfort from the host government above the concession. Lenders will often insist on an important piece of quasi-security of host government

---

[40] R McCormick, 'Legal Issues in Project Finance' (1983) 1(1) *Journal of Energy & Natural Resources Law* 21–43, noting how the concession is the one asset over which security is not normally created effectively by the security instrument alone. This is because the host government which has granted the licence is able to revoke it in circumstances over which the lenders have little or no control or say. This means that other forms of security and assurance will be required, such as the host government support agreements discussed in this section.

support through which the government will give specific assurances that are clearly framed by reference to the underlying concession. This agreement is driven by the financiers' desire to reduce the political risk associated with a project and to secure particular contractual commitments over certain aspects of the project. Those assurances will generally include a statement confirming that the host government is aware of the financing and has no objection to it, or, positively approves it.

Interestingly, support may extend to an agreement that there will be no change of law that will have a material adverse effect on the specific project; for example, through the introduction of new laws which require changes to the specifications of the project. This type of provision is called a non-discrimination clause, and is often the compromise struck with governments who object to having their hands tied over future policies through, for example, broad stabilisation of law clauses. The compromise is that the government will agree to constraints on its powers on a non-discriminatory basis; that is, it will not, in exercising its legislative powers, discriminate *against the project or the project company* on an *individual basis*, and will therefore be free to pursue any generic human rights- or land-related policies that it desires as part of its normal legislative powers. Whilst this type of private mechanism is not comparable to a blanket stabilisation of law clause that freezes laws applicable to the project to those in place at the date of signing the investment agreement, it can still have a deterrent effect. This is because of the ability of a project-specific non-discrimination clause to support a disciplining effect on the state, much like stabilisation of law clauses but through a project-targeted private mechanism. Here, the state is contractually regulated against making any legal or regulatory changes that could recognise alternative claims to land around the project site, thus 'discriminating' against the specific project through the operation of the contractual term.

From this examination of concession contracts we can observe that contractual terms matter for land rights issues and that practice in this field is hidden, changing and of a slippery nature. Private terms give a high degree of priority and insulation to developers, with provisions that discipline the state towards supporting the concessionaire's vision of private development. Whilst private terms do provide some social regulatory protections through the incorporation of DFI performance standards into contracts, more transparency around the terms of these contracts is needed as well as greater efforts to rebalance power asymmetries. As discussed, this could be done through domestic legislation or regulations that compel the inclusion of clauses that by default, recognise indigenous rights in contexts of development, giving them a veto right prior to construction. Subsequently if the project goes ahead with community support it should require the incorporation of FPIC strategies as a matter of course into concessions and without qualification against the rights of the investor. The renegotiation of older contracts so that they meet these higher standards is also required. DFIs are in a privileged position to spearhead this movement, but the level of economic conflict of interest they face within these projects and the limits of their constitutive mandates are not conducive to such an outcome. In this case, development institutes like the United Nations Development Programme or the Department of International Development might offer more space to promote the renegotiation of contracts for fairer and more rights-compliant outcomes.

Having analysed documentary issues pertaining to the development stage, I now consider how private mechanisms in the financing and construction phases can impact upon indigenous peoples' rights to land.

3.5   The Construction and Financing Stages: Raising the Red Flag

The end of the long development stage will dovetail with the start of another long process: the financing stage. This will see the negotiation and production of the finance documents, the full development of project documentation if not previously done, and amendments to the project documentation if changes are required as a result of the lenders' bankability assessment. Once the company has secured the necessary financing, the construction phase begins.[41] This would, therefore, be a good interface point for the financing syndicate, the environmental and social specialists within the financiers' operations teams and the financiers' lawyers to continue to apply pressure on the borrower for information about competing land claims. In reality however, the construction period constitutes a period of intense financial risk as the lenders have disbursed funds to build the project at a point where none of the assets that will generate return on their investment have been constructed. This results in a heightened need for financing documents to be completed so that money can be disbursed to start project construction. Debt instruments for project

---

[41] Through the concession contract, the project company will have already secured from the government the right to site acquisition as well as permits and licences to ensure site acquisition, access and ability to construct.

financing will contain concrete mechanisms to enable this forward movement and thus pose an overlooked red flag for rights recognition.

At the same time, the construction period presents a special dilemma for land rights issues. This dilemma revolves around the participants' desire to satisfy the conditions for loan disbursement so that money can be quickly released for land clearance and construction and taking the time to build trust and recognise the rights of an indigenous community, who could be entitled to special measures such as FPIC and benefit-sharing arrangements under relevant performance standards. Conducting strategies that satisfy social commitments towards indigenous communities have the potential to slow down construction and operation, eat into the project's bottom line and increase project costs and its risk profile at the most sensitive phase of a project financing: the construction phase.

At this stage, the concessionaire can make determinations about land clearance and, possibly in conjunction with any social consultant it has hired, determine whether indigenous peoples' performance standards will apply. Of course, this may have already happened a few years prior, shortly after the concession contract was negotiated. The point is that day-to-day decision-making around the implementation of standards is concentrated in the hands of sponsors who are guided by a singular motivation to construct the project. This can incentivise the cursory implementation of standards or their entire dismissal, even in situations where it is very clear that investment is being made into a situation of ongoing local conflict and land legacy disputes, some practical examples of which are discussed in the case studies that follow.

For now I build on the kind of private mechanisms that during this stage can work against the recognition of indigenous peoples in a project area, squeeze out the implementation of any preventative but time-consuming trust-building processes with local communities and in a worst case, incentivise eviction processes and increase vulnerability. Specifically, in the construction and financing phases, I am concerned with how commercial interest rates, provisions for liquidated construction damages and completion guarantees (which constitute the main exception to the non-recourse nature of PF) can interface with the recognition and implementation of rights. I also analyse positive and negative aspects of an important mechanism used within all engineering, procurement and construction contracts called the completion certificate. This certificate is drafted by the project company and contains specific factual requirements that the construction contractor must verify, to the satisfaction of the lenders, before the contractor is released from liability and the borrower takes over the constructed facility. Finally I analyse how IFC policy performance standards on land and indigenous peoples' are implemented within the loan agreements.

3.5.1   The Impact of Interest Rates and Liquidated Construction Damages

One customary device for softening the increased commercial risk during the construction phase is for lenders to insist on higher interest rates up to the end of that period with rates ratcheting down during the less risky operation phase. As noted in the complaint letter from the Bujagali project referred to in the preface, the incentives created by these types of debt mechanism can increase the vulnerability of communities to expeditious eviction processes and contribute to a diluted resettlement process, as sponsors become focused on getting through completion quickly so that interest rates can reduce.

Another major preoccupation for sponsors and lenders during financing and construction is ensuring that project costs do not spiral out of control as they will have to procure more funding to fill any gaps. One way they will achieve this is through targeted financial mechanisms that incentivise the construction contractor to meet key dates for construction. So-called liquidated-damage penalties are triggered within the construction contract if the contractor does not complete on time and within price. They constitute an expensive daily rate comprised of all additional debt costs arising from an extended construction period, reasonably foreseeable contractual damages payable by the project company under any sales contracts, fuel supply contracts and other project contracts,[42] and can easily amount to hundreds of thousands of dollars daily.

Designed to compensate the project company for the costs it incurs for delay and ensure the predictable and stable continuation of the project under delay circumstances, the prospect of these hefty liabilities can deter the contractor's focus away from anything that can delay the forward motion of the project, such as talking with communities on the ground and informing the sponsors of any discussions. That these contractual incentives to complete materialise during the period in which land needs to be physically cleared for construction, make them a feature that will weigh against the recognition of indigenous communities within

---

[42] Hoffman, supra n. 17, 178.

development sites and contribute to their land vulnerability when faced with these projects.

I now go on to analyse some of the more specific private mechanisms during this period starting that with a mechanism for mitigating construction risk: the negotiation of a limited form of recourse to the sponsors during the construction period called a completion guarantee or debt service undertaking.

3.5.2   The Hidden Dynamics and Dilemmas of Completion Guarantees

One mechanism that actively contributes to the sponsor's single-minded focus on completion is the completion guarantee. Under this agreement, lenders negotiate a degree of financial recourse to the shareholders. Shareholders will agree to pay the financiers a predefined percentage that is due under the loan agreement in the event that completion does not occur by a specific long stop date.[43] The guarantee covers the lenders in the case of any construction delay or failure as the lenders' agent will be able to call under the guarantee to have the sponsors repay the lenders' outstanding sums upon failure to complete. Given the enormous contingent liability that the guarantee would present on a sponsor's balance sheet and the corresponding impetus for sponsors to reach completion so that the guarantee can be released, the mechanism creates hidden incentives for construction.

A closer look at who might be providing a completion guarantee illustrates how the structuring of a project can directly interfere with rights recognition. As discussed previously, it is not uncommon for the state to be a minor equity participant in the project. This minor equity shareholding can result in major tension between a state's legal or moral responsibility to recognise indigenous rights at the crucial construction period and the myriad of contractual commitments it has made to support the project. Furthermore, when it comes to providing a completion guarantee the financiers will actively treat the state like any other corporate sponsor. For example, as a minority shareholder in the project the sponsors could require the state to financially guarantee a substantial

---

[43] Part of this payment will of course be passed through from any liquidated damages paid by the construction contractor to the project company as discussed in Section 3.5.1. However, a guarantee is of more comfort to the financiers as it is an entirely separate and directly enforceable legal obligation on the sponsors towards the financiers to pay a predefined sum which equals the lenders' debt-service cost.

part of the debt service up to completion. A particularly troublesome example from a completion guarantee for a liquefied gas pipeline project illustrates how the state holding a minor equity interest is required to guarantee 51 per cent of outstanding debt. In parallel, a well-known, deep-pocketed Dutch sponsor with a higher equity stake is required to provide a significantly lower guaranteed percentage. The hidden dilemma that this documentation creates over the state's choice to recognise rights to land or expedite completion so that the guarantee can be released, should not be overlooked in considerations of vulnerability and rights incompatibility.

3.5.3   Completion Certification

An essential part of the debt service completion guarantee discussed in Section 3.5.2, will be the delivery of a completion certificate certifying that all of the requirements of project completion have been satisfied. Delivery of that certificate and the satisfaction of its contents will release the construction contractor from liability under the construction contract and transfer the constructed facility to the project company ready for operation. In this regard, the project completion certificate contains a comprehensive list of technical conditions that the construction contractor needs to satisfy before it can be released from liability. It will include guarantees regarding production testing and statements that all infrastructure has been physically and mechanically completed, for example. Within that certification will be statements about the project being designed and constructed and maintained in accordance with 'environmental and social commitments'[44] which are defined to include the project company's requirements under the loan agreement to eliminate, reduce and monitor the environmental and social impacts of the project in accordance with lender performance standards. Inclusion of these issues within the completion certification is a welcome addition. However, on closer inspection the financiers can, in their sole discretion, determine that the borrower's non-compliance with these social commitments is not material enough to delay construction and can waive those socio-economic requirements as a condition for completion.[45]

Moreover, it is imperative that, if communities agree to the project, time and finances for consultative processes are factored into the project design and the certification process. At present there is a failure for PF

---

[44] Reference to a common terms loan agreement for an oil pipeline project.
[45] Ibid.

documentation to include resettlement costs as a line item in project costs[46] thereby ensuring that resettlement issues are costed into initial project design.[47] As seen in the Mozambique concession analysed in Section 3.4.1.2, costs of resettlement are externalised from the project by passing them onto the government – a practice that is entirely consistent with PF incentives that are focused on pushing risks away from the project company, keeping costs predictable and as close as possible to their initial predicted amounts. Including costs associated with resettlement, such as for the hiring of local experts and mediators and associated legal costs, into the project budget could be one practical way of internalising resettlement and agreement-making costs into the project at an early stage. Ways in which this could be achieved are suggested in Chapter 8.

Section 3.5.4 will analyse the interface of performance standards on indigenous communities and land within the finance documents.

3.5.4   The (Un)happy Interface of Finance Documents with Lender Performance Standards

Given that financiers and concessionaires frequently highlight environmental and social loan conditionality as being a key method through which they conduct due diligence and contribute to the Sustainable Development Goals, an analysis of how policy goals relating to land and indigenous rights interface into finance documentation and the behaviours that guide that interface, is overdue. First, an obvious flaw is the practical reality that DFIs will frequently enter into a project late into the development stage and at a point where the sponsors may already have conducted a resettlement and removal process. Even if a DFI commits funds early on in the project life cycle, it is not clearly understood how and where those policies are implemented into the documentation and what technical and behavioural factors will weigh on their application. I have considered some of those factors in

---

[46] A typical definition of Project Costs taken from a sample common terms agreement reads 'all costs and expenses incurred by the Company in connection with the development, design, engineering, procurement, construction, commissioning and financing of the Project', with no mention of costs incurred in satisfying social performance standards.

[47] This was a recommendation of the African Development Bank in the 'Review of the Implementation of the African Development Bank's 2003 Involuntary Resettlement Policy', Chapter 2, supra n. 24. The World Bank has accepted this point on resettlement costs forming part of project costs within consultation processes; however, the recommendation has not yet been agreed within the environmental and social policies.

Section 3.5.3 on completion certification, but others exist in the important pre-construction period.

3.5.4.1 Promising Compliance through Lender Performance Standards

Environmental and social performance standards will interface with and weave through the landscape of the finance mechanisms, appearing at various junctures throughout the financing phase of a development project. In this section, I explore whether key moments in the debt instruments adequately incorporate the requirements of these policies within the loan so that indigenous rights are recognised and implemented in clear and rights-compliant ways. Those key moments include the specific conditions (called 'conditions precedent') which, when satisfied, automatically mean that the lenders become contractually obliged to make an advance to the borrower. Other key interface moments include the numerous representations of fact made by the borrower to induce the lenders into disbursing funds at various stages throughout the project. The borrower is also required to honour multiple covenants within the debt instruments. These serve as a mechanism for lenders to ensure the continued soundness of its asset, that is, the loan, and to give the lenders specific inside information on, and limited control over, the business of the concessionaire. Loan agreements will contain a generic clause requiring the project company to 'comply or cause compliance with the Applicable Lender Environmental and Social Policies and Guidelines'.[48] Throughout the life of the loan the borrower will make periodic (quarterly or semi-annually) covenants about its compliance with applicable lender environmental and social policies and guidelines, providing ongoing feedback, learning and engagement with the lenders about the implementation of performance standards.

Through standards on land and involuntary resettlement the borrower is expected to avoid resettlement or where avoidance is not possible, to actively incorporate affected communities into projects, to make positive contributions to development[49] and, at a minimum, to do no harm to

---

[48] Reference is made to conditions precedent within numerous common terms agreements for liquefied gas and mining projects.

[49] EBRD 2014 Performance Requirement 5 on land and involuntary resettlement. Its objective is to avoid and mitigate adverse social and economic impacts from land acquisition and to restore, and where possible, potentially improve, standards of living and/or livelihoods. IFC Performance Standards 2012 contain a similar provision requiring that in addition to compensation for lost assets, economically displaced persons

local communities. IFC Performance Standard 7 on indigenous peoples expands consideration of their specific circumstances through developing mitigation measures for the acquisition of land subject to traditional ownership or under customary use. For indigenous peoples the preference is for avoidance. If avoidance is not possible, compensation should be land based or in kind,[50] and the company should offer rights to continued access to natural resources or as a last option, compensation and identification of alternative livelihoods if project development results in loss of land access.[51] Other rights include the fair and equitable sharing of benefits associated with the use of resources central to the identity and livelihood of affected groups,[52] and development of a special indigenous peoples' plan or broader community development plan with separate components for indigenous peoples. In principle, should the borrower fail to comply with the 'applicable policies' on the ground, the lenders' contractual remedy is loan termination, or calling an event-of-default, the implementation of which I also consider.

Compliance with social performance standards will routinely appear within debt mechanisms and will be guided by the routine decision-making of financiers. Appreciating the contractual conditions through which financiers implement social policies tells us about the real ability and effectiveness of these policies to protect indigenous communities' rights to land. Is the implementation of social standards hindered by the placement, timing, motivations and contractual remedies surrounding the financial documentation? At this stage, a few general observations can be made that set the scene and give a flavour of the highly regulated and insulated nature of these policies and the light touch surrounding their implementation within the financial documentation.

In projects in which a DFI is lending in parallel with multiple commercial lenders and other DFIs and thus plural safeguarding policies could apply, the lenders' agent, in consultation with the DFIs, would advise its client on how to coordinate those policies and comply with them all, in line

whose livelihoods or income levels are adversely affected will also be provided opportunities to improve, or at least restore, their means of income-earning capacity and standard of living.

[50] IFC Performance Standard 7 on Indigenous Peoples provides land-based compensation or compensation in kind in lieu of cash compensation where feasible. EBRD's Performance Requirement 7 contains a similar provision.

[51] IFC Performance Standard 7, 14

[52] Ibid and IFC Performance Standard 7, 9.

with an internal coordination agreement.[53] It is then up to the client, usually in conjunction with an appointed private consultant, to make final decisions on implementing those policies on the ground. The relevant set(s) of applicable guidelines are then fleshed out within an environmental or social plan that is developed and drafted by the environmental or social consultant hired by the sponsors and paid for by the lenders.

As I illustrate in the following case studies, the sponsors, on the advice of the consultant they have hired, will exert unfettered control over the determination of important issues such as whether to apply the indigenous performance standard to the policy or to rely on the standard relating to involuntary resettlement which would not require FPIC strategies or the negotiation of special benefit-sharing agreements. If a gap analysis is being conducted, the same applies but given the lack of independence of the consultant that analysis may only serve to justify the sponsors' prior actions. We can appreciate how this technical-legal process ultimately streamlines the set of legal norms that can apply to the project, displacing references to common, customary or constitutional norms that might have appeared within the concession contract, for example, in favour of the self-regulatory praxis of lender performance standards.[54] One set of agreed standards will then become, through the defined terms, clauses within the debt instruments and behind-the-scenes advice of the financiers and decisions of the concessionaire and its private expert, the exclusive standards for disciplining the borrower throughout the project.

Other illustrations of this insulation and disciplining are already visible. We have seen how concession agreements typically only contain references to the property rights of the concessionaire with some more modern concessions referring to World Bank IFC guidelines or resettlement plans, all of which are under the control and influence of the concessionaire. Finance documents continue this demarcation within covenants and representations that require the borrower to comply with a set of lender environmental and social standards throughout the life of the project and over which the lenders and their client have overall control. This position thus works, through practice, to diminish the visibility and influence of local and international law and debunk the

---

[53] Discussed in informal conversations with an IFI interlocutor and further analysed in the context of the Oyu Tolgoi Project in Chapter 5.
[54] Referring back to the illustration from the Mozambique concession contract in Section 3.4.1.2.

DFI's own policy that their clients must meet performance standard requirements and also comply with national law and laws implementing host country obligations under international law. Given the problems with the formal legal regime explored in Chapter 3, it could be argued that the availability of lender standards is, at least, a positive practice. That said, the practices through which land-related considerations interface with the finance documentation at key points, eradicates the practical effectiveness of these standards.

3.5.4.2 Conditions Precedent   Standardised model clauses require the borrower to make a representation that it has satisfied specific conditions – 'conditions precedent', which when fulfilled, mean that financiers become contractually obliged to make an advance to the borrower (the holder of the concession). Conditions precedent provide an insight into what are the most important conditions for the lenders to know before lending substantial funds. In this way, they tell us a lot about lenders' priorities and what they consider to be the core elements for a feasible project that has an excellent chance of viability.

Typical conditions will include delivery of information representing the sound legal condition of the borrower (evidenced through certified copies of the project company's constitutional documents), certified copies of its opening balance sheet to show it has no existing liabilities, details on the economic viability of the project (supported by copies of the executed finance documents), its technical advancement (evidenced through copies of the material project agreements like the concession agreement, host government guarantee, insurance arrangements, for example) and information on project authorisations. There are always specific conditions requiring the lenders to deliver copies of all 'material access rights, water rights, property rights and third party consents or agreements necessary for development, construction or operation or maintenance of the Project'.[55]

To further illustrate, a set of conditions precedent for a fertiliser plant in Oman refers to types of industrial, building, governmental approval required for supply of gas or others feedstock and tax exemptions. There are also provisions for the delivery of specific environmental licences applicable to the company, and of national heritage and cultural approvals, but no specific requirements for the delivery of independent reports on

---

[55] Reference is made to conditions precedent within numerous common terms agreements for liquefied gas and mining projects.

land-related issues or certification that communities have been consulted. In the event that the project is taking place within a country, such as Australia, that contains heritage protection laws and a specific native title regime legally requiring companies to consult and enter into agreements with communities prior to land disturbance, it is likely that those domestic requirements would enter into any financing documents at this stage. Financiers would want to ensure these are negotiated in accordance with legal requirements before drawdown as an insurance against native title claims competing with their private property rights. However for legal regimes with no domestic law requiring private actors to consult with indigenous communities, there are no watertight private mechanisms within the financing documents for socially disciplining lending activities at this crucial pre-drawdown and pre-construction stage. The company could be required to deliver a representation, the content of which is suggested in Chapter 8's recommendations. These types of measures could provide a tangible entry point into an area of legal practice that is highly concentrated in favour of private financial incentives.

Of course, these issues should be seen as part of a chain which brings the same issues into the development stage by making their reporting mandatory requirements of the PIM document that is given to lenders by sponsors early on in the project life cycle. Tracing issues of indigenous recognition and FPIC back to this early development stage through the documentation might encourage all parties to think about them as a core part of the project life cycle. Moving further downstream, thinking must go into how to attach land-related issues to the pre-land divestment stage arise and later on, into financing documentation. In Chapter 8, I describe some national legal and institutional policy reforms that can mobilise this including laws that give indigenous communities the initial right to veto a project and thus place a freeze on land disturbance pending community consent.

3.5.4.3 Event of Default Lite   The main remedy for a breach of covenant is the lenders' right to accelerate the loan, making all outstanding debt and interest immediately due and payable. In the event of a project default,[56] event-of-default provisions will permit the lenders to

---

[56] For non-payment of principal, interest and fees; misrepresentation; consistent non-compliance with specific covenants; failure to reach construction by a certain date; bankruptcy of a major project party such as the construction contractor; state expropriation; and revocation of permits or governmental authorisations.

stop additional loan advances until the problem is resolved, to retain funds within the accounts of the borrower and force them to make prepayments with those funds or permit the lenders to enforce their security. Whilst lenders may point to this remedy as a measure of how seriously they adhere to compliance with environmental and social performance standards, there is no obligation on the financiers to stop funding in the event of such a default. The loan agreement will, instead, as analysed earlier in this chapter, contain mechanisms through which a borrower's non-compliance with lender performance standards is silenced through a forced prepayment or, as is more common, negotiated around in order to bring the borrower back into compliance. The later remedy is meaningless for communities removed from ancestral land that has been built on. It makes nonsense out of the minimum standard in these policies to do no harm and in the indigenous persons' policy, the preference for land-based compensation and continued access rights to natural resources, discussed in Section 3.5.4.1.

Moreover, as compared to other types of default the grace period for remedying a breach of the safeguarding policies is much lengthier. Failure to comply with covenants under the loan, such as ensuring the company's continued access to land or water necessary for the construction of the project, will constitute a far more serious event-of-default with no long grace period. The discrepancy between how the two types of land interests are prioritised within the financial contracts illustrates the real priority of lenders to issues of social policy. This inconsistency substantively undermines the commitment of financiers to policy adherence as a key tool for contributing to sustainable development outcomes and goals. It would not be unreasonable for breach of such social covenants to be treated with the same level of seriousness as failure of the borrowers to obtain access rights for the project's construction – an event which would certainly make lenders think twice about advancing funds.

As has been seen there are multiple structural factors within the debt instruments that code and advance capital and at the same time, dilute the effectiveness of policy standards. First, the overall incentives of PF and the private contractual mechanisms that prioritise these incentives over issues of public interest, discussed at length in this chapter. Second, contractual mechanisms exist but appear too far upstream in the project life cycle to have meaning for indigenous rights. Third, when those mechanisms do appear, lenders pick and choose whether to waive safeguarding protections in the loan agreement requiring the borrower to deliver information, if, for example, delivery of a social-impact assessment or resettlement plan were to hold up disbursement of funds. In circumstances where lenders are keen for money to go out the door to start construction and sponsors are equally keen to release an expensive completion guarantee, it would, from their perspective be reasonable for them to waive the requirement for a resettlement plan or indigenous peoples' plan as a means of conducting their economic functions and staying true to their mandate.

Fourth, there is gap in thinking about how indigenous peoples' reports (and by extension, social-impact assessments) that require the company to implement FPIC processes, early community partici-pation and the negotiation of land access and benefit-sharing agree-ments can be turned into a meaningful condition precedent for first disbursement of the loan and monitored through a specific ongoing covenant on the borrower for the duration of the project loan. The study of the Barro Blanco case in Chapter 5 illustrates a reluctance among DFIs and their counsel to think about how existing financing mechanisms can be tailored to better address these issues. This is because at this point the incentives are simply too loaded in favour of the project going ahead.[57]

Fifth, the resettlement plan or any indigenous peoples' report is pro-duced through an organisation or independent consultant that the bor-rower commissions and the lenders pay for. There is little transparency and therefore public input and scrutiny into the obvious ethnical tension in this private arrangement, its terms and scope. This means that issues around how legal, policy and governance failures contribute to indigen-ous vulnerability will likely only come under scrutiny when things go wrong in a project and the hurdles to a successful ombudsman process have been surmounted by those adversely affected as illustrated in the following case studies.

For a financier whose ultimate duty is to its shareholders and not third parties, it is enough that loan agreements contain mechanisms that incorporate due diligence requirements and attached to them is a loan termination remedy. This type of thinking empowers a culpability-and-discharge model of thinking rather than one that considers how

---

[57] This raises the larger question of whether the finance documents are, in fact, the best point of interface for issues of land and indigenous' peoples or whether more should be done much earlier in project development and certainly pre-financing stages, such as the permit/concession grant stage and the PIM stage. A good solution could be a series of interfaces at all of these stages and thus throughout the project ecosystem.

financiers and their clients can collectively use their power and leverage and the blank slate of the special purpose vehicle to deliver progressive and preventative measures for earlier, independent and thus more human rights–compliant consultation. Going any further than this tick-the-box mentality to reflexively question the whole project design as well as the contractual terms and how issues of sequencing and socially driven incentives are crucial for good practice around policy implementation, is not seen as part of a lenders' formal legal duty. Moreover, looking at these issues and making alterations to development finance practice by proactively working with their clients and governments on these issues, will carry a high risk of affecting a financiers' bottom line of getting money out of the door so that the project can be constructed and thus begin repayment of the lenders' principal and interest under the loan. As highlighted in Chapter 2, prevention means context and context costs time and money.

There is also a backlash amongst lawyers advising companies and lenders against advising their clients to look into how private contract-ual mechanisms are working in practice and how they might be improved to make them more socially compliant. This backlash might result from an overall apathy or fatigue towards issues of human rights among their financier and concessionaire clients. Nonetheless, there is an obvious tension between this reluctance and the job of a legal advisor to actively guide its client through a new legal field, to see problems before they arise and to design contractual mechanisms that work in a preventative rather than reactive (termination) way. There is much secrecy around the contractual conditions and incentives through which DFIs and their clients will implement or de-implement social policy goals. This lack of transparency and reluctance to openly discuss these technical interfaces extends perfect conditions through which power will dictate rights outcomes. So, whilst the addition of these performance standard mechanisms into the loan agreements provides comfort to lenders that they are adhering to human rights and sustain-able outcomes, they are derailed by the proverbial elephant in the room – contractual mechanisms.

PF mechanisms produce a remarkably secure, clear and predictable rule-of-law compliant set of outcomes for developers and in parallel, a weak rule of law in terms of unclear legal outcomes for indigenous communities. The structures extend a silent hierarchy within develop-ment projects in which private norms are automatically prioritised over domestic and international legal norms during the implementation of a project. As they currently stand it is unlikely that technical PF mechanisms will fill the lacunas in the legal framework on development projects and have the real potential to increase the vulnerability of indigenous groups to development projects. Chapters 5 and 6 illustrate three case studies that contextualise this phenomenon, showing how financing mechanisms have impacted upon rights recognition and implementation on the ground for communities in Mongolia, Panama and Uganda.

5

Discretion, Delegation, Fragmentation and Opacity

Impacts of Financing Mechanisms in Mongolia and Panama

This chapter explores how aspects of the project finance (PF) mechanisms analysed in Chapter 4 impact upon the recognition and implementation of communities claiming an indigenous connection to land. Analysis of case studies in Mongolia and Panama examine how various project financing contractual and policy mechanisms impact on the ground with indigenous land rights recognition and implementation, in both positive and negative ways.

Sitting behind each of the case studies are aspects of the weak and fragmented legal framework discussed in Chapter 3. For example, Mongolia and Panama have all ratified the non-binding UNDRIP but display an inconsistent voting record on the ILO Convention 169 and the UNDRIP.[1] The legal framework is also patchy at a domestic level. Mongolia does not have domestic recognition of indigenous peoples whilst Panamanian law does contain some statutory recognition as I will highlight. The point is that regardless of these legal variations, each of the transnational development projects have – through a combination of an enterprise-led state, the PF mechanisms that push forward those enterprises and associated behaviours of the financiers and concessionaires that implement those activities – overshadowed those legal frameworks, such that development projects go ahead on land upon which groups assert indigenous status.

As the studies demonstrate, regardless of the legal framework, PF mechanisms and the contracts underpinning them interface with local and international indigenous rights systems. Consequently, the behaviours of concessionaires and financiers become deeply implicated in the recognition and implementation of indigenous land rights. These opaque mechanisms, and the interfaces and behaviours they create, ought to be

---

[1] Neither Mongolia nor Panama have ratified the ILO Convention, perhaps because of its legally binding nature for states that ratify it, whereas they have adopted the UNDRIP.

given more consideration for the way in which they work hard at prioritising the rights of concessionaires and financiers (discussed more broadly in Chapter 4) and in contrast, the dangers they pose for rights implementation and equitable rule-of-law outcomes under conditions of highly concentrated power. The technical regimes explored in this chapter contextualise some of those in the previous one, examining their implementation in the contexts of indigenous rights claims and vulnerability. They include some of the core project documents in a PF transaction such as the concession, the debt finance mechanisms and the implementation of DFI social policy standards within loans[2] as well as the mechanical and predictable stream of decision-making behaviours that operationalise those contracts and policy tools. These studies give valuable context for illustrating the highly fragmented legal regime applicable to transnational development projects as they interface with indigenous peoples' land rights. Looking at these studies and the technicalities in Chapter 4 reminds us that it is always useful to follow the money (and think around financial streams) in order to understand more about the implementation of rights in contexts of development projects.

1   The Oyu Tolgoi Project in Mongolia

The *Oyu Tolgoi* gold and copper mine is a large transnational development project in Mongolia. Situated in the Southern Gobi region approximately 550 kilometres south of the capital Ulaanbaatar and 80 kilometres north of the Mongolia–China border (the 'OT Project'), the mine has been developed, financed, constructed and operated through a special purpose private project company called Oyu Tolgoi LLC ('OT'). OT is owned 66 per cent by Turquoise Hill Resources, with Rio Tinto owning a controlling share in Turquoise of 51 per cent. The remaining 34 per cent of

---

[2] Given that credit approval was granted to both of these projects prior to 2012, both of the studies analysed here adopt the 2006 IFC Performance Standards and for the Oyu Tolgoi Project, the 2008 EBRD Environmental and Social Policy. Neither of these policies had a clear requirement for free, prior and informed consent involving a process of good faith negotiation, through a mutually acceptable process that is evidenced through agreement-making. This more substantive definition of FPIC was brought into the DFI policy mechanisms through the revised 2012 IFC standards. Nonetheless, the policies on indigenous peoples used in these projects were moving towards recognising FPIC, as they contained mechanisms requiring early and informed community participation in developing a project, ongoing community engagement throughout a project's lifecycle and requirements for good faith consultation.

the project is owned through a minority equity stake held by the Government of Mongolia (GoM) through which it takes royalty and dividends upon successful project construction and operation.

Since 2010, Rio Tinto has also managed the OT Project and during this period, unilaterally conducted the resettlement of 89 herder households prior to the involvement of the PF lenders (which included the IFC and the EBRD),[3] and thus the application of two sets of performance standards on land and indigenous peoples. This resettlement process became the subject of two complaints filed by those herders to the IFC in 2012 and 2013. Those complaints detailed how herders self-identify as indigenous,[4] practising nomadic lifestyle and culture and with sacred relations with water resources such as the Undai River, based on which they claim a right to access the land and water resources. Moreover, the herders claimed that diversion of water resources has 'violated their human rights guaranteed by Mongolian and international legislation, specifically: water rights, pasture rights, livelihood rights...and historical and cultural heritage protection rights'[5] in contravention of the IFC's social safeguarding policies. Nonetheless, by 18 May 2015, up to three years after resettlement, OT's shareholders had agreed upon a plan to progress to the next stage of underground development. By the end of 2015, the PF agreements were signed and following final board approvals, construction began during 2016. First production from the mine is expected for 2020. This brief socio-financial history signals a number of things.

First, Rio has, in this case, unilaterally conducted activities of public interest involving the resettlement of indigenous people, in an ambiguous

---

[3] OT financed the project through a $4.4 billion project finance facility: one of the largest in the mining industry. The facility comprised a syndicate of international financial institutions including the IFC and the EBRD, and export credit agencies representing the governments of Canada, the United States and Australia, and numerous commercial banks.

[4] The complaint states that 'we are Indigenous people who practice nomadic lifestyle and culture, and make livings from herding livestock that are heavily reliant on pastureland yields and capacity. We are legitimate owners of the pastureland with historical rights supported by traditional customs. However, the company does not accept it, yet it provided no justification to further their position. The company thinks we are not ethnic minorities so that we have no right to claim land access. Pasture rights are essential to support nomadic lifestyle and livelihoods infrastructure, but violations of pasture rights protection lead to collapse of traditional lifestyle based on pastoral nomadism'. Second Complaint of herder groups resettled in the Oyu Tolgoi Project, 11 February 2013.

[5] Excerpts from Second Complaint, supra n.4.

legal and regulatory context. Without examining the contracts, policies and related reports, it is not clear under what legal or regulatory instruments Rio has conducted resettlement. Has Rio implemented resettlement through generic provisions in the concession that have delegated legal authority for land issues to the company?[6] As the DFIs did not enter into the project timeline until years after resettlement, was Rio using any policy or regulatory framework to guide its local interventions and were those interventions independently monitored or were they taking place within a legal and regulatory black hole? The concession agreement was signed in 2009, so there was at least a five-year period between the end phase of exploration, the development phase and the start of financing during which time Rio had become so economically sure of the project that it had cleared the project site.

This timeline also tells us something about the breakneck speed at which the project reached financial close and started construction. Whilst this aggressive timeline is routine for lawyers working on these types of project, the economic incentives for lawyers and their clients to negotiate financing documents and start construction are behaviours that will negatively impact upon the implementation of indigenous performance standards in a rights compliant manner. At the same time, a period of five years is a good amount of time in which resettlement and consultation measures can be conducted if factored into the project design much further upstream and not front loaded into the project life cycle – by which time, these sensitive issues can be held hostage to multiple factors. These include internal economic and political pressures to reach financial completion, and an 'approvals culture' in which safeguarding standards are implemented too late, if at all, and are often weighed (in a losing battle) against the financial rewards linked with gaining project approval[7] and getting money out of the door.

This critique is highly relevant for PF mechanisms when land and indigenous issues tend to appear downstream in project design and

---

[6] As illustrated later, clause 5.3 of the investment agreement for the project expressly delegates all matters relating to the reclamation of land to the full responsibility of the investor.

[7] Sarfaty, *Values in Translation*, Chapter 2, supra n. 23 and G Sarfaty, 'The World Bank and the Internalization of Indigenous Rights Norms' (2005) 114 *Yale Law Journal* 1791, referring to the 'approvals culture' which disincentives engagement with social policies that can slow down project approval. Some DFIs are slowly opening up to implementation deficits within their own standards – see the report compiled for the AFDB referred to in Chapter 2, supra n. 24.

within a setting of highly polarised economic incentives as illustrated in Chapter 4. The OT Project study adds new context to these observations bringing them into sharper focus through discussions around the specifics of the project's legal and regulatory framework, or, the constellation of project law that brings the financiers, concessionaire and their lawyers to this brink.

1.1 Connecting Project Finance with the Political Economy of Development in Mongolia

Analysing how technical aspects within PF mechanisms impact upon the recognition and implementation of herders' rights in this case requires some explanation. Over the last two decades, legal reforms in Mongolia have produced a clear and predictable backdrop for investors' rights and a shadowing effect on the state, creating the condition for the entry of private-sector development in the form of transnational development projects. World Bank Group reforms promoted the benefits of private-land ownership by foreign entities in order to mobilise economic development and industry creation in Mongolia through the exploitation of its natural resources. This narrative created the conditions for entry of development projects in Mongolia and associated PF mechanisms.[8]

Consequently, the GoM entered into a catalogue of legal reforms to promote the so-called development policy. These reforms resulted in the state being placed in a precarious position in terms of its future ability and incentives to recognise and implement any rights to land, particularly indigenous/customary rights that might compete with the surge in mineral development and extraction. Reform included the new 1992 constitution permitting land, for the first time, to be held privately and exclusively.[9] The privileging of private, exclusive land rights was further codified into the 2002 Law of Mongolia on Land with article 30 granting rights to business entities and organisations to lease state-owned land for

---

[8] For a good review of development practices in this period see D Sneath, 'Land Use, the Environment and Development in Post-Socialist Mongolia' (2003) 31 *Oxford Development Studies* 441.

[9] Article 6 creates the default position that land, except that in private ownership of the citizens of Mongolia, including land subsoil, forests, water resources and fauna, is the property of the state with article 6(5) permitting for the first time, foreign nationals and legal persons to exclusively use the land for a fee during a specific period of time.

up to 60 years with the possibility of extension. The 2006 Mining Law provides a further formal layer of legal certainty for mining investors specifically by regulating the ability of the state, as owner of all mineral resources naturally occurring on and under the earth's surface in Mongolia, to grant exploration and mining rights to private entities. As is typical for mining laws, the 2006 law sets out the requirements for state grant of an exploration or exploitation licence and guarantees investors the right to enter into an investment (or concession) agreement through which it can make a direct private bargain with the state for exclusive property rights.

This legal framework has been transplanted over the specifics of the historic context of customary land access and non-exclusive co-operative mobile pastoralism in Mongolia,[10] in which local authorities accepted herders' customary rights to land even though they were not formally registered.[11] So whilst Mongolia has adopted numerous international legal instruments, the most directly relevant being the non-binding UNDRIP, domestically it does not recognise its large population of pastoralist groups as indigenous, instead considering them a part of mainstream society.[12] Other ratified instruments include the ICCPR and the ICESCR pursuant to which the state guarantees 'collateral' land rights in the form of rights to culture, food and water.[13] Ostensibly, these instruments provide a robust protective legal framework, but a closer look at the technical aspects of the financing and project documents shows that public law obligations and considerations fragment out and fail to appear in a clear and convincing manner within key project documentation, such as the investment agreement and the project's due diligence social assessment. Whilst consideration of human rights[14] is now a feature of IFC Performance Standards, these factors are, as I assess, only given fleeting examination within the behaviour of those that implement PF documentation.

---

[10] Sneath, supra n. 8 discusses the historical system of collective customary farming and mobile pastoral land use that had developed into part of a larger socio-political system characterised by public land access and non-exclusive co-operative mobile pastoralism.

[11] Reference is made to interviews and conversations with resettled herders in October and November 2015 (translated from Mongolian to English).

[12] Ibid.

[13] Article 10 of the Mongolian Constitution directly incorporates treaties into domestic law.

[14] IFC 2012 Performance Standard 1, 4.

1.2   The Oyu Tolgoi Investment Agreement

Signed in 2009, positively, Rio agreed to make the concession public.[15] Provisions within the contract clarify the rights of Rio over the contract area relating to matters of property, land and water. Concrete terms require that the GoM provide support to the investor in obtaining the permits necessary for the use of land required for project implementation. This includes land needed for locating roads, energy generation facilities or networks for energy transmission, water supply, railroads and communication facilities in accordance with the laws and regulations on land. Clause 5.3 then expressly delegates all matters relating to the reclamation of land to the full responsibility of the investor, thus clarifying the question at the start of this case study about the legal authority under which Rio had conducted resettlement post 2010. This one clause has blurred rights and obligations with respect to land between the state and developer to create the legal conditions for the investor to clear land in an unmonitored and unfettered manner.

A positive addition to the Oyu Tolgoi investment agreement is a generic boiler plate clause providing that any relationship which is not governed by the agreement is to be regulated by the effective laws and regulations of Mongolia, and the international treaties to which Mongolia is a party. The likely aim of this generic contractual mechanism is to prevent arguments on how state–investor agreements constitute odious public law black holes because by adding this clause and making the contract public, the parties have opened themselves up to public scrutiny and potential accountability. However, in the context of indigenous peoples' land rights, this type of contractual mechanism has restricted value as it would not catch the UNDRIP, which does not constitute an international treaty, and Mongolia has not ratified ILO Convention 169.

1.3   Aligning the Implementation of Lender Performance Standards with Market Thinking

As the project moved into the financing stage, governance processes for recognising and implementing indigenous people and their land rights automatically flowed into the debt instruments. Through loan conditionality, OT is contractually required, through a fragmented contractual process within the PF mechanisms that acknowledge a role for

---

[15] Clause 15.21 of the concession agreement states that the agreement shall be made public.

private-sector responsibilities,[16] to take an active role in the planning, implementation and monitoring of resettlement issues, especially in contexts in which government capacity is limited. Given the presence of IFC, EBRD and Equator Principle Financial Institutions co-financing the project, plural sets of safeguarding policies are applied. In the now common practice of co-financing, a number of questions arise. In a syndicate of lenders applying two or more performance standards, how are those standards harmonised? Or if not harmonised, which standard takes priority? And who is making crucial decisions on which policies to apply at this stage and under what parameters?

On the harmonisation point, in the OT Project, in theory, three sets of policies are applied: the Equator Principles, IFC and EBRD policies. Whilst thought has been given to the unclear practices around harmonising policies,[17] the reality is that financiers will expect their clients to comply with all policies applicable to the project.[18] To the extent that there is an inconsistency between those policies, the lenders' agent, in consultation with the DFIs, would advise their clients on how to coordinate those policies through a coordination agreement, as discussed in Section 3.5.4.1 of Chapter 4. Should a commercial bank subject to Equator rules come into the financing plan later on, it can request that the DFIs share due diligence upon payment of a fee.

Having received advice from the lenders' agent on how to coordinate safeguarding policies, it is then up to the company, usually in conjunction with an appointed private expert, to make final decisions on implementing those policies on the ground. At this juncture the dynamics around who is making decisions becomes very opaque. In 2012, after resettlement, Rio Tinto engaged an independent company to retroactively conduct an environmental and social impact assessment (a gap analysis) as a means of satisfying all of the applicable environmental and social requirements relevant to the project. That Environmental and Social Impact Assessment (ESIA) provides insights into the translation and application of the legal framework bearing on the project.

---

[16] Discussed in Chapter 2.
[17] Cernea, 'The "Ripple Effect"', Chapter 1, supra n. 14, AFDB Safeguards and Sustainability Series, Chapter 2, supra n. 24.
[18] For example in the OT Project, as discussed later, Rio's consultant, in principle, looked to satisfy all sets of policies. Also confirmed with informal conversations with an IFI interlocutor.

The ESIA acknowledges the IFC standards as the de facto international environmental and social performance benchmark for project financing,[19] thus prioritising them over any other source of law. In parallel, the ESIA contains no mention of the specific human rights treaties to which Mongolia is party, with the majority of references to mining laws and regulations constituting the legal framework for the project. There are, however, two references to grazing and water rights that might be acquired through customary practices developed over time through accepted patterns of behaviour within societies that become accepted as law within such communities. In this context, the ESIA contains one short paragraph on how customary land and water rights will need to be addressed in the event of displacement or resettlement of herders.[20] The paperwork then unilaterally advises the company that 'PS7 on indigenous people does not apply'.[21] The rationale given is that herder communities are part of the mainstream of Mongolian society from an ethnic and cultural perspective and should be considered as a 'vulnerable group' given the pressures being placed on their traditional lifestyle by economic development and social changes.[22] This technical advice formed the unquestioned basis for Rio's determination that no indigenous people existed in the project area.

This is an almost algorithmic outcome that supports the economic motivations in the crucial construction phase of a project financing, but entirely contradicts local realities illustrated through the herders' complaints that they are indigenous people and ought to benefit from special legal strategies. These legal strategies could take the form of a legally documented agreement requiring the company to consult with herder communities prior to any future project activities taking place on their land, giving herders continued access to special land and water resources and containing benefit-sharing arrangements which provide a higher quantum of compensation. That compensation should reflect the herders' special indigenous relationship to land. Moreover, the poor scheduling and discretionary decision-making through which experts and the concessionaire have determined serious issues of indigenous

---

[19] Environmental and Social Impact Assessment 2012, Oyu Tolgoi Project, 21. http://ot.mn/media/ot/content/page_content/commitments/ESIA/1_ESIA/Introduction/ESIA_OT_A1_Introduction_EN.pdf.

[20] Ibid, 7.

[21] Stating that Performance Standard 7 is not applicable as there are no indigenous peoples impacted by the project.

[22] Supra n. 19, 23.

status and resettlement after the act of resettlement, demonstrate a lack of care towards local communities. These implementation practices look more like new exercises in PF externalisation in which risks are pushed away from the project.

Equally insightful are the behaviours and arguments of the financiers who later invested into the project and were charged with addressing the herders' complaints and translating their calls for indigenous recognition into compliance with the financiers' own performance standards. Discussions with DFI staff reveal institutional tensions and a contradictory approach to questions over what constitutes human rights, poverty alleviation and justice and how those values sit against PF mechanisms and institutional mandates.

It is frequently cited that the political prohibitions within the mandate of DFIs preclude human rights considerations and prevent the implementation of the do-no-harm and human rights narratives within performance standards.[23] Whilst the objectives of the indigenous policy are to do no harm and ensure that the development process fosters full respect for the human rights, dignity, aspirations, culture, and natural resource-based livelihoods of indigenous peoples, neither IFC nor EBRD policy refers to the applicability of the UNDRIP. When this contradictory legal-institutional approach is translated into practice and aligned with institutional mandates, the most decisive consideration for steering the implementation of any human rights and free, prior and informed consent–based policies appears to be economic functionality.[24]

Interlocutors noted how management is aware of the ambiguity between promoting performance policies that speak to the full spectrum of human rights: civil, political, collective, cultural and green rights, and the practical reality that only civil and political rights are directly relevant to the development of market economies and will, therefore, be actively promoted. There is also a superficial insistence that performance standards be referred to as 'requirements' as opposed to 'standards'. The idea is that the terminology of 'requirements' signals a harder internal approach to public policies than milder 'standards', even though regardless of terminology, both policies are subject to the same discretionary

---

[23] Referring to a World Bank Group webinar in which the author participated on 'The Evolution of Safeguards: The Proposed Environmental and Social Framework', on file with the author.

[24] In this section references to conversations refer to informal discussions with financial institutions.

standards, blunt monitoring requirements and event of default remedy discussed in Chapter 4.

Decisions over policy operationalisation are typically based on an economic, new public management method of implementation. Conclusions over whether to make positive development contributions or simply do no harm, will have a direct correlation with the sum the institution is investing in the project and its amount in relation to other lenders as a means of leveraging influence. This socio-economic trade-off is present within IFC standards which state that the level of bank engagement is determined by the nature and scope of the proposed investment.[25] This sentiment was echoed within discussions with interlocutors in which commitment to public policy issues was said to be dependent on project economics and even the type of development project undertaken. The understanding here is that road projects are more development-friendly because communities can use roads, and mines are 'dirtier' and thus require a higher level of social engagement. Thus the scope of social engagement within a development project appears inconsistent and arbitrary, with decisions around whether to trigger a policy and to what extent being routinely balanced against the economics of the project and the relative power of a DFI *vis-à-vis* the other international finance institutions participating in the project. The implementation of these rights recognition and implementation tools are, therefore, deeply intertwined with power and economy.

The effect of these power dynamics for the clear and stable implementation of indigenous rights to land is further seen in a growing trend of financial investors to factually demarcate 'who' is indigenous in the light of poor national legal protection for land-connected groups. PS 7 makes indigenous determination within the project area a matter for the IFC or EBRD's private client who may seek input from competent professionals conducted through the ESIA mechanism.[26] That these private mechanisms set up a governance regime in which private experts (as illustrated in the OT Project), are made crucial for determining this status under contractual terms paid for the concessionaire is concerning for a transparent, rule-of-law based approach to implementing these projects.

---

[25] IFC Performance Standard 1, 19.

[26] IFC Performance Standard 7, 8 'the client will identify, through an environmental and social risks and impacts assessment process, all communities of Indigenous Peoples within the project area.'

Follow-up conversations with financiers on this issue, reveals that they follow the lead of international law when applying its policy on indigenous people. When pushed for details on exactly how they translate that legal position, investors focused on the complexity and fragmentation around indigenous definitions citing the sheer number of interpretations around the definition, some of which I have discussed in Chapter 3. Investors tended to discuss international law on indigenous rights around characteristics of ambiguity, fragmentation and its non-binding quality, and used those characteristics as a guiding logic for conducting their own analysis of indigenous peoples in the project area. One interlocutor translated the UNDRIP's silence around the definition of indigenous peoples (which from a human rights perspective protects a wide number of people that self-identify as indigenous regardless of formal legal status) as legal support for attributing their own policy and institutional definition to the term for a given project. The result is that power and economics can steer decision-making around which groups are indigenous rather than a generous, human rights–compliant application of the rule based on self-identification in favour of those that it is designed to protect.

Taking the example from the OT Project, common to the IFC and EBRD indigenous standards is the use of the term in a generic sense to refer to a distinct social and cultural group possessing the following characteristics in varying degrees: self-identification, collective attachment to geographically distinct habitats and distinct language. The EBRD also classifies as indigenous, people with descent from populations who have traditionally pursued non-wage (and often nomadic/transhumant)[27] subsistence strategies and whose status was regulated by their own customs or traditions. Despite EBRD's classification, Rio, supported by the IFC and EBRD, made the internal decision not to apply the indigenous peoples' performance requirement to the OT Project but to instead classify herders as vulnerable.

Both PS 7 policies contain the provision that indigenous peoples do not lose their status because of dispossession or because they might live in mixed or urban communities visiting their land on a seasonal basis. Yet, interlocutors prefer to use the term vulnerable rather than indigenous to denote those who – by gender, ethnicity, age, physical or mental disability, economic disadvantage, or social status – are more adversely

---

[27] EBRD Performance Requirement 7, 4.

affected by displacement than others.[28] This is justified, perhaps ironic-
ally given the level of erosion of state power achieved through the
contractual mechanisms, on the basis that it (a) protects national sovereignty (in which DFIs do not wish to 'meddle') and (b) avoids further
legal fragmentation within international legal definitions. There was also
the suggestion that indigenous peoples' use of mobile phones means that
they are no longer indigenous and contributed to the overall institutional
choice to classify herders as vulnerable, as confirmed within the project's
ESIA. In practical terms this legal manoeuvring has the effect of short
circuiting some important legal rights that attach to indigenous status,
such as FPIC and the requirement to enter into benefit-sharing arrangements with communities under PS7.

Categorising groups as vulnerable clearly suits the commercial
imperatives of a project financing. There is no need to think about
implementing time-consuming and expensive FPIC process for prior
consultation, benefit-sharing and negotiating compensation, all of which
will result in the delay of money leaving the door for project construction,
potential knock on project delays and cost overruns for the project
company. The practical result is a process that creates highly certain legal
outcomes for developers' rights and correspondingly uncertain legal outcomes for communities. It is likely that similar investor determinations
will be made in future investments within Middle Eastern countries such
as Morocco and Jordan, which contain communities self-identifying as
nomadic and into which future investments are planned.[29]

The OT Project illustrates how technical and behavioural aspects of PF
mechanisms matter for understanding rights implementation and recognition gaps in contexts of vulnerability. Significant recognition and
implementation gaps arise when power is concentrated through PF
mechanisms, placing the legal framework in the shadow. One rule that
is discernible in the transnational normative field of development projects is a sorting and ranking of norms in favour of the concessionaire
and financiers and the overall expeditious forward motion of a project
financing.

---

[28] EBRD Performance Requirement 7.
[29] G Sarfaty, 'The World Bank and the Internalization of Indigenous Rights Norms', supra
n. 7, examining World Bank behaviours around implementation of its indigenous policy
in Morocco, which does not formally recognise Berbers that self-identify as indigenous.
See the wind, waste, solar and power projects project financed by the EBRD in Middle
Eastern countries such as Jordan www.ebrd.com/work-with-us/project-finance/project-
summary-documents.html?1=1&filterCountry=Jordan.

Positively, the IFC ombudsman mechanism through which resettled herders filed their complaints have, years later, been successful in placing pressure on the financiers' client, resulting in the successful mediation of an agreement with resettled herders, the content of which is analysed in Chapter 7. Yet the overall picture tells a story of how voluntary policy norms, contractual terms and economic behaviours routinely sideline human rights norms and indigenous recognition to further entrench existing vulnerability. The lack of open discussion among financiers around the types of embedded structural and behavioural inequities highlighted in this study undermines the effectiveness of their own ombudsman mechanisms through structural alterations to these governance arrangements that might prevent harm from taking place from the outset.

2 The Barro Blanco Project in Panama

The Barro Blanco Hydropower Dam Project in Panama provides a further illustration of PF mechanisms impacting upon indigenous rights implementation. The dam is located on the Tabasara River in the Chiriqui Province of Western Panama. Developed by Generadora del Istmo S.A, a Panamanian developer, the project provides energy for downstream copper mines. German and Dutch development financiers, the Netherlands Development Finance Company (FMO)[30] and the German Investment Corporation (DEG),[31] provided a PF loan of approximately US$50 million with agreement to finance reached in August 2011. Since financing, construction of the project has gone ahead on indigenous territory without the consent of communities, resulting in the flooding and eviction of the indigenous Comarca Ngäbe-Buglé people, one of the seven indigenous groups in Panama. The Panamanian government has actively supported the project despite Panama's ratification of the UNDRIP[32] and domestic law specifically requiring consultation with

---

[30] The FMO is a bilateral development finance institute that is jointly owned between the Dutch government and corporate investors, including numerous large Dutch banks.

[31] The DEG is a privately owned subsidiary of KFW – the Credit Institute for Reconstruction which was formed as a state-owned enterprise as part of the post-war reconstruction Marshall Plan. DEG specialises in long-term loans, project financing and equity investments and has a business model similar to the IFC.

[32] Although Panama has not ratified ILO Convention 169 and thus presents an inconsistent legal policy towards indigenous peoples that is, perhaps, easily sidelined for political and economic expediency.

the Comarca regarding projects which are located within Comarca territory.[33] Complaints lodged with DEG and FMO's ombudsman brought to light how poor implementation within PF mechanisms of DEG and FMO's own environmental and social standards, especially on FPIC, resulted in the lenders failing to comply with their own policies on land, resettlement and indigenous people. This contributed to negative impacts on livelihoods and territories, forced eviction and inadequate resettlement.[34]

In 2014, a group of local and international NGOs[35] in conjunction with a general council comprised of the members of the Comarca Ngäbe-Buglé, lodged a complaint with the independent complaints mechanisms of FMO and DEG stating that the lenders should have ensured that the project respected the rights of the indigenous community, in particular the right to FPIC. They argued that the lenders had failed to comply with standards of direct application to them and in so doing had neglected to ensure the project's compliance with international human rights standards. These lender standards include IFC's performance standards which, for FMO, are the primary standard in guiding client relationships and FMO's implementation of the Dutch banking sector agreement for international responsible business conduct regarding human rights.[36]

---

[33] Law 10 from 1997 requires that specific consultation requirements apply to projects which are located entirely within Comarca and Law 72 of 2008 declares that indigenous land outside the Comarca also have the status of collective land and requires government authorities and private actors to coordinate with the traditional authorities of the indigenous peoples in order to obtain free, prior and informed consent to use the land.

[34] FMO-DEG Independent Complaints Mechanism Panel report No. 1, Barro Blanco Hydroelectric Project Panama, May 2015 www.deginvest.de/DEG-Documents-in-English/About-DEG/Responsibility/Barro_blanco_final_report_EN.pdf.

[35] A group of NGOs were involved including a local movement called M10, and Dutch NGOs SOMO and Both Ends.

[36] FMO Statement 'FMO takes further measures to respect human rights' September 27, 2017 www.fmo.nl/news-detail/816a6094-74a6-4f21-8cc7-a1383375e144/fmo-takes-further-measures-to-respect-human-rights. Since the signing of the Dutch Banking Sector Agreement in 2015 in which the banking sector agreed to increase their responsibility to respect human rights in their investment activities, the FMO has introduced a number of position statements setting out concrete steps for strengthening its human rights policy. These include introducing an early warning system for risk of oppression or violence towards human and environmental rights defenders and strengthening provisions for verifying broad community support and FPIC from people that might be significantly impacted by FMO investments; for example by requiring the organisations to which FMO lends to consult in a meaningful manner with anyone that may be affected by the project. Nonetheless, it is still not clear how these measures are concretely implemented, especially in light of the level of discretion lenders have for waiving covenants (discussed in

The panel assessment is insightful for how it translates and harmonises the growing number of public and private law standards that can bear on investment. Acknowledging that the network of European DFIs (which would include FMO and DEG) has given broad commitments to the UDHR and ILO Core Conventions, the assessment goes onto note the 'complexity of directly applying these instruments to the private sector scenario'.[37] It then swiftly concludes that the lenders' application of the IFC Performance Standards was the appropriate way to align project performance with both the UN Guiding Principles on Business and Human Rights and the OECD Guidelines for Multinational Enterprises.[38] In so doing the panel has placed the IFC Performance Standards on a higher plane in which those standards are held out to automatically provide a rights-compliant policy that subsumes a host of public and private human rights norms. This is a bold position to take in light of the many complaints around the implementation of these standards.[39] This begs the question of whether these standards can, without fundamental changes to the governance frameworks through which they are implemented, ever be human rights compliant in a local context given the routine nature of policy failure in this field.[40]

Chapter 4) and the lack of information on land and indigenous issues that lenders have at the financing stage, despite having the power and leverage to ask their client to produce this information. As for early warning systems, it is unclear how these are implemented in light of the continued investment of FMO into high-risk projects such as the Honduran hydro project linked to the murder of activist Berta Cáceres in 2016.

[37] Supra n. 34, 11.

[38] Noting how it 'feels that it is appropriate to use the framework of the UN Guiding Principles on Business and Human Rights – which were adopted shortly before the project agreement in this case – to assess the degree to which the lenders acted to support or respect the relevant human rights principles contained in these instruments'. The panel then sets out a number of administrative procedural steps for implementing the UNGPs which include identifying and assessing human rights impacts, integrating findings, taking action and conducting effective due diligence and monitoring processes.

[39] The website of the IFC Ombudsman is a growing database of complaints lodged by communities affected by IFC financed projects and is a good source of information on the routine violation of the IFC's own policy standards www.cao-ombudsman.org/.

[40] This also raises the question of exactly who these independent accountability mechanisms are ultimately designed to serve: communities or the 'client' of the panel members, the DFI. Clearly, the procedures around the appointment of IAM members are crucial for ensuring the independence and legitimacy of the mechanism, as discussed in Chapter 4. In this regard it is worth recalling that unlike the IFC CAO, the FMO/DEG mechanism contains no selection process involving civil society or other external stakeholders. With all of these mechanisms it should be noted that the DFI pays the salary of the panel members.

What followed was a review of whether DEG and FMO had fully complied with those polices. This required an analysis of the ways in which the IFC's indigenous safeguards policy had been implemented within the project financing. Specific gaps in timing and substance were found in relation to the appraisal of issues around land acquisition and the use and the quality of consultations with affected communities that jeopardised the recognition and implementation of the Comarca Ngäbe-Buglé's customary land rights.

2.1   Deficient Lender Due Diligence, Project Financing and International Law

As documented in the timeline to the project within the panel assessment, lenders were aware of basic issues relating to indigenous people and resettlement as far back as 2009. This is evidenced through various internal bank memos to FMO's investment committee and board minutes released to the panel members. In this paperwork, the project was acknowledged as involving business activities with potentially significant adverse environmental or social risks and/or impacts that are diverse, irreversible or unprecedented (called a Category A project under the performance standards).

Whilst classifying the project as Category A, the memo goes onto suggest that this poses 'no significant issues',[41] and as a remedial measure simply suggests that an indigenous peoples' report should be a condition precedent to first disbursement. Further letters from the FMO board disclose the necessity of 'comfort'; that the 'NGO issues'[42] have been satisfactorily addressed and agreed in a protocol between lenders. The panel report also refers to several local protests that started in 2011. These included a blockade of the Inter-American Highway in front of the project area and contestations over the lack of clarity over whether the land concession had considered the traditional land rights of the Comarca of Ngöbe-Buglé and had not been granted through the correct authorities within the community. A few months later, a letter from DEG further acknowledged serious concerns with indigenous communities and the existence of issues around an agreement with traditional authorities.[43]

[41] Supra n. 34, 14.
[42] Ibid.
[43] Ibid.

Produced in 2011 as a condition to funds, that legal due diligence report was basic in nature and failed to consider important issues over consent and land. Aware of the report's shortcomings, the lenders commissioned a second report from an independent advisor. This report considered key issues of legal approvals on land, indigenous authorities, power structures in indigenous communities and the possibilities of participating in the project as well as recommendations for improving participation and stakeholder engagements. Whilst having the foresight to commission the report was a positive due diligence step, its value was entirely eroded as a result of its scheduling. The report was received four days after the lenders had made a first disbursement under the loan,[44] the proceeds of which would be used to construct the project. Tensions around the dam continued and despite four visits from lenders to the project site since July 2011 and a UN dialogue table, the lenders continued with financing despite having full information and overlooking ongoing serious conflict. The result was that the lenders had invested into a 'very antagonistic situation'[45] which was further impressed on them through the direct involvement of the UNDP and the UN special rapporteur on indigenous peoples, James Anaya, who, in a 2013 report (two years after financial completion), concluded that there had been no adequate consultation in respect to the project.

2.2   The Ombudsman Panel: Translating Applicable Law and Creating a Legal Black Hole

An interesting feature of this project is the way in which the ombudsman panel members have dealt with and translated each normative layer that bears on the project to produce a legal result in which the project, in the opinion of the panel, operates in a legally unregulated black hole.

First, the panel notes that there is no provision in the lenders' policies that FPIC itself was required. IFC PS7, in the 2006 version that applied to this project, did not require consent to the project, but free, prior and informed consultation. Whilst this may be the case on paper, the logic behind this opinion defies any long-term common sense and sustainable approach in light of the continued local opposition to the project. The

---

[44] Ibid, 15. The overview of project due diligence demonstrates how first disbursement was made on the 7 April 2012 with the second indigenous peoples' report delivered on the 11th.

[45] Ibid.

interpretation that FPIC simply does not apply to the project as it was not a concrete requirement of the 2006 IFC version, does not conform to the spirit of the 2006 policy on indigenous people. That policy was moving closely towards FPIC by, for instance, requiring the lenders to comply with aspects of free, prior and informed consent (without using that exact term) by necessitating that clients conduct early and informed community participation and good faith community engagement throughout the project life cycle.

Against the real backdrop of the local tensions around the project that the lenders had notice of, the panel's narrow interpretation is questionable for its self-serving nature. So whilst the panel notes land and cultural issues were important, it sidesteps the issue of whether the lenders have conducted adequate due diligence by relying on parochial reasoning. The result is to place the project in a legal black hole and pave the way for the company to construct and operate the plant according to its own short-term lending commitments, oblivious to local laws and realities.

Second, the panel's translation of the formal legal requirements applicable to the project also supports a policy of placing the project in a legally unregulated space that crowds out local realities and 'NGO concerns' when they endanger the mobilisation of the project financing. The panel reinforced its view that whilst FPIC was important, it did not apply to the project. First, because Panama has not ratified the ILO Convention 169 and second, as according to the panel 'there was nothing in Panamanian law which required FPIC to *the design and implementation* of the project as a whole'. This is a remarkably short-sighted view to take when there is a key provision of national law, identified by the panel, requiring that specific consultation requirements apply to projects which are located entirely within Comarca territory,[46] even though that law may not clearly and concretely refer to project design and implementation as a whole.

The panel's third reason for not applying FPIC was in relation to international human rights standards. Specifically, those set out in the decisions of the Inter American Court on Human Rights, stating that the requirement for FPIC at the time of project approval only applied in respect of 'large-scale development or investment projects that would have a major impact within [the community's] territory', a term that is not defined in the judgment.[47] Perhaps seizing on this lack of clarity, the

---

[46] Supra n. 34.
[47] The panel referred to the case of *Saramaka People* v *Suriname*, Chapter 3, supra n. 14.

panel took the view that this was not the case in relation to this project,[48] regardless of the fact that the Barro project was classified as a Category A project subject to NGO activism for several years and had involved investigations from various UN bodies. That an independent ombudsman mechanism, in which members may or may not have legal training, is unilaterally interpreting and applying or choosing not to apply human rights standards to development projects, poses a real issue for the recognition and implementation of human rights standards in contexts of development. More generally, this practice can cast into doubt the ability of the global regime of independent accountability mechanisms to deliver independent and effective accountability for communities.

Given that the panel had already interpreted the IFC standards to be the most appropriate way to subsume and align project performance with the UNGP and OECD standards, the above behaviours continue along this trend that ultimately relegates local and international norms to project performance and project mechanics. A further illustration is seen in the way that lenders relied on the 2008 contested agreements between the company and the indigenous elected Cacique General as evidence of an appropriate and legally binding agreement, despite being aware of the local tensions surrounding the legitimacy of those agreements at the time of first disbursement.[49] So, instead of insisting that the company conduct fresh and updated legal assessments and diligence, the financers relied on an outdated and contested paperwork trail. These illustrations show how the financiers (with the later support of the panel) have strategically manoeuvred around the uncertainties of domestic and international legal norms to create a situation in which they can unilaterally determine and implement the project's legal framework.

The project also raises red flags over the quality of the lenders' local legal due diligence assessment. In project financing it would be standard and routine practice for the lenders to obtain a legal opinion from local lawyers and in respect of English law finance documents, from international law firms. Opinions are addressed to the lenders and delivered to them for their sole benefit. They serve as a vehicle for giving assurances that the agreements have been executed with due and proper authority; the counterparties have necessary capacity, power and authority to conclude and perform their contracted obligations; and the

[48] Supra n. 34, 18.
[49] Supra n. 34, 20.

agreements are legal, valid, binding and enforceable. In new or untested jurisdictions, the most important reason for using an opinion will be to signal and mitigate legal issues well before the documents are signed. Issues that are sometimes well visible within local law that have a bearing on the project, will come to light during the process of preparing a legal opinion and to this end, the lenders' international legal counsel will prepare questions for local legal counsel to opine on.

Issues around land and potential land conflicts around the concession area would certainly fall under the logical scope of an opinion and it would be reasonable for the lenders' counsel to pose these questions to local counsel at the outset. Against this background, it is suboptimal that, in the Barro project, the opinion simply comprised of a 'combination of notes and emails from lawyers – most issued prior to disbursement that have been taken to constitute the required legal opinion'.[50] That the lenders failed to order an independent legal opinion from lawyers with defined expertise in indigenous rights and the local Panamanian legal context is another iteration of the short-term and low-priority treatment of indigenous issues in this case.

Failure to commission a formal legal opinion should be a red flag for conducting human rights–compliant due diligence that satisfies the UNGPs and IFC Performance Standards, as that opinion provides some evidence that the lenders have been fully appraised of all social risks at the time of lending. Of course, whether the company implements the findings in the opinion will depend on the types of issues and behaviours discussed in this chapter and Chapter 4. However, ordering a local opinion is well under the lenders' control and so neglecting to commission one should, of itself, constitute a policy implementation failure.

Having analysed the general trend of discretionary decision-making in Chapter 4, this chapter has given some context to how loan mechanics and short-term ideologies surrounding them will actively contribute to the failure of lenders to comply with their own safeguarding policies, impact upon indigenous peoples' rights and the application of local and international legal regimes. In the Barro case a number of poor due diligence measures were taken, including a narrow approach to applying domestic and international norms to the project, failure to commission a formal independent Panamanian legal opinion, unsatisfactory scheduling of the second indigenous peoples report and, related to this, the

---

[50] Supra n. 34, 21.

superficial annexing of that report as a condition of signing. These behaviours provide crucial insights into how lenders are implementing performance standards as just another part of the ordinary and mechanical stream of decision-making that is a mundane part of 'doing the paperwork' for project financing and with a tick-the-box, no culpability approach towards satisfying NGO concerns. This is even the case when investing into a Category A project with significant and potentially irreversible social risks, as this project was.

Through case studies in Mongolia and Panama, I have illustrated that PF mechanisms are, in practice, not helpful in filling international and national legal protection gaps for the recognition and implementation of indigenous peoples' rights to land, and result in more fragmentation to the legal framework surrounding these projects. The hidden behaviours of financiers and concessionaires involved in PF are deeply implicated in the recognition and implementation of indigenous peoples' rights to land. As the studies show, fragmented PF mechanisms, the incentive structures they create, short-term mentality and high levels of discretion that guide those mechanisms – in sum, the constellation of development project law and practice – will create the conditions for important fact-finding and information around land and indigenous people to be ignored and displaced.

In context of an enterprise-led state that is entirely invested in the project's success, there is a trend for states to sit back and transfer powers regarding land acquisition and even the demarcation of indigenous status to concessionaires and financiers, through private contractual arrangements and policy standards. This results in the creation of more substantial gaps for implementing domestic and international indigenous rights norms within development projects in addition to those 'hard' legal lacunas explored in Chapter 3. Subsequently, development projects can be conceptualised as spaces for the production of highly controlled legal, political and economic structures that will routinely impact on the formation of fair, accountable and clear legal outcomes for communities.

In Chapter 6, I explore the Bujagali Hydropower Project discussed in the opening preface. Through this study I illustrate how salient terms and behaviours around public-private power purchase agreements matter for issues of indigenous recognition and poverty reduction strategies in the context of the Sustainable Development Goals and the growing wave for 'people first PPPs'.

6

Pricing for Poverty

Project Finance, Power Purchase Agreements and Structural Inequities in Uganda

The Bujagali Hydropower Project on the Victoria Nile in Uganda has been one of the most controversial dam projects in modern times. It is the largest investment into East Africa and private power project in Sub-Saharan Africa. The government approved the hydropower dam on the River Nile in 1994 as the lowest cost option to increase power production and address the serious power shortages, delays and inaccessibility of electricity in Uganda. In 1999, the Government of Uganda (GoU), in an effort to address its serious energy problems, contracted with Nile Power (AESNP), a privately owned consortium, to build the hydropower project and the related interconnection project.[1] Having secured financing, which included assistance from the World Bank's International Development Association which offers concessional loans and grants to the poorest countries, AESNP then withdrew from the project before construction began, but after it had completed economic, social and environmental assessments of the project and resettlement. Political impasse followed but the government revived the project and in 2005, it awarded a contract for the hydropower project to Bujagali Energy Ltd, who then submitted an application to the African Development Bank (AFDB) for partial funding. Completed in 2012, the project has been widely censured for being a questionable investment given its environmental and social impacts, its expense and the resulting high cost of electricity for local Ugandans.[2] Despite these environmental and social concerns and like the projects in Chapter 5, DFIs categorised the project as Category A for its serious and irreversible environmental and social risks. The GoU approved the project which then attracted project finance (PF) from a

---

[1] The objective of the interconnection project is to provide the transmission infrastructure to evacuate power from the hydro project to distribution companies.

[2] Case Study, The Bujagali Dam Project in Uganda, 2017, Centre for Public Impact. www.centreforpublicimpact.org/case-study/bujagali-dam-project-uganda/.

consortium of international financial institutions, commercial banks and export credit agencies.

In June 2002, the World Bank's independent investigative unit, the Inspection Panel, found that under AESNP, the project had violated five bank policies, including those on involuntary resettlement and environmental impact assessment. Some of the urgent social concerns included the shallow, short-sighted and short-term focused management of the resettlement of approximately 8,700 people.[3] There were claims that the flooding of homes had irreversibly impacted on the major water spirit in the culture of the indigenous Basoga Kingdom, resulting in the dam being postponed for years because of fierce disputes between healers claiming to be the water spirit's representatives.[4] The project has also had serious financial repercussions on communities because once fully operational, energy prices in Uganda actually increased, making access to energy unaffordable for many Ugandans. In 2008, the AFDB acknowledged that the project will fail to meet the needs of 95 per cent of Ugandan households that currently do not have access to electricity, and that the electricity pricing formula needs to be evaluated through a poverty and social impact analysis.[5]

In this chapter, I explore how aspects of the PF structure including the contractual mechanisms within the power purchase agreement (PPA)[6] between the project company as generator of electricity and the GoU as purchaser, have contributed to poor rights implementation and increasing poverty. Compared to the studies in Chapter 5, this is the most remote in its direct connection to the implementation of customary rights to land as it does not focus on contractual or policy instruments that invoke indigenous interests per se, such as the performance standards discussed in Chapter 5 or direct agreement-making in Chapter 7. Nonetheless, as demonstrated in the preface through the letter lodged by the indigenous community member, the complex pricing terms of the PPA, accepted by the host government to facilitate access to international

---

[3] Ibid.

[4] More project information can be found in the African Development Bank (AFDB), Independent Review Panel Compliance Review Report on the Bujagali Hydropower and Interconnection Project, June 20, 2008. www.afdb.org/fileadmin/uploads/afdb/Docu ments/Compliance-Review/30740990-EN-BUJAGALI-FINAL-REPORT-17-06-08.PDF.

[5] Ibid, 65.

[6] A power purchase agreement is a long-term, complex contract between a generator of electricity and a purchaser which defines the terms of sale between the power producer and purchaser.

loan markets, can have real implications for increasing the overall vulnerability of already marginalised and impoverished groups. The fact that the negotiation of specific terms within the Bujagali PPA has led to spiralling electricity costs and an overall bad deal for local communities is an important interface for understanding deficits in rights implementation and increasing vulnerability in contexts of globalisation and development finance.

1   Background to the Project

Structured as a long-term thirty-year project, the construction, feasibility analysis and operation of the plant was undertaken as a public-private partnership (PPP) operated by a special purpose company Bujagali Energy Limited (BEL), with the GoU taking a minority shareholding.[7] BEL secured project financing of the power station through a complex syndicate of financiers including the private-sector arm of the World Bank Group, the IFC, with additional contributions from other government development finance agencies. These included national DFIs such as the FMO (the Netherlands Development Finance Company) and regional ones such as the AFDB and the European Investment Bank. Government export credit agencies contributed, providing government-backed loans, guarantees and insurance to companies from their home country investing in the project. The project also benefited from a $115 million twenty-year partial-risk guarantee from the World Bank's insurance arm, the Multilateral Insurance Guarantee Agency (MIGA), to insure lenders against the risk of the government breaching the terms of the PPA. Moreover, a syndicate of commercial banks invested into the project, incentivised by the high level of DFI backing.

Hydropower projects carry some very specific risks for investors because of their vulnerability to site-specific factors such as high geological and hydrological risks. They also require significant land area, with commensurate mitigation and compensation for environmental and social impacts. In addition, the construction phase for hydropower facilities is unpredictable and lengthy, and represents a significant project risk. From a financing perspective, lenders will only finance these types of project if it is structured in ways that insulate the project company from

---

[7] Shareholders in Bujagali Energy Limited include the government, a privately owned insurance company with a majority stake, a private Norwegian renewables company and the Aga Khan Fund for Economic Development.

risk, passing as much of those risks away from the project company as is possible. Whilst this type of behaviour is, as discussed in previous chapters, typical for PF, this mentality will be heightened in a hydropower project, as illustrated by this chapter's analysis of the PPA terms and the structure of the project.

To mitigate these risks, as part of the bankability analysis, lenders in the Bujagali project procured numerous financial comforts and supports to protect the financial streams and repayment of the PF loans against any payment default by the electricity buyer, the Ugandan Electricity Board (UEB). DFIs are fundamental to providing this support in their ability to structure the transaction in a way that makes investment attractive to the private sector. The lack of any commercial debt financing without the extensive support of multilateral or bilateral financing institutions reflects the poor creditworthiness of the government. Consequently DFI support alleviated much of the risk of investing into a hydropower project in a developing country, in which the buyer, the UEB, has a poor credit rating. So, the presence of a number of DFIs in this project offers risk mitigation to commercial lenders due to the level of access DFIs have to governments, being themselves comprised of states. Benefits also flow from the IFC's ability to provide commercial lenders with a guarantee of being preferred creditors over all other government payments in the event of any debt freeze in a local jurisdiction.[8]

In addition to DFI involvement, other private mechanisms that will lower the risk of investing into a developing country include the provision of risk guarantees. The provision of these guarantees serves a key commercial function as they increase the amount of time left for the project company to repay the loan – up to a period of 30 years, thus far beyond the typical 15-to-18-year loan tenor for a non-hydropower PPP. This longer repayment period is better aligned with the more complex and longer life cycle of operating a hydro project, but obviously carries corresponding risks of payment default as the 'life' of the loan is longer. A risk guarantee will insure the lenders against the occurrence of risks specified in the insurance contract. In the Bujagali project, the MIGA guarantee insured lenders against any potential government payment default under the PPA during that long repayment period. This type of security comes at a substantial cost to the lenders. As I discuss later, the

---

[8] Discussed in Chapter 2.

high insurance premium paid to MIGA is ultimately passed through to the government as a debt cost and included as part of the capacity payment it has to pay for purchasing electricity under the terms of the PPA. In addition to the MIGA guarantee, the lenders also required a sovereign guarantee against payment default as well as numerous other financial mechanisms discussed in this chapter.

This type of over-structuring to insulate the project company from the risks of doing business in a developing country raises serious questions about the sustainability of these so-called development financial mechanisms and structures; not least in their hidden ability to divert resources away from vital public services in poor countries. As I analyse, the ways in which the project has been structured, the terms within the PPA and the implementation of the social safeguard standards, cast doubt on the IFC's claim over the added value of its involvement in the project and its role in alleviating poverty. For the IFC that added value[9] functions to make the project more commercially bankable to lenders and contributes to national development plans.[10] This is typically achieved through, for example, the structuring techniques discussed in this chapter (which include the adoption of environment and social safeguard standards). All of these technical aspects function to ensure that the project is then able to access the international loan market, reach commercial operation, and create impacts that will somehow trickle-down and translate into poverty reduction.

---

[9] Project Appraisal Document on a Proposed International Development Association Partial Risk Guarantee in the Amount of up to US$115 Million for a Syndicated Commercial Bank Loan, and on Proposed International Finance Corporation Financing Consisting of: An 'A' Loan in the Amount of up to US $60 Million, A 'B' Loan in the Amount of up to US $40 Million, And A Risk Management Instrument in the Amount of up to US $10 Million for the Bujagali Hydropower Project in The Republic Of Uganda, November 14, 2001, 19. For the IFC that added value typically comes in the form of structuring the proposed project to ensure proper risk sharing amongst the parties as well as providing Uganda with access to the international loan market, providing advice on the power sector, ensuring the adoption of appropriate environmental and social safeguard standards and contributing to poverty reduction. http://documents.worldbank.org/curated/en/307371468760804260/pdf/multi0page.pdf.

[10] Ibid. For a recent example see the World Bank Group's investment package to fund the Nachtigal Hydropower Project in Cameroon. The project is said to help the country reach its goal of providing access to electricity for 88% of its people by 2022 and thus supports the Government of Cameroon's Vision 2035 to achieve shared growth, reduce poverty, address poverty traps in rural areas and create jobs through increased industrialisation. www.worldbank.org/en/news/press-release/2018/07/19/cameroon-world-bank-group-helps-boost-hydropower-capacity.

2   The Relationship between the Power Purchase Agreement, People-First PPPs and the Sustainable Development Goals

The relationship between the PPA, rights implementation and sustainable development is an important conversation to have as the demand for energy continues to rise and many countries, especially those in Africa, face inadequate access to affordable and reliable modern energy.[11] In Uganda, for example, only 1.2 per cent of the total population has access to grid-supplied electricity, with even lower access in rural areas.[12] The critical importance of providing affordable electricity to the people of Uganda is an integral element of national development and of Uganda's poverty reduction efforts.[13]

Finding solutions for these developmental deficits has led to an uptick in the development and construction of hydroelectric projects globally in China, India and Africa. Development banks have targeted the potential of power projects as a cleaner and greener energy source,[14] even though the sustainable and human rights–compliant nature of hydroelectric projects is questionable, as the Bujagali project and many others illustrate.[15] At the same time, the UN-endorsed Sustainable Development

---

[11] The Nachtigal Hydropower Project in Cameroon, supra n. 10. Also see plans for the Africa–EU partnership on power generation in the West Africa Power Pool which includes Mali, Senegal and Mauritania and is co-financed by the European Investment Bank and the World Bank Group. www.africa-eu-partnership.org/en/success-stories/ clean-reliable-hydropower-mali-mauritania-and-senegal. On the uptick in hydropower and the renewed involvement of DFIs in projects across Sub-Saharan Africa see F Pearce, Will Huge New Hydro Projects Bring Power to Africa's People? (2013) *Yale Environment 360.* https://e360.yale.edu/features/will_huge_new_hydro_projects_bring_power_to_africas_ people.

[12] World Bank Sustainable Energy for All Database. https://data.worldbank.org/indicator/ eg.elc.accs.zs.

[13] National Development Plan of Uganda, 2010/2011, 2014–2015, Poverty Reduction Strategy Paper, IMF Country Report No. 10/141, 33, www.cabri-sbo.org/uploads/files/ Documents/uganda_2010_formulation_external_prsp_ministry_of_finance____imf_region_ english_.pdf.

[14] The Africa–EU partnership refers to hydropower as a source of clean energy. www.africa-eu-partnership.org/en/success-stories/clean-reliable-hydropower-mali-mauritania-and-senegal.

[15] Supreme Court of India, *Narmada Bachao Andolan* v *Union of India*, 18 October 2000, writ petition (civil) No.319 of 1994, AIR (2000) SC 3751. The 2015 joint complaint from UN special rapporteurs on food, water, sanitation, indigenous rights, human rights and transnational corporations, to the UN regarding Chinese hydropower investments in Cambodia, especially the Lower Sesan 2 and Stung Cheay Areng Hydropower Projects. https://earthrights.org/wp-content/uploads/documents/submission_to_special_rapporteur_ on_hydropower.pdf; B Mayer, Judicial Review of Human Rights Impacts of Hydroelectric

Goals has given a high priority to public-private partnerships as a vehicle to achieve those goals. Much attention has been given to various forms of partnership: public, public-private and civil society partnerships, with more attention given to public-private partnerships as potential solutions for mobilising the vast amounts of capital needed to provide basic energy to meet demand in developing countries. Intergovernmental bodies have now taken a renewed interest in PPPs under the catchy phase of forming 'people-first PPPs'[16] under which people, not the private sector, are the main beneficiaries. In this vision, the focus is on using PPP projects to promote access to food, water, energy and transport through projects that are equitable, sustainable, work for all and are designed to improve livelihoods.[17]

It is imperative that new people-first-PPP projects do not recreate the mistakes of Bujagali. Whilst I do not argue that the Bujagali project was designed as a people-first PPP, some of the reasons for its failure to address the massive energy shortages in Uganda[18] are rooted in the early stages of project design and the standardised, boilerplate contractual terms that are negotiated to mitigate the risk of doing business in developing countries. These conditions actively work against principles of equity, sustainability and inclusive development. Examining these contractual-community PPP linkages is, therefore, an important conversation to have in the context of the SDGs and the limitations of traditional forms of PPP financing.

3   What Can We Learn from the Bujagali PPP?

In Bujagali, the PPA comprises of a thirty-year contractual arrangement between the project sponsor (BEL) as an independent power producer, and the government's state-owned entity in charge of transmission, as purchaser. The project is built through a structure that is typical for PPPs in which BEL will build, operate and own the plant for a defined period and then transfer it to the government at a nominal cost of $1. This structure itself incentivises a short-to-medium-term view of the project

---

Projects, Legal Working Paper Series on Legal Empowerment for Sustainable Development, Centre for International Sustainable Development Law, 2012. www.cisdl.org/wp-content/uploads/2018/05/Mayer_Judicial_Review.pdf.

[16] UN Economic Commission for Europe, International PPP Centre of Excellence. www.uneceppp-icoe.org/#/home.

[17] www.uneceppp-icoe.org/people-first-ppps/what-are-people-first-ppps/,

[18] AFDB Independent Review Panel Compliance Review, supra n. 4, 7.

as investors know that the project will be transferred to the government after thirty years.

The level of government support in the Bujagali project is considerable. It has a minority equity stake in the project although it has agreed not to have representation in the governance of the project company and has also agreed not to receive any shareholder dividends until the debt is fully paid back.[19] In addition, the government is the purchaser of power under the PPA and is responsible for the related interconnection project, meaning that it has legally undertaken to guarantee purchase and interconnection. These contractual features result in significant power asymmetries in which construction and operations risks are passed on to the government, making it similar to the private stakeholders, singly focused on project completion and operation.

Further aspects of the PPA create incentives that compromise rights recognition, implementation and will actively work against poverty reduction. The following two subsections focus on two such aspects: resettlement delegation practices and pricing terms under the PPA.

3.1   Delegating Resettlement to Private Actors: Links between Law, Policy and Vulnerability

Pursuant to the PPA, BEL was required to update the resettlement action plan for the hydro project. In 2006 BEL passed on this obligation to prepare the social and environmental assessment (SEA), including the resettlement action plan, to private consulting companies, RJ Burnside International Ltd. Guelph, Canada, and Frederic Giovannetti, Consultant, France.[20] Burnside also prepared the SEA for the related interconnection project. Neither of these assessments considered that the project area was inhabited by peoples with customary ties to land.

---

[19] AFDB Independent Review Panel Compliance Review, supra n. 4. This type of provision under which shareholders agree (under the shareholder agreement) to defer dividends until after the lenders are repaid is a common aspect for making a project financing bankable to lenders. In the context of a developing country which is already providing multiple levels of support to the project as analysed in this chapter, the point is whether this type of provision is fair and equitable when compared to other shareholders who are deep-pocketed commercial entities that can mitigate the impact of deferred dividend payments. This provision for deferred dividend payments should also be seen in light of the presence of the MIGA risk guarantee under which the time for loan repayment for the lenders is considerably extended. Clearly, as a consequence of this structuring, the government entity will have to wait for a long time to receive any dividend returns.

[20] AFDB Compliance Review, supra n. 4.

Positively, in 2006, the AFDB then posted a summary of the SEA and the resettlement action plan on its website and submitted the SEA to the bank's board of directors in January 2007. The SEA and resettlement plans were also presented in public meetings organised by the Ugandan Ministry of Energy and Mineral Development and the National Environmental Management Authority.

In 2007, after signature of the loan agreements and construction contract, but prior to the start of construction, a group of Ugandan NGOs – the National Association of Professional Environmentalists, lodged complaints concerning AESPN's legacy resettlement activities. BEL agreed to resolve these issues prior to commencing activities through SEA commitments for compensation, land titling, addressing concerns about the quality of the housing provided to the resettled community and the creation of employment and income-generating opportunities for the resettled community. The NGO complaints focused on the unfair treatment of the Basoga people, who, they argued, should have been treated as indigenous given their special connection to the land and natural resources and vulnerability to land loss. NGOs claimed that BEL's resettlement was not adequately completed and there remained outstanding issues over loss of livelihoods, under-compensation, lack of adequate consultation, inability to obtain secure land titles and requests to share in project benefits.[21] In response, BEL appointed a local NGO, Inter-Aid, whose primary function was to monitor the implementation of the resettlement process under the SEA. Inter-Aid was also charged with implementing a grievance procedure in which it, along with other actors, hears complaints arising from the resettlement and seeks to resolve those issues.

A number of observations can be made with respect to the impact of these delegation practices for the recognition and implementation of indigenous rights in this case.

First, a high level of discretion is granted to private consultants to determine issues of customary rights. Second, there is a potential link between that private determination and the state as the decision that no indigenous people were present on the project site follows the level of formal legal domestic recognition of indigenous people in Uganda. In the Bujagali project, as in the Oyu Tolgoi project, financiers and their advisors, appear to have taken the lead from domestic legal norms that

---

[21] AFDB Compliance Review, supra n. 4, 23.

support non-recognition. In Uganda, the government does not implicitly recognise any group as indigenous in the 1995 constitution,[22] a position that is representative of many African states.[23] This sidelining or non-observance of local realities at the state level is one aspect that has provided a policy pretext for the AFDB not to develop a stand-alone policy on indigenous people. In so doing, the AFDB has created a regulatory and policy deficit that reinforces the legal lacunas for the protection of indigenous rights in development project contexts.

Responses from the AFDB on the issue of indigenous peoples in Africa reveal this harmonisation of policy with domestic law. These responses provide further illustrations of how financial actors think about indigenous people and domestic laws on indigenous rights in the context of large development projects. In the African context, it was not until 2016 that the AFDB recognised that addressing issues of inclusive growth meant addressing the concerns of marginalised groups such as indigenous peoples in its operations.[24] This resulted in the bank carrying out a specific assessment of the issues affecting indigenous people in Africa to understand 'who they are, where they are and how they can be better accommodated in the bank's quest to ensure inclusive growth'.[25] Some of the reasons cited for conducting the review included slow but increasing

---

[22] While Article 32 of the constitution promises 'affirmative action for those who have been historically disadvantaged', it has been primarily invoked for the protection of children, women and people with disabilities. No domestic law expressly recognises or protects indigenous people. Uganda has not ratified ILO Convention 169 which guarantees the rights of indigenous people but has adopted the non-binding UNDRIP. Independent Work Group for Indigenous Affairs. www.iwgia.org/en/uganda.

[23] University of Pretoria: "Overview Report of the Research Project by the International Labour Organization and the African Commission on Human and Peoples' Rights on the Constitutional and Legislative Protection of the Rights of Indigenous Peoples in 24 African Countries" (2009): illustrating the still very limited constitutional recognition of indigenous groups in Africa but noting some piecemeal positive developments in Cameroon, Gabon and the Democratic Republic of Congo that have arisen in response to World Bank operational policies relating to infrastructure programmes such as road-building programmes in the DRC, and generally noting how whilst recognition has grown on the international and regional plane, there is very little domestic constitutional or legislative recognition of rights in the African context. www.ilo.org/wcmsp5/groups/public/—ed_norm/—normes/documents/publication/wcms_115929.pdf. Also, Report of the African Commission's Working Group of Experts on Indigenous Populations/Communities (2005). www.iwgia.org/images/publications//African_Commission_book.pdf

[24] African Development Bank Group's Development and Indigenous Peoples in Africa 2016, 1(2). www.afdb.org/fileadmin/uploads/afdb/Documents/Publications/Development_and_Indigenous_Peoples_in_Africa__En__-__v3_.pdf, 4–5.

[25] Ibid.

domestic legislation recognising indigenous people in Africa, the growth of the indigenous movement globally, pressure from civil society and a need to keep up with other development banks working in Africa. Arguably the lack of constitutional domestic protection in Africa was at least one factor that has supported the bank's policy of not giving special attention to these issues through the implementation of a safeguard policy. Positively however, the growing recognition of rights at the international level has started a process whereby the bank has been forced to consider these issues in local and regional contexts.

A lack of domestic legal recognition means that DFIs are, in contexts of poor state recognition, increasingly following each other's lead and the advice of private experts, in matters of indigenous rights recognition. For instance, in Bujagali, the AFDB simply relied on the findings of the World Bank Inspection Panel's investigation report that agreed that the indigenous peoples' policy should not have been triggered as there were no minorities involved.[26] This in turn, followed advice from RJ Burnside International that the Basoga are not an indigenous group but a disadvantaged and vulnerable one. In light of the similar conclusion reached in the Oyu Tolgoi project, the imposition of a lighter, vulnerable policy standard appears to be a default policy solution for managing issues of indigenous peoples where there is no state recognition.[27]

Two final points can be made with respect to the delegation of resettlement practices that is common in PF scenarios. There is concern over the proximate relationship between Inter-Aid and BEL and the contractual dynamics under which BEL pays Inter-Aid. Whilst it is a positive outcome that the project company hired an NGO to oversee resettlement, the terms of this relationship make it challenging to convey with certainty that the NGO was an independent interlocutor. Related to this were concerns over the processes through which Inter-Aid was selected which were not based on a truly open and competitive hiring but instead, a pragmatic continuation of the role that the NGO had played in the first stages of the Bujagali project.[28] The second concern involves the mechanisms whereby Inter-Aid is responsible for the grievance procedures relating to resettlement. Given its role as a witness of the

---

[26] AFDB Compliance Review, supra n. 4, 245.

[27] Although as the Barro Blanco Project demonstrates in Chapter 5, there is also the possibility that local laws can be entirely ignored through an interpretation that supports the project's right of way.

[28] AFDB Compliance Review, supra n. 4, 34–35.

resettlement process and it having to potentially defend its own conclusions as a witness in any future grievance process, a potential conflict of
interest arises.[29]

The following section moves onto discuss how specific terms in the
PPA can increase vulnerability and poverty.

3.2   The Nexus between Power Pricing and Poverty

The provisions discussed in this section are standard for PPP-structured
project-finance-funded power-project transactions but are, for the
reasons discussed below, questionable in the context of a highly indebted
developing country. An essential part of the PPA is the power tariff paid
by the UEB. All tariff costs are paid in US dollars – a mechanism which
passes on the entire risk of exchange-rate fluctuations to the UEB.
Broadly speaking, the government pays a tariff consisting of a capacity-
based payment. As discussed in Chapter 4, the underlying rationale
within any project financing is to pass as much financial, commercial,
legal and political risk away from the project company. So, just as a
construction contractor that fails to complete on time will pay an amount
in liquidated damages to the company that is proportionate to debt
financing costs,[30] which is then passed onto the lenders under the terms
of the loan agreement, in a PPA scheme, the power tariff is similarly
comprised of a financial element that equals the lenders' debt and interest
payments.

The tariff cost is therefore comprised of an amount that is equal to
all the lenders financing costs. Those will include all costs associated with
the repayment of debt (principle and interest), the repayment of equity,
the return on equity, and operation and maintenance costs.[31] It is
common practice for lenders lending into a country with a low credit
rating to offset that risk by negotiating higher costs of loan and financing

---

[29] Ibid.

[30] Discussed in Chapter 4.

[31] The Bujagali Power Purchase Agreement – an Independent Review, November 2002,
Prayas, Energy Group, Pune, 12–13. The main components of any power tariff will
include the following elements: construction costs (which include all interest that has
to be paid during construction which may typically be compounded in this period due to
the higher risk during this period for PF lenders), pass-through costs (i.e. costs such as
customs duties, payment of fees to government authorities etc.), financing fees (i.e. fees
and commissions paid for raising debt and risk guarantees etc.), and amounts that the
lenders keep reserved for specific project risks in a debt service reserve account.

fees with the project company. The Bujagali project is no exception and is notable for its eye-watering costs of export credit agency loan and financing fees which are, through the payment of the tariff, ultimately passed onto the government entity. For example, the export credit premium alone amounts to about 20 per cent of the actual export credit support, with the premium accounting for about 7.5 per cent of the total project costs.[32] As the sole buyer, the UEB is, therefore, bound to bear, in US dollars, the brunt of the project financing costs as part of the power tariff it pays to the project sponsor under the project financing structure.

It is, however, customary (and logical) that at the end of the construction period tariff payments will decrease substantially, as part of the tariff includes an amount equal to the compounded interest costs payable to the lenders under the debt instruments for that riskier period. It would therefore be typical for the project company to pay a lower interest rate to the lenders after construction and for that saving to pass through to the power purchaser through a lower tariff charge. This de-escalation does not take place under the Bujagali PPA. What is particularly unusual about the Bujagali project is that the PPA contains no mechanism whereby the buyer, here a government entity, can control or cap the financing terms.[33] The inequitable results of this formula mean that the risks of spiralling debt services costs are passed through to the government, who is in turn forced to pass on those increasing costs to Ugandan customers.

Another surprising feature of the PPA is that UEB's tariff payments are fixed, based on the production capacity of the project and are thus, not commensurate with actual generation from the plant. As a consequence, if power demand in the country is lower than expected, generation from Bujagali may also be lower, but the production capacity upon which the tariff is pegged is the same, resulting in a higher tariff payment than amounts recouped under tariff costs in lower demand. Similarly, if the water flow is lower, for example, due to climatic changes, generation will be lower, but the UEC's tariff will still remain high as it is fixed on a modelled production capacity.

---

[32] Ibid, 31.

[33] This, along with its lack of representation in the governance of the project company discussed earlier, illustrates some of the structural inequities in the PPA in which much of the costs and risks are passed through to the government whilst the government has no control over those terms.

Whilst the PPA allows deferrals of capacity payments for certain 'act of God' events, those deferrals come at a high cost. Deferments are allowed in the case of a hydrological force majeure which is defined as being a level of water flow of the Victoria Nile that is less than the assumed base flow.[34] However, such a deferral attracts an interest rate of nearly 20 per cent, and in such case the deferral has to be repaid immediately when the water flows return to the assumed discharge.[35] The option of deferral under the Bujagali PPA is prohibitively expensive and is designed to keep UEB out of formally getting into payment default. However, the impact of these provisions for climate change and basic fairness are enormous.

In order to prevent any deferrals and to keep water flow at the prescribed level, the government will be perversely incentivised to make as much water as needed available for the dam (perhaps extracting more water using unsustainable practices) including in the driest years[36] to keep production capacity at an optimum level. This would place the UEB in a better position to fully recoup tariff costs through electricity charges (although this also depends on demand which, as shown, is also a government risk). Given that Uganda is highly exposed to the risks of climate change with the River Nile's hydrological condition deteriorating due to global climate change,[37] climate change could render the project uneconomic in the long term. This will leave the government locked into an enormously expensive project that is actually contributing to the country's climate change exposure and placing that risk on communities that are least able to bear it.

Another questionable characteristic of the capacity payment under the PPA is that it is formulated on an actual cost basis, as opposed to a maximum ceiling charge. This means that the PPA provides that actual interest will be charged in the tariff payment with no ceiling or maximum level to those debt costs. The introduction of an actual cost-based formula represents a significant shift in risk away from the project investors and lenders to the government entity. This in turn increases the possibility that the UEB will have to either increase tariff payments

---

[34] Supra n. 31, 14. Specifically if the water flow of the Victoria Nile is less than an assumed base flow of 700 cubic meters/sec in 1999, linearly decreasing to 450 cubic meters/sec in 2015.

[35] Ibid.

[36] AFDB Compliance Review, supra n. 4, 11.

[37] National Association of Professional Environmentalists, The Unresolved Issues in the Bujagali Dam Project in Uganda, 2007. www.nape.or.ug/publications/energy/45-the-unre solved-issues-in-bujagali-dam/file.

under the PPA or the GoU will need to make payments under its government guarantee[38] potentially incurring huge debts.

Lastly, aspects of the project's contractual security arrangements conflict with poverty reduction; in particular, the funders' need for multiple security mechanisms to invest in the project results in high costs. Whilst it is routine for investors to seek multiple payment security mechanisms in projects such as Bujagali, the costs of these multiple layers are questionable given that an indebted country will bear them until all of the debt is repaid – a considerable time. The level of security demanded from the government in this case is excessive, driven by commercial fears that have resulted in an imbalanced and inequitable contractual structure. Consisting of at least three levels, it includes a liquidity facility under which the UEB has to maintain at least $20 million (about two months of tariff payment under the PPA) in a separate bank account until the entire debt of the project is repaid, as well as a debt service reserve of around $50 million. A second layer is made up of an escrow facility under which the UEB is required to top-up and replenish those two debt service and liquidity accounts immediately and, if necessary, by directly depositing electricity export revenues in them. The third level of security comes in the form of the government guarantee and the partial risk guarantee from MIGA. Through the guarantee agreement, the GoU guarantees all of UEB's payments. In case of payment default, the government will immediately pay the project company any unpaid amounts. This guarantee will be applicable as long as any part of the project debt remains to be repaid or until the buyer utility obtains an 'investment grade' rating from an internationally reputed credit rating agency. The MIGA guarantee then provides a further layer of security if the GoU fails to make these payments. A more equitable approach to this contractual structure might have involved eliminating the liquidity and debt service reserve, thereby considerably reducing the project costs and consequently, the capacity payments under the PPA.[39]

The net result of this series of contractual conditions is to place the government in an unsustainable financial, social and environmental condition that contradicts principles of poverty reduction and sustainable development and violates DFI operational safeguarding.

---

[38] Supra n. 9, Bujagali Project Appraisal Document, 9. This is because under the guarantee the GoU bears the risk of the UEB's payment default under the PPA.

[39] Supra n. 31, 24 which could have reduced the capacity payment by about $9 million in the first year, and by an average of $4.3 million per annum during the lifetime of the PPA.

Remarkably, another feature of the project contracts contains a condition relating to the privatisation and restructuring of the UEB.[40] This
demonstrates how modern World Bank Group–funded independent
power plants can use private contractual devices to influence policy
decisions on developing countries. In the long term, the project and its
hidden private financial terms have the real potential of increasing the
debt burden of a highly indebted country and contribute to long-term
behaviours under which the government is incentivised to sideline the
implementation of issues of wide public interest.[41] As this study illustrates, these include indigenous peoples' recognition, sustainable
hydrological and electrification practices and even the development of
climate change measures, as a direct result of the contractual mechanisms within the project.

The previous three case studies have analysed the multiple ways in
which PF structures and mechanisms will interface with international
and domestic indigenous rights norms, resulting in impacts on
vulnerability and poverty. Other illustrations can be found within the
numerous complaints lodged with DFIs. For example, a 2014 complaint
lodged with the IFC concerned a cement plant in northeast Bangladesh
operated by a subsidiary of the multinational corporation Lafarge.[42] The
plant was supplied with limestone from a quarry in a neighbouring
Indian state that had a conveyor belt connecting the two sites built over
indigenous-held land. The case again flushes out aspects of how PF
mechanisms tangibly interface with and adversely impact upon the
recognition and implementation of indigenous peoples' land rights in
local systems. Specifically how the IFC's loan and equity contributions to
Lafarge and the procedures for loan approval and policy implementation
have contributed to violations of government and customary laws on
land ownership, as well as the IFC's policies on indigenous peoples and
involuntary resettlement that were applicable to the loan. The case again
highlights how implementation and monitoring of the IFC performance
standards was deficient because the lenders were not fully apprised of

---

[40] Supra n. 31. 26.

[41] For a review of resistance to privatisation practices see D Hall, E Lobina and R de la
Motte, 'Public Resistance to Privatization in Water and Energy' (2005) 15(3–4) *Development in Practice* 286.

[42] IFC CAO Assessment Report regarding local stakeholder concerns in relation to IFC's
project with Lafarge Surma Cement (#8035) in India, 2014. www.cao-ombudsman.org/
cases/document-links/documents/LafargeSurmaCementAssessment_Report_FINAL_
May2014.pdf.

land and indigenous issues when the board approved the project. The panel noted an inadequate review of the Indian social impact assessment at the crucial time of project approval and much ambiguity over whether the IFC adequately supervised its client's commitment to carry out a process of independent external monitoring of resettlement under the Indian social impact assessment.

Having examined how PF mechanisms interface with issues of indigenous land rights norms, Chapter 7 comparatively analyses how concessionaires are directly entering into mediation processes with indigenous communities resulting in firm contractual arrangements. These contracts constitute an important and typically hidden part of the fragmented legal framework relating to transnational development projects involving indigenous people analysed in Chapter 3. I analyse the positive and negative aspects of these contracts. Might they address some of the lacunas in the legal framework of indigenous peoples' rights to land in development circumstances to provide fairer and more certain legal outcomes for communities? Or, do aspects of these contracts and the behaviours surrounding them further fragment the legal framework with damaging consequences that increase the vulnerability of indigenous communities to development projects?

7

Negotiating Land Outcomes

A Comparative Look at Concessionaires, Indigenous
Peoples and Power

The previous chapters have analysed how project finance mechanisms and the incentives surrounding them will impact the recognition and implementation of indigenous peoples' land rights. In this chapter, I continue to develop my theme of examining how private mechanisms interface with the recognition and implementation of indigenous peoples' rights to land by analysing how contractual arrangements between indigenous groups and concessionaires can directly interface with indigenous land rights norms. Specifically, I explore land-related contractual entitlements such as land access provisions; free, prior and informed consent (FPIC) processes; compensation payments; and forms of apology, to illustrate whether contractual clauses dealing with these issues could fill the gaps in the formal legal framework analysed in Chapter 3.

As discussed, those gaps are varied and include an international legal order that speaks primarily to states and is punctuated with a poor record of recognising and enforcing judgments in the face of the economic and political interests of transnational development projects in which the state is itself an economic beneficiary. Nonetheless, businesses do have a responsibility to respect human rights and the rights of indigenous peoples through the UN Guiding Principles on Business and Human Rights.[1] Respecting human rights means that companies must employ due diligence, independent to whether it is conducted by the state, to ensure that the company's actions do no harm to indigenous peoples' human rights, including rights over land and resources. In the previous chapters, I illustrated how project finance (PF) mechanisms will work to further fragment the recognition and implementation of indigenous peoples' land rights. Consequently, I have argued that the analysis of these mechanisms and the contracts underpinning them must be a core part of a company's due diligence exercise.

---

[1] Discussed in Chapter 3.

There is, of course, a link between PF mechanisms and the development and implementation of private contracts as the extent of any mediated contractual arrangements can be shaped by the quality of social impact assessment ensuing from a DFI loan conditionality covenant. By extension, failure to flag land rights issues upstream at the land divestment stage and then through the project life cycle and documentation in addition to the poor implementation processes within PF mechanisms analysed in the previous case studies, will fragment out the availability of baseline information for entering into contractual agreements. Put simply, the structures, documentation and behaviours around earlier stages of PF in which the borrower's delivery of social impact assessments can be traded off for reasons of project timing, schedules and lender discretion, create more lacunas and fragmentation that can hinder the development of potentially more participatory measures such as full-blown mediated arrangements with groups. Project developers and lenders that take their social obligations seriously at this stage and have delivered social impact assessments dealing with issues of indigenous land claims over the project area, will arm themselves with useful baselines upon which contractual entitlement on FPIC, for instance, can be designed, scoped and negotiated. Failing to have this data can aggravate on the ground practices for implementing agreements with communities.[2]

1   The Problematic Conditions around Agreement-Making

There are certainly serious concerns with an approach to indigenous land rights that relies solely on negotiated contract-making. These include: the lack of publicly available agreements that provide details of privately negotiated land terms along with a willingness of concessionaires to talk about the thinking and decision-making that has gone into the process. I have come across this reluctance on numerous occasions. Whilst I have been fortunate enough to obtain access to contracts and discussions with interlocutors, I have been struck by the lack of transparency from

---

[2] This was a finding of an independent study of human rights experts that was commissioned by Newmont Mining for the Merian mine in Suriname discussed later in this chapter. J Anaya, J Evans and D. Kemp (2017), 'Free, prior and informed consent (FPIC) within a human rights framework: Lessons from a Suriname case study'. RESOLVE FPIC Solutions Dialogue: Washington DC.

concessionaires who prefer to keep their cards close to their chest. Yet, at the same time, interlocutors present a real desire to know what their corporate counterparts are doing on similar issues. There are, of course, legitimate reasons for keeping details confidential, such as if the community desires this for fear of abuse if details become public or a wish to keep the location of sacred sites secret. However, this should not stop companies from providing more details about the processes, principles and general arrangements they are using in this regard and even producing specially redacted agreements in which all sensitive information is removed prior to publication.

Lack of transparency is not the only concern for the overall legitimacy of these private arrangements. Overriding concerns about negotiated arrangements include the high concentrations of power in the hands of private concessionaires. As illustrated in this chapter, this can result in insecure and non-human rights–compatible outcomes as the negotiation of contractual arrangements and their content can be tied to, and translated around, exogenous considerations. This can result in concessionaires agreeing to negotiate better terms with groups only when, for example, commodity prices are high, making indigenous rights recognition contingent on economics or a project has attracted consistently high-profile NGO publicity.

Contract-making can arise as a result of multiple factors, a position which itself casts doubt on the reliability and predictability of these mechanisms as a panacea for rights recognition and implementation. The lack of international regulation on contractual arrangements also means that the practice of private contracting becomes highly fragmented, subject to a number of variable factors that are not easily replicated elsewhere and can be subverted for economic interests. For example, we will see from revisiting the Oyu Tolgoi case that contracts were forged as a result of sustained NGO pressure combined with the strategic use of a DFI grievance mechanism. Contract-making might also stem from an ad hoc organisational decision. For example, where a company knows that a community claims indigenous status but is not recognised as such under national law, as was the case with Newmont Mining in Suriname discussed in Section 3 of this chapter. It might also arise from domestic legal requirements, as is the case in Australia, or as an outcome of the PF-lending covenants discussed in Chapter 4, requiring the borrower to enter into a social management plan. These types of covenants can result in the company entering into contracts with indigenous peoples.

Contracts can also result from a non-binding recommendation from a state-based non-judicial mechanism such as the national contact point mechanisms under the OECD Guidelines for Multinational Companies, as was the case for the Norwegian hydropower company Statkraft.[3] In the Australian example discussed in this chapter, Rio Tinto actively uses its policy of agreement-making in Australia[4] as a means of showing that it is promoting the rule of law and equity in areas of high social conflict and where the state is itself, conflicted. The fact that companies are using the language of the rule of law and equity demonstrates how agreement-making is a paradigm that has the power to impact upon the rights of communities in a tangible way. The overall point is that these arrangements are happening for a variety of unpredictable reasons, that they have consequences for communities and indigenous land rights norms and should therefore be engaged with as a potential means to mitigate conflict around land and natural resource extraction in development project contexts.

2   Gaps in Existing Studies

There are few existing studies that focus specifically on how private developers implement land-related covenants into their projects, the behaviours and decision-making that guide this implementation and an analysis of how these contractual mechanisms interface with domestic and international norms on indigenous peoples' rights to land. This is largely a result of the severe lack of transparency and openness in available contractual information on issues of land access, compensation and the processes through which investors translate FPIC values into their practices.

There is, however, fruitful literature on community development or social impact agreements entered into between communities and companies with the goal of promoting community development. This literature is vastly differentiated between communities, location and regulatory context and can encompass a universe of benefits including

---

[3] Referring to recommendations of the Swedish national contact point in *Jijnjevaerie Saami village* v *Statkraft* for the company Statkraft to enter into private agreements with indigenous Saami communities relating to a windfarm over traditional land. https://complaints .oecdwatch.org/cases/Case_280.

[4] Interviews with manager of agreement-making and acting manager of indigenous employment, business development and planning, Rio Tinto, on file with author.

financial, employment, business development, education and community welfare projects.[5] Those benefits constitute a broad universe of ancillary or 'good neighbour' contractual benefits that any local community should benefit from in the context of a large development project.

These benefits are not the focus of this enquiry, which is more focused on a small part of community development or social impact agreements that are crucial for land-connected groups. Those arrangements include covenants within agreements that specifically relate to land access, compensation quantum and private processes that seek to translate FPIC principles into practice. More concretely, I identify a practice whereby private developers are applying the free, prior and informed consent principle which relates specifically to *land* consent *prior to any land disturbance*, to other, more generic, benefits. For instance, developers are stating that they have obtained FPIC from communities but on closer inspection, that FPIC relates to housing and education projects that have been developed during or after project construction and land disturbance. [6] This interpretation of FPIC is a misuse of its fundamental legal meaning, which is to give indigenous peoples a chance to consent to the use of their land and resources prior to resource development taking place. For developers, such a human rights approach grounded in the provisions of the UNDRIP requiring FPIC processes prior to the approval of any project,[7] would potentially require costly changes to project design that respect continued access to traditional land and also ameliorated compensation for exchange of land holdings.

In this chapter I analyse aspects of the contractual interfaces taking place between transnational concessionaires and local indigenous actors within negotiated agreement-making where those interfaces relate to land rights issues. My primary case study is the participation agreement[8]

---

[5] J Loutit, J Mandelbaum and S Szoke-Burke, 'Emerging Practices in Community Development Agreements' (2016) 7(1) *Journal of Sustainable Development Law and Policy*, http://ccsi.columbia.edu/files/2016/07/Emerging-Practices-in-Community-Devel opment-Agreements.pdf. M Tysiachniouk, L Henry, M Lamers and J Tatenhove, 'Oil and Indigenous People in Sub-Arctic Russia: Rethinking Equity and Governance in Benefit Sharing Agreements' (2018) 37 *Energy Research and Social Science* 140–152.
[6] As illustrated in the Newmont and Sakhalin studies in this chapter.
[7] Discussed in Chapter 3.
[8] Drawing on the RTIO and [ ] People Claim Wide Participation Agreement between Hamersley Iron Pty Limited, Robe River Mining, Hamersley HMS Pty Ltd, Hamersley Resources Ltd and the [identity is subject to confidentiality provisions] People (PA). Rio provided other information in the form of emails, books and interviews with key stakeholders including the principal legal officer of the native title representative body

made between concessionaire Rio Tinto and aboriginal traditional owners relating to an iron ore project in the Pilbara region of Australia. These agreements apply the statutory Australian Native Title legal framework of agreement-making post *Mabo v Queensland (No. 2)*[9] into a transnational field of a large development project. Some interesting aspects of these direct agreements between Rio Tinto and aboriginal communities relate to land access rights over culturally sensitive areas, consultation mechanisms and compensation payments through profit-sharing formulas in the form of mining-benefit payments. I analyse whether aspects of this negotiated arrangement, in which indigenous communities are seen as stakeholders in the project, work to fill in some of the lacunas within the formal legal framework; specifically, relating to poor compensation and generally, whether the agreement can provide a degree of certainty in rights recognition and implementation that fills in the patchy, site-specific and anti-development judicial statements on indigenous rights in common law jurisprudence discussed in Chapter 3.

3   Concessionaire Mischief: Illustrations from Agreements in Russia and Suriname

To give context to my primary study, I open this chapter with a short illustration of some other contemporary negotiated agreements with indigenous communities. I explore the scope of benefits awarded and specifically whether they relate to difficult issues around land rights, and if so, how those agreements translate legal norms on indigenous rights to land into private mechanisms.

The first illustration is from one of the world's largest integrated oil and gas projects – the Sakhalin-2 in Russia. Sakhalin-2 is a consortium led by the operator Sakhalin Energy, headquartered in Yuzhno-Sakhalinsk, Russia. Three companies founded Sakhalin Energy Investment Company Limited in 1994 – Royal Dutch Shell, Mitsui Co. Ltd, and Mitsubishi Corporation – to develop oil deposits on the northeastern shelf of Sakhalin Island.[10] Shell sold its once controlling stake in the

---

for the Yamatji and Pilbara regions, within RT business including legal counsel, and senior managers on indigenous agreement-making.
[9] [1992] 175 CLR 1 (HCA).
[10] For a good overview of the project and its social impacts see 'Oil and Indigenous People', supra n. 5.

company to a state-owned Russian company, Gazprom, although Shell, through a subsidiary, Shell Sakhalin Holdings BV, still owns 27.5 per cent of the project.[11] Through Sakhalin Energy, Shell took the lead in designing and launching the benefit-sharing agreement with indigenous communities.

Local and international NGOs protested over the environmental impact of the project, particularly its impact on the endangered Western grey whales, but also around the project's impact on the recognition of indigenous communities within the project area. As a result of NGO action which culminated in the blockade of road access to the project construction sites, since 2006 Sakhalin Energy has implemented a partnership programme called the Sakhalin Indigenous Minorities Development Plan (SIMDP).[12] The plan notes that whilst indigenous rights are protected under constitutional, federal and local regulatory laws for the Sakhalin Oblast area, those rights remain poorly defined and their presence does not translate into practice, remaining mostly paper declarations.[13] It is interesting that non-recognition and insecurity of indigenous rights under domestic law has been raised in the SIMDP. This entry might imply a correlation between the level of recognition and security of indigenous recognition under national law and the amount of benefit sharing that will be made available from the company. I revisit this point in the agreement in Suriname discussed later in this section.

A look at the scope of the SIMDP reveals some positive and negative aspects. Positively, that Sakhalin Energy has publicly adopted numerous global standards, including the UNGPs and the UNDRIP in its operations.[14] Next, that the project company has budgeted annual project funds to the tune of $320,000 for indigenous benefit-sharing arrangements. This point demonstrates that the earmarking and allocation of

---

[11] The circumstances around the sale of Shell's controlling interest in the project were highly political. As a result of sustained environmental lobbying against the project, the Putin government terminated the project in 2006 citing numerous breaches of Russian environmental laws. Due to these pressures, the consortium was forced to sell Shell's controlling stake in the project to Russian owned Gazprom.

[12] In collaboration with the Regional Council of authorised representatives of the Sakhalin North indigenous peoples' and the Sakhalin Oblast Government, Sakhalin Indigenous Minorities Development Plan, 2011–2015, Sakhalin-2 Project, http://simdp.com/uploads/files/FIN_SIMDP%202_eng%20.pdf.

[13] Ibid, 17.

[14] In the SIMDP these include the UN Global Compact, UN Guiding Principles on Business and Human Rights, ILO Convention 169, the UNDRIP, IFC Environmental and Social Sustainability Standards and World Bank standards on Indigenous People.

funds from the project budget or elsewhere is entirely possible in a transnational development project. It also cuts through arguments that such earmarking of costs for undefined and uncertain purposes is too complicated in large projects, and certainly for those involving project finance where costs need to be clearly and predictably quantified upfront. Aspects of the SIMDP show how the private sector can make small positive steps towards filling in some of the lacunas from judicial mechanisms that take a regressive view towards socio-economic and cultural rights of indigenous peoples.[15] For example, the focus areas of the SIMDPs, and the related tripartite cooperation agreements[16] that mobilise the SIMDPs, revolve around good neighbour provisions. These include the creation of ongoing social and cultural development programmes such as education, healthcare and cultural heritage programmes. There is also a traditional-economic-activities support programme for the sole purpose of reviving and developing customary economic activities such as dog breeding and reindeer herding.

Another positive aspect is that the SIMDP envisages that the company will communicate and consult with communities using methods and processes that respect their traditional practices and do not seek to replace them. The fact that the tripartite cooperation agreements also lock the local government into the process is a considerable achievement for engaging all-powerful stakeholders in the process. Sakhalin Energy has also set up a grievance mechanism whereby communities can lodge complaints directly with the company about any aspects of the SIMDP. Information on grievances are fed back to the lenders periodically as a result of covenants within the project finance loan agreements requiring the borrower to inform the lenders of social and environmental events, although as I considered in Chapter 4, lenders will not cease lending for this type of default but rather trigger a mandatory prepayment of the loan so it can exit, or, as is more likely, negotiate specific actions with the company to bring it into compliance.

Whilst these provisions offer some tangible benefits to communities, they are limited in their ability to recognise and implement secure access to the most important resource for indigenous communities: land. This is

---

[15] Discussed in Chapter 3 and specifically the judicial tests around continuous cultural connection that work to restrain indigenous peoples' development.

[16] Between the Sakhalin Oblast Government, Sakhalin Energy Investment Company Ltd., and the Regional Council of the Authorised Representatives of the Sakhalin Indigenous Minorities.

a negative aspect of these types of indigenous benefit-sharing agreements that concentrate only on general benefits. In this context, the company's use of the international legal standard of FPIC is striking and shines a poor light on the practical methods through which it claims adherence to and implements global legal standards in its operations. In the SIMDP, FPIC is not used in the way in which it was intended when drafted, which is the process through which indigenous peoples must be informed about and give their consent for a prospective project to go ahead *prior* to potentially irremediable project construction activities taking place.[17] Instead, the SIMDP applies the principle to indigenous consultation around the varied good neighbour projects envisaged under the SIMDP.[18] This is an erroneous use of the term in a context in which it was not originally written. The SIMDP tells us nothing about the customary mechanisms through which the indigenous communities affected by the Sakhalin-2 project can communicate and consult with the company over potential alterations to the project design as the project continues to operate over the coming decades. Neither is there any mention of compensation amounts for loss of traditional land. The use of FPIC in these circumstances reveals how transnational companies are, at an operational level, translating and shaping international legal standards at their discretion to suit the practical realities of a now fully commercially operational project, resulting in non-rights–compliant outcomes.

The next illustration comes from the Merian mine involving transnational corporation Newmont Mining. The Merian mine is located in Suriname, in northeast South America, and on the traditional land of Maroon peoples. The Pamaka, one of the country's six Maroon tribes, claims customary ownership of the land on which the mine is located. Suriname Gold Project CV, a Surinamese limited partnership owns the mine. Newmont Suriname, LLC, (previously known as Suriname Gold Company, LLC) is a fully owned subsidiary of Newmont Mining Corporation, which operates the mine on behalf of Suriname Gold Project CV, a Suriname limited partnership. Newmont Suriname is the managing

---

[17] The rationale behind this being that the most adverse impacts of a project on indigenous peoples' territories are mainly during the construction of a project thus highlighting the importance of mobilising the FPIC process long before construction begins.

[18] Referring to the consistent use of the term FPIC in the SIMDP and the cooperation agreement in the context of consultation for the community projects envisaged under the plans.

partner, owning a 75 per cent interest in the limited partnership, and Staatsolie Maatschappij Suriname NV, Suriname's state-owned oil company owns the remaining interest. In February 2016, Newmont commissioned an expert panel comprising indigenous rights expert James Anaya and NGO Human Rights Watch, to interrogate whether and, if so, how the company has applied and implemented FPIC in its dealing with the Maroon community in Suriname from a human rights lens. The investigation resulted in a report on the implementation of FPIC at the mine (the RESOLVE Report).[19]

The context to the Newmont case is an interesting one that again illustrates the interfaces between local and international norms on indigenous peoples' rights together with the implementation-related behaviours of a private actor in the broader context of a rights-incompatible state. There have been multiple judgments[20] from the Inter-American Court affirming the collective rights of the indigenous and tribal peoples of Suriname over lands and natural resources on the basis of the guaranteed rights under the American Convention on Human Rights. Through these rulings the court has made clear that FPIC is one crucial safeguard that will contribute to respect for the rights of indigenous and tribal peoples. Notwithstanding this international legal backdrop, the government has failed to recognise the rights of these communities and has not complied with the core aspects of the legal judgments including the demarcation of land and implementation of domestic law to implement that process. According to the RESOLVE Report, there is a direct link between the complexity of the state not recognising the land and resource rights of the Maroon tribes and the level of ambiguity around how

---

[19] In 2012, RESOLVE, Newmont, BG Group, Oxfam and other companies and civil society organisations established the FPIC Solutions Dialogue to learn from site-based experience, work together on test cases, and develop guidance and tools to help operationalise FPIC in practice. Newmont offered the experience at its Merian mine as an opportunity to gain new insights, identify lessons, and improve practice, with a focus on implementation. See the RESOLVE Report, supra n. 2.

[20] *Moiwana Village* v *Suriname*, IACTHR [2005] Series C. No. 124, *Saramaka People* v *Suriname*, Chapter 3, supra n. 14 and *Kaliña and Lokono Peoples* v *Suriname*, IACTHR [2015] Series C, No. 309. As the RESOLVE Report notes the Saramaka case holds particular relevance for the Merian mine. The Saramaka is one of the largest Maroon tribes, comprising an estimated 42 per cent of Maroon peoples in Suriname. In the mid-1990s, the Government of Suriname granted timber and mining concessions in Saramaka territories without consulting traditional authorities. The Saramaka took their case to the Inter-American Court. Building upon its jurisprudence in the 2001 landmark case of *Awas Tingni* v *Nicaragua* (Chapter 3, supra n. 36) the Court affirmed the collective rights of the Saramaka and ordered the Government of Suriname to recognise those rights.

Newmont approaches the issue of land rights.[21] So whilst the company has in general terms declared that Merian is operating on Pamaka land,[22] in real terms the company has operated and negotiated as if it is operating on state land, not traditionally held land. As analysed below, the scope of the benefits offered demonstrates this practice.

Aspects of the Suriname report display similar characteristics to that of Sakhalin in Newmont's approach to FPIC and the content of benefit-sharing agreements. Similar to Sakhalin Energy, Newmont states that its community engagements at Merian are based on the principles of FPIC but it does not claim to have obtained the FPIC of the Pamaka prior to starting construction. Newmont has instead, similar to Sakhalin Energy, negotiated a set of good neighbour agreements which include a general set of benefits. Through a cooperation agreement which defines each party's roles and responsibilities, the agreement implements specific projects, on infrastructure improvement and maintenance, preferential local employment and procurement, participatory environmental monitoring and community health and safety, all of which have the potential to contribute to the social and economic development of the community. The agreement also refers to establishing a complaints and grievance mechanism, communication and information sharing, and outlines the parameters for the creation of a Pamaka community development foundation. The report also notes positive steps that address the inherent power imbalances between the Maroons, the state and the company, through company provision of independent legal, anthropological and geographic expert advice to the community.[23]

Nonetheless, as the report notes:

> When companies recognize customary land ownership, the nature of consent agreements are stronger because the terms become tied to those rights. This moves beyond achieving good relations with local people and applying the principles of FPIC to the degree that a company chooses. At Merian, recognition of customary land ownership could facilitate a form of consent premised on the full extent of the Pamaka's land rights. While the cooperation agreement did include preferential employment and procurement for the Pamaka, infrastructure improvement and maintenance, a complaints and grievance mechanism, community development funding, and several other benefits, it did not go far enough to create a

[21] RESOLVE Report, supra n. 2, 17.
[22] RESOLVE Report, supra n. 2, referring to a letter of intent entered into between the company and communities prior to the cooperation agreements.
[23] RESOLVE Report, supra n. 2, 27.

truly equitable benefit-sharing agreement that reflects customary ownership interests of the Pamaka. The Pamaka may have consented to community development projects on their territories, but they did not have an
opportunity to consent to resource development, or to negotiate to secure
tangible benefits from the project in exchange for access to their land
holding.[24]

Similar to the Sakhalin project, a major issue is that the mine was, by this
stage, in advanced stages of construction and the community did not
have the chance to voice its concerns and consent to resource development prior to construction taking place, which is the foundation for a
human rights–based approach to FPIC. This raises the question of the
legal basis on which Newmont has negotiated benefits. The negotiation of
benefits from the position of legally recognised rights would result in, as
the report notes, truly equitable benefit sharing. This might take the form
of a right for the community to better compensation, consultation prior
to construction and flowing from this, changes to project design and
build so as to entirely avoid specific areas decided in consultation with
communities, although as the law currently stands the community would
not be able to veto development. The scope of benefits provided by both
Newmont and Sakhalin and their approach to FPIC as applying to the
negotiation of good neighbour benefits suggests an approach that does
not satisfy a human rights–based approach to FPIC that is negotiated on
the basis of land ownership, but rather a company based approach
to FPIC.

The Sakhalin and Newmont studies illustrate some important points
about the relationship between local, international and private remedies.
They signal a link between the quantity and quality of benefit sharing and
the strength of domestic legal recognition of customary rights. In other
words, the level of ambiguity or fudge in a company's recognition can
mirror the uncertainty and lacunas in the legal framework. The studies
also illustrate mischief in how companies are implementing FPIC into
their projects in a manner that does not take seriously FPIC rights as
legally recognised rights and processes that are owed to communities
before any private land impact can take place. The reason for this
mischief also correlates with the ambiguity of international and domestic
law to effectively police and implement these rights at the state level.

---

[24] RESOLVE Report, supra n. 2, 18.

4   The Rio Tinto Approach in Australia: Communities as Project Stakeholders

In 2011 Rio Tinto signed a series of agreements with aboriginal traditional owners relating to an iron ore project in the Pilbara region of Australia. These agreements are different to those negotiated in the Suriname and Russian studies as they are divided into one set of good neighbour benefit agreements relating to issues such as education, housing and general development for the communities contained in a set of 'regional standard agreements', and another set of entitlements under a 'participation agreement' that relates solely to land rights. The positive and negative aspects of the latter participation agreement are the subject of this analysis.

Many examples of agreement-making have come from Australia[25] where there is domestic legal recognition of indigenous groups and related legal requirements for companies to negotiate and enter into agreements with groups. Australia's Native Title Act 1993 (NTA) requires companies that have been granted any lease or licence to negotiate with aboriginal communities that have a legally recognised interest in the land as native title holders or registered native title claimants. As discussed in Chapter 3, after Mabo, jurisprudence on the scope of traditional rights has been disappointing. Courts have chosen to frame traditional rights as narrow site-specific rights and interests such as hunting or fishing rights, ceremonial rights and access rights and have limited the ability of communities to develop those rights beyond a specific site, in order to secure their long-term economic and cultural survival. Moreover, whilst numerous legal systems have specific statutory or constitutional provisions[26] recognising so-called informal and indigenous rights to land, there are, as has been highlighted in Chapter 3, significant blocks to the implementation of those mechanisms.

For instance, as discussed in Chapter 3, in countries where a right to consult or compromise is enshrined in statutory or constitutional norms, that right is limited because the domestic legal framework gives communities a right to negotiate, typically for a prescribed period.[27] During that time there will be a moratorium on any economic activities and parties

---

[25] C Faircheallaigh, 'Negotiating Cultural Heritage? Aboriginal– Mining Company Agreements in Australia' (2008) 39 *Development and Change* 25.

[26] Chapter 3 provides examples.

[27] Under section 35 of the Native Title Act the period is six months.

are required to negotiate in good faith. In Australia, legal consultation rights do not constitute a veto[28] but a legal obligation to consult with, listen to or 'compromise'[29] with traditional owners and for communities to gain a seat at the negotiation table for a minimum period of six months. However, if no agreement is reached within that period, the relevant minister will make a determination based on requirements set out in the NTA such as national interest. This is a legal position similar to eminent domain.

So, whilst one of the fundamental legal rights provided in the NTA scheme is of consultation with registered native title claimants having the right to negotiate with companies on indigenous land-use agreements, this right must be viewed against a larger context of what would happen if no agreement is reached and which set of power dynamics and property rights will take precedence in a default no-agreement situation.

Against this legal context, the participation agreement contains some positive features. First, as I will show, they go further than good neighbour entitlements and give detailed focus to the issue of land rights, elaborating on legal processes of consultation and compromise. Another positive point is the starting point of the agreements, especially when contrasted with the findings of the Merian study. Through specific clauses the agreement expressly recognises indigenous land ownership as the foundation for agreement-making. That ownership might flow from a positive native title determination, a common law determination of native title or from the group claiming to have rights or responsibilities under aboriginal law that fall within the agreement area. There is also clear recognition that groups that are the subject of the agreement have 'Traditional Responsibility'[30] for land and waters in the agreement area

---

[28] As assessed in Chapter 3, the Australian position informs the position under international law.

[29] *Brownley* v *State of Western Australia* [1999] FCA 1139 states that the intention of Parliament is that a government party engage in negotiation with a native title claimant with an open mind, willingness to listen, and willingness to compromise, to reach an agreement under which the native title claimant will agree to government doing the act it proposes.

[30] In the contract this is defined as Aboriginal Persons with (a) either a genealogical connection to the Aboriginal Persons in occupation of the Agreement Area at sovereignty, or another form of connection to the Agreement Area (including through adoption, incorporation or historical circumstances) or (b) persons with rights and responsibilities under Aboriginal Law and customs in respect of the Agreement Area.

even if those rights are not formally recognised by the laws of Australia and the state.[31]

There are clauses recognising that previous governments, companies and other persons may have, in the past, tried to use the agreement area to secure economic benefits for themselves without paying compensation. Other clauses confirm the company's commitment – through the agreement, to improve its relationship with the group, confer mining-related benefits that will empower the socio-economic circumstances of the group and facilitate ongoing traditional cultural life. The overall result is that benefits are negotiated from a starting point based in legal recognition. From this base there is a possibility, at least, for deeper and more equitable benefits that relate not only to good neighbour benefits but also translate into better outcomes for the recognition and implementation of customary land rights.

Next, the process of agreement-making is, as is required under the NTA, taking place prior to land incursion, resulting in a more human rights–compliant interpretation of consultation than seen in other examples. The primary method through which pre-construction stage agreement-making and consultation is satisfied within the agreement is through requirements relating to rights-reserved areas. The basic principle behind the consultation process is that traditional owners will support Rio Tinto's operations only if it follows the procedures contained in the agreement. This involves a process in which native title property rights are, by default, reserved in favour of traditional owners. The reservation of specific sites is undertaken through a process in which traditional owners work with the company to identify cultural sites and sites of special cultural interest. Through this process, if traditional owners designate a site as of significant cultural importance with traditional property rights, the community and company then work together to ensure that the site is entirely avoided so that groups can continue to have access to that land. If the site cannot be entirely avoided, steps to mitigate adverse effects are negotiated so that the company will have the group's consent prior to lodging a mining application. This mitigation might involve modification of the project design to avoid sites of cultural significance with specific provisions in the agreement relating to this.

---

[31] Clause 4.2 (Recognition).

During negotiations, traditional owners identified areas as being of high cultural importance to them.[32] Based on confidential information provided by traditional owners, it was agreed that certain types of moratorium could be placed on specific areas such that groups can retain access. These mining restrictions are embedded within the agreement in the form of several layers depending on the type of land restriction agreed. The manager of indigenous agreements[33] described that Rio Tinto agreed to move boundaries back in some areas so that significant aboriginal sites were not disturbed, to bend pipelines around specific areas and to exclude entirely from the exploration licence sites of high cultural significance that are sitting on substantial iron ore reserves.[34] Rio Tinto's land geographic information system then embeds data relating to those restricted land access points. This means that any future mining tenements remain on notice as to the restrictive covenants over those culturally significant land interests, ensuring that groups retain access over these sites. Interlocutors conceded that forging consent and agreement making was one of the most difficult aspects of this process. Central to this difficulty was the multidimensional aspect of consent requiring input from legal, anthropological and sociological advisors that often ran against project schedules and time constraints. It is a positive development that in this case the company took the time to develop and implement a process of agreement-making that has taken place prior to incursions on land. That said, the practice of implementing agreement-making for these agreements reveals some negative aspects.

Rio Tinto's response to the complexities of dealing with traditional decision-making processes, conflicts amongst groups and an overall lack of familiarity amongst communities with decision-making processes, was to introduce the concept of representative bodies. In this scenario, implementation takes place through the incorporation of local representative bodies incorporated as corporate vehicles. Whilst a former legal advisor to Rio acknowledged the challenges of training groups to work within western concepts of board meetings, shareholder decision-making, quorums and appointment of directors to make decisions, the

---

[32] Interview with former legal counsel to Rio Tinto on agreement-making, on file with author.

[33] Interviews with manager of agreement-making and acting manager of indigenous employment, business development and planning, Rio Tinto, on file with author.

[34] In the agreement one such area over culturally significant land and traditional land rights was excluded as 'outside the boundary of explorations licence Z'.

company view remains that corporate structures are the best and only model to provide for communal agency action. Whilst corporate models are indeed effective for the corporation, it is highly dubious that retrofitting these models onto the norms and practice of indigenous groups serves their interests effectively.[35] This practice can be compared with the Sakhalin and Merian examples in which both companies agreed that all issues of decision-making and consultation will be conducted in accordance with customary practices.

Another interesting feature of the agreement lies in its scheme for compensation payments, called mining-benefit payments. Legal counsel for groups explained that they fought hard to obtain both forms of land access and financial compensation. The rationale for this legal approach involved:

> Looking at development as binary and saying groups do not want anything or want only compensation misses the point. They recognise that answers are not simple and it is not practical to turn away: they now live in two worlds where mining will go ahead but they also want some benefits and the ability to stay and protect their country. In reality they would want both: compensation and the ability to access and protect country.[36]

The payments constitute compensation for current mining operations and are linked to groups providing consent for operations and access to land. Payments have a dual purpose. According to the company, they form part of a process of socio-economic empowerment to develop life skills rather than entirely relying on Rio financially[37] and are also aimed at providing business certainty.[38] In terms of quantum, the contracts fill in a lacuna that I discussed in Chapter 3 on the difficulty courts had in the *Timber Creek* case[39] with awarding damages for extinguishment of non-economic rights to land. So it seems that at present, $1.3 million is the quantum for non-economic loss, although it is likely that corporations will appeal that amount. Interestingly, Rio Tinto is well aware of

---

[35] L Godden and M Tehan, *Comparative Perspectives on Communal Lands and Individual Ownership: Sustainable Futures* (Routledge 2010).

[36] Interview with legal counsel to aboriginal groups, on file with author.

[37] Supra n. 33.

[38] Clause 14: the purpose of the financial payments is to provide certainty to Rio that amounts paid constitute final compensation for everything Rio has done previously and is allowed to do under the agreement in future, excepting negligent acts and contractual breach.

[39] *Northern Territory* case [2019], Chapter 3, supra n. 63.

the law's ambiguity on how much compensation would be given for traditional land, noting that the compensation regime set out in the agreement would certainly exceed any amount awarded under the native title regime.[40] Compensatory norms are quantified within the agreement; however, the precise amount is confidential. Whilst some companies have buffers through the provision of price floor and ceilings above and below which payments cannot move, the agreement does not contain such a process. Payments under the agreement are designed to work like a partnership or benefit-sharing model in which the parties, as stakeholders, share gains and losses. Rio Tinto will then make those payments into a trust for a shifting class of beneficiaries (the traditional owners). That trust is set up under the agreement pursuant to which funds will be invested according to a set formula. Whilst this partnering approach may have positive empowerment benefits, there are several problems, which I now analyse.

Overall, this approach to compensation signals that the company views groups as project stakeholders with legal entitlement to land rather than as targets of corporate social responsibility. This is a position with positive and negative effects. Whilst it may have positive results in that groups can negotiate deeper and more equitable benefit sharing, it is not clear what factors have contributed to this approach giving this practice a quality of unpredictability. It may purely be the specific Australian context that operates as a stick that urges companies to operate on this basis and provides communities with some power and leverage to demand better benefits. Looking back at the more good neighbour set of generic benefits offered by companies in the Sakhalin and Merian cases, in which the level of state presence and recognition was low, a stakeholder approach based on legal entitlements may well be linked to domestic legal recognition and related regulations requiring agreement-making.

At the same time, rushing to make indigenous communities project stakeholders should be treated with caution as it fails to give adequate recognition to the structural and intense historical vulnerabilities upon which communities are entering into agreements. Indeed the term stakeholder has an inherently commercial meaning which manifests in the Rio contract: communities are held on an arm's-length basis with the contract making it clear that no fiduciary or special relationship is created

---

[40] Supra n. 33.

between the company and the community. There are deliberate and carefully scoped out sets of entitlements that cannot be easily renegotiated and provisions that mean that benefit payments are linked to overall project losses and gains. Indeed, once communities are made 'stakeholders' by signing the agreement, they become vulnerable to the risk of all contractual benefits being pegged against the price of ore. As a lawyer to the aboriginal groups noted:

> My work at the Yamatji Marlpa Aboriginal Corporation is driven by the price of iron ore. During the 2006-2010 mining boom when the price of ore dropped and China's appetite was immense, YMAC was courted by a number of companies including RT, Hancock Prospecting Pty and BHP Billiton looking to seek access to country.. ..due to the low price of ore and massive Chinese demand companies may have been more willing to spend time and money on agreements.[41]

Thus, a negative aspect that comes out of the agreements is a signal that companies merge compliance with domestic and international law on indigenous rights through contractual arrangements that make communities business partners to a project. This is a position that needs to be treated with extreme care given the inability of traditional communities to operate in a private market-orientated fashion and the asymmetrical power dynamics in such a paradigm.

The PA illustrates some positive aspects showing how, through carefully worded agreements that are negotiated from a basis of recognition of customary land rights, there might be some positive outcomes for communities. As discussed, these include human rights–compliant consultation processes that occur prior to construction, enhanced compensation and consultation processes that maintain access rights and impose mining restrictions for special cultural sites. These contractual measures go beyond what is required under the formal legal framework. There are, however, multiple negative outcomes not least in the power dynamics at play, consultation processes that do not reflect customary practices and the problems of making indigenous actors commercial stakeholders who are exposed to falls in commodity prices, which can result in further vulnerability. It is not acceptable that indigenous communities should share in the negative turn of a project. A more equitable arrangement for a company with as deep a pocket and leverage as Rio Tinto should be to

---

[41] Supra n. 36.

plan and budget for keeping communities financially protected in the event of any cyclical market downturn.

5   Leaving Your Principles at Home? A Comparative Look at Rio in Mongolia

The final illustration of agreement-making comes from the Mongolian Oyu Tolgoi project discussed in Chapter 5, also involving Rio Tinto. Comparing this project with that of the behaviour of Rio Tinto in the Pilbara project, shows vastly different behaviours and uneven practices when corporations interface with differing domestic local contexts with varying levels of indigenous recognition. The lengths that Rio Tinto went to in the Pilbara project to take preventative measures, expend time and commit considerable financial resources in early agreement-making is sharply contrasted with the Mongolian study, where no such measures were taken. Instead, NGOs had to work hard to overcome the significant power imbalances, consistently pushing Rio through the grievance mechanism of the IFC to enter into a mediation process which culminated in a written agreement.

In 2017, Rio entered into an implementation plan of agreed actions, to be monitored by the IFC, to resolve the complaints of local herders.[42] Aspects of this agreement provide further insights into the frequently hidden interfaces and connections between private agreements, international law and domestic courts. First, Rio states in the agreement that the herders claim indigenous status. This position shows the strength of the herders' customary legal claim despite the lack of formal recognition under Mongolian law. Second, amongst the boilerplate dispute resolution clauses, the parties agree that to the extent any dispute cannot be settled amicably, it can be elevated to a court. This is a remarkable undertaking given that it opens the door for any future dispute over the terms and implementation of the agreement to be heard in court. It would also mean that a court could give its view on whether the herders are indeed indigenous, thereby opening the door for wider social debates and activism around this issue. In such a case, some of the wording within the publicly available agreement could become persuasive. For example,

---

[42] Herders' Complaint Resolution Agreement, 9th May 2017, between the Khanbogd Soum Government, Elected Representatives of Khanbogd Soum Bagh Herders and Oyu Tolgoi LLC. www.cao-ombudsman.org/cases/document-links/documents/OT2_CompaintReso lutionAgreement2_ENG.pdf.

the project company has provided the herders with a letter of apology appended to the agreement, which expressly acknowledges the herders' long customary connections to the land and Undai River and the hasty work the project company undertook along the river without consultation.

Third, the scope of the remedies are far-reaching and constitute a mix of the good neighbour benefits seen in the Merian and Sakhalin cases with some land-specific remedies similar to the Pilbara agreement. For example, the contract contains a formal letter of apology, discussed above, more complete compensation and provisions for consultation over the redesign of the project to avoid sacred sites located within the mine-lease area. There are also good neighbour benefits which include the injection of financing for socio-economic and cultural projects on vegetation, development of traditional herder knowledge and livelihood practices, including the creation of supply chains for livestock raw material producers, and projects that connect herders' deep wells with renewable-energy initiatives. The NGO involved in the complaint, Accountability Counsel and members of the herders involved in the mediation, have commented on how the tripartite councils set up under the agreements that included herder communities and their elected representatives, local government and the company, overcame significant power imbalances with the help of Accountability Counsel.[43] Of course, the effective implementation of these agreements must be continuously monitored.

Negatively, as Rio does not formally acknowledge herders as indigenous, the basis for the negotiation of these benefits is the ongoing dispute with the herders and not formal recognition under domestic and international law, as is the case in the Pilbara agreement, which offers a more extensive range of benefits, not least ongoing mining-benefit payments. The herders have not been awarded any compensation for loss of their ancestral rights to land in the form of a trust arrangement, for example. Positively, however, the content of the Oyu Tolgoi agreement demonstrates how advocacy and the use of private ombudsman mechanisms can, with NGO pressure and a DFI complaint mechanism, be an effective tool for the recognition and implementation of indigenous peoples' rights in a situation where a state is not rights compliant.

---

[43] Accountability Counsel website. www.accountabilitycounsel.org/client-case/mongolia-south-gobi-mining/#impact.

A comparative look at all of these cases illustrates an alarming level of fragmentation and uneven treatment of vulnerable groups that share the same experience of dispossession and vulnerability when faced with large development projects. For example the differing behaviour and outcomes of Rio Tinto in the Australian and Mongolian projects illustrates how a transnational company operating in a mature legal system with statutory recognition of indigenous rights can leave its manners and principles at home when it conducts similar large development project operations in another location, but where there is no recognition of indigenous peoples' rights. It has also taken many years for herders to reach a resolution agreement, with the mechanics of the project financing producing enabling conditions through which Rio and its financiers could effectively sideline the voices of herders claiming indigenous status.[44] These results run contrary to assumptions about the ability of private grievance mechanisms to help communities with limited access to the formal justice sector. The above examples also demonstrate how corporate practice on agreement-making can, in situations of low or no state regulation, work to corporatise the meaning of FPIC and de-root the principle from its legally intended meaning, i.e., as a consent process specifically relating to land which must be undertaken prior to land disturbance/construction.

Whilst some positive aspects to agreement-making exist, as illustrated, corporate policy around agreement-making and its subsequent quality will turn drastically on disparate factors. These include the economics of the project, individual corporate commitment, local resistance, the level of recognition, commitment and enforcement of domestic and international law that is shown by the state, and even the presence of a voluntary private complaints mechanism. Consequently, the overall fragmentation of rights across contracts secretly negotiated under disparate conditions and with no outside regulation makes it challenging for communities in comparable situations to build a scientifically informed, uniform minimum baseline of rights through a bank of precedents that could facilitate advocacy around the better recognition and implementation of traditional rights to land in development project contexts.

---

[44] Discussed in Chapter 5.

Moving Forward

The preceding chapters have investigated ways in which transnational development projects constitute a unique regulatory challenge for the development agenda, efforts around rights recognition and implementation, vulnerability and contemporary dynamics for social expulsion. Sitting at an idiosyncratic juncture of law, economics, institutions and vulnerability studies, it is useful to recall the core themes that have brought this study together: power (lessness), fragmentation, state remoteness, delegation, fairness and integration. These themes signal that development projects constitute slippery regulatory targets that upset traditional legal thinking, structures and organising logic around the way in which the law operates in globalised settings. Critique should be constructive in order to have value. In this spirit, some of the previous chapters have made suggestions on how to regulate these projects so that they provide clearer, more predictable and fairer 'rule-of-law'–compliant outcomes for the recognition and implementation of indigenous peoples' rights to land and thus begin to redress some of the huge power imbalances within these projects that can find unhappy conclusions in land-grabbing scenarios. In this final chapter, I summarise the findings by bundling them into themes and I conclude with some recommendations for an overall remedial agenda.

1 Regulatory Deficit

At various points it has been argued that the legal architecture around development projects fails to adequately recognise and regulate for indigenous peoples' rights – deprioritising them in favour of a larger political economy of land commodification that has, in turn, been supported by the rules that sustain global capital investment and the global financial architecture – contract and private property rights. At the moment, practice around the recognition and implementation of indigenous rights to land in these projects is, by and large, taking place within a shielded zone which prioritises the projects' creditors and shareholders, to the obvious benefit of concessionaires and financiers and the detriment of communities. The result for those communities: repetitive injustices and exclusion.

This points at a systemic legal failure in which traditional state-centred legal orders have been unable to cope with and counteract the growth of the extralegal nature of norms in the global financial market-place of transnational development, and the highly specialised legal disciplines that enable that market and unseat state power itself, such as project finance and direct commercial agreement-making. At the same time, traditional legal orders are deeply implicated in furthering those projects at the cost of alternative claims to land and the develop-ment of indigenous peoples' land rights in development project con-texts. This systemic failure has been illustrated through jurisprudence which displays embryonic and limited legal strategies for regulating this hyper-plural legal field and values that defer to neoliberal logic. This is highlighted in the lack of a legally binding right that fully delivers on article 32 of the UNDRIP, providing indigenous communities with the right to say no to development prior to the occurrence of any land incursions. Without this right, what is the current legal standard of consultation and compromise for?

On a macro level, international law struggles to reel in the enterprise-led state and account for the plurality of norms, actors and institutions that constitute the main protagonists in these projects. One can lament international law's role in forming institutions such as the World Bank Group and other multilateral development finance institutions that are endowed with the economic and technical mechanisms assessed in the previous chapters that will, through their development agendas, become deeply intertwined with a local historic political socio-economy. At the same time as forming and clothing these institutions, international law has not provided the legal tools for addressing the conflicts and human rights impacts that would flow from their operations. The instrumental use of international law in facilitating the creation and operation of these key players in the club of global development finance, its meaningless allegiance to public and private law binaries in the hyper plural socio-legal field of development project finance and the limited legal treatment of indigenous peoples' rights when confronted with development projects and capital expansion all have something in common. They provide further illustrations of the role of international law in the 'legal rendering of immiseration'[1] in the global economy.

A fundamental problem in these activities, as was illustrated in Chapters 4, 5 and 6, is the routine blurring and informal delegation of legal roles and responsibilities between the state and private actors that occurs in the shadow of formal law. Rights implementation will thus take place in confused, conflicted and largely unaccountable ways. Processes for rights recognition and implementation are shaped through standards designed by financiers who are not on the ground, implemented by their clients who are on the ground and private experts that are hired by the company and paid by the lenders. All the while, the state sits in the shadows and becomes enterprise led, and frequently enjoys a shareholding in the project itself. In other situations, concessionaires might enter into confidential legally binding private agreements with indigenous communities as illustrated in Chapter 7. A black box is formed in which formal legal standards can become invisible, or, removed from their original legal meaning to suit where concessionaires are in a specific project schedule.

Equally, the promise of accountability and redress for communities that is offered through the growing network of financial ombudsman mechanisms has, whilst being a good start, been inherently compromised by the structural technicalities of a project that are well-formed and shielded by the rules of private law: its underlying standardised contractual terms, incentives, scheduling, discretionary behaviour and over-reliance on privately hired experts. These contractual and policy mechanisms produce conditions that will query the inherent ability of ombudsman mechanisms to deliver on accountability, whilst these structures remain so deeply entrenched within paperwork and mindsets. Moreover, currently there is neither independent domestic or international regulation around these private financial mechanisms nor have they been given sufficient policy and research attention. The result is, as I have illustrated, that significant gaps have opened up in which private arrangements and clauses will automatically privilege the private property rights of the concessionaire, displacing the rights of indigenous communities through automatic and almost contractually automated

---

[1] See J Linarelli, ME Salomon and M Sornarajah, *The Misery of International Law: Confrontations with Injustice in the Global Economy* (Oxford University Press, 2018).

ways. All of these synergies can sow the seeds for future social conflict. The same can be said about the growing practice of concessionaire–community agreement-making and the lack of regulation around it. The lack of information around the conditions and content of these practices, scholarly hesitance to see them as part of an ever-growing, rich, international economic legal order and the demarcation of these agreements as purely private contracts, are crippling barriers to regulation and real-world legal thinking.

Another major gap is seen in current due diligence practices not addressing the ways in which a development project and its contractual matrix and behaviours around them can contribute to poor recognition, implementation and vulnerability. Furthermore, in the highly fragmented legal framework on indigenous rights to land in development projects and the irreversible effects of getting things wrong in this setting, it is not good enough to talk about due diligence as a voluntary compliance responsibility rather than an obligation. A responsibility-based, rather than an obligation-based, approach as in the UNGPs is not hard enough to encourage companies or financiers to conduct due diligence and deliver fairness to groups that are powerless against the numerous hidden layers of legal and policy orders, practices and behaviours bearing on them in a development project scenario. The language of responsibility makes common sense for developers and financiers that do not want to become caught up in litigation, conflict and complaints. Thus, systemic legal change is required to tackle these deficits, starting at the national level and then, through codes of practice, directly engage with policy and contracts. These efforts can be buttressed by research and advocacy that touches on some of the under-researched aspects of development projects discussed in this book. Recommendations on what this could look like are detailed below.

As can be seen, regulatory deficits in the recognition and implementation of indigenous peoples' rights to land in development projects exist along an entire chain of law and 'non-law' or extralegal mechanisms and involve multiple types of actors from plural disciplinary fields; thus redressing these gaps requires a multi-actor approach. There are however some positive developments which I will start with.

First, there has been a growing recognition and development of indigenous rights over the last twenty years with some increasing focus on indigeneity as a transnational global movement. With the success of the UNGPs, the business and human rights community has developed into a stand-alone legal field that has certainly spurred advocacy in legal fields of direct relevance to accountability of development projects such as the recent *Jam* case discussed in Chapter 3. These movements have made significant inroads into addressing the legal gaps discussed in that chapter and thus regulate private actors in transnational development finance contexts. It does, however, remain to be seen how effectively the proposed binding treaty on business and human rights and the *Jam* case will translate into practice and eventually, due diligence strategies. Another positive development is the work of NGOs such as Accountability Counsel, SOMO, Earth Rights and Both Ends, in conjunction with local NGOs, that brought development projects into public focus and, as illustrated, have helped to broker legal outcomes.

The last ten years has also seen an increasing agenda amongst financiers for environmental and social compliance resulting in the growth of specific internal environmental and social teams and the mushrooming of grievance mechanisms. As analysed in Chapter 4, there are some positive aspects within existing financial instruments that already recognise the existence of alternative claims to land, and the growing practice of agreement-making does illustrate some useful developments for plugging the gaps in the current legal framework. At the same time, we must not fall into the trap of thinking that the development of safeguarding standards, grievance mechanisms and agreement-making are silver bullets for addressing the major deficits in the legal and political regulation and power asymmetries that have captured this field.

As we have seen, opening the mysterious box of development finance institutes to analyse the contractual and policy framework they apply that governs relationships between their client concessionaires and local communities as well as the behaviours around the implementation of that framework, will frequently vitiate the implementation of indigenous rights and impair any human rights–compliant approach. This is concerning given the secrecy around the implementation of these policies and contracts, and the lack of measures to independently oversee these practices. It is, therefore, crucial that the existing private mechanisms are exposed for their shortcomings and substantially amended. Given the importance being placed on private finance and public-private partnerships in the push to meet the Sustainable Development Goals, this is timely. Within this constellation of regulatory deficits, some major areas of concern are visible. More advocacy work could be undertaken to bring the relevance of these issues into view for the law (broadly conceived) and development agenda.

2   Contractual Clauses

At various points in the preceding chapters it has been argued that the fundamental structures of project finance do very little to close the lacunas in the formal legal framework. Those structures can, in fact, make matters worse for indigenous communities in unexpected ways as they work to amplify a short-term culture that is obsessed with shareholder return. That culture places utmost pressure on the project participants, which often includes the government, to ensure the predictability of revenue streams and prevent any external factors from piercing the project's special purpose ring fence. Consequently, financiers and concessionaires focus on securing a bankable project in which as much endogenous risk is pushed away from the shell project company in order to keep revenue streams consistent and at a pre-modelled optimum amount of return. Given that in a limited recourse project finance context, debt and equity payments are made upon from sale of the asset or service produced by the project, the construction phase presents a highly precarious stage for lenders and communities. This is because lenders and sponsors have lent to a project and are thus fully exposed and sensitive to risks that could damage project construction and operation and, thus, their financially modelled future debt service. The heightened sensitivity and drive for predictability interfaces with the need to clear land to start the construction process. Inevitable clashes with holders of customary land rights and the potential for large-scale forced eviction can, therefore, be accentuated by these contractual preoccupations.

A number of features can impact upon the recognition of alternative land claims and drive or pre-dispose the concessionaire and financiers towards actions that result in rights violations. These features include a thirst for algorithmic contract standardisation and the negotiation of contracts that protect and prioritise the developers' property rights and thus future income flow. More specifically, many of the core project documents, such as the concession contract through which the state divests land, are negotiated during the early development stage. Examination of current practice shows that existing mechanisms fail to adequately grip onto the governance framework and thus recognise and make provision for alternative claims to land within contractual arrangements. At the pre-construction and construction phases, and specifically the grant of permit and negotiation of concession stage, both of which are hotspots for indigenous rights due to the risk they pose for irremediable land clearance, information is missing, not considered or if considered, moulded within contractual clauses to further the interests of the developer.

For instance, host support agreements entered into at this stage will frequently contain non-discrimination provisions which have a similar effect as stabilisation of law clauses. Completion guarantee structures in which the state guarantees a large percentage of the debt, will also encourage the state to see like an enterprise at this point of rights vulnerability. As has been assessed, it will be standard practice for interest rates to be higher during the construction phase to reflect the increased risk to project finance lenders. This financing practice motivates the project company to get through this stage as quickly as possible so that interest rates will ratchet down. Clauses for liquidated damages in the construction contract as well as the lack of information on indigenous issues and consent in the completion certification will all reinforce the forward motion of the project during this hotspot stage. And whilst clauses exist for implementing environmental and social safeguards into the loan agreements, the incentives and culture of the financiers and concessionaires that advise on and implement these measures can render any due diligence a purely formalistic and paperwork process. As illustrated in the Panama case this rigid culture can defy common sense and certainly obfuscate a human rights–compliant approach to the recognition and implementation of indigenous rights to land.

Concessionaires may argue that they simply do not have enough time for consultation and rights-compatible implementation. However, as illustrated in the previous studies there is often a considerable time-lag between exploration through to financing which can often stretch up to a decade, this argument holds little sway. In fact, the consideration of these issues in the earlier development stage would be the ideal period as the heightened incentives towards construction that kick in during the financing stage do not still exist. Financiers can still, at this stage, decide not to fund the project. If at this moment, concessionaires (through leverage from their financiers) are forced to inject a progressive, long-term and upstream mentality to implementing safeguarding standards, it could be possible to sequence mechanisms and actions for recognition, implementation and trust building at this pre-construction period and gain community approval. Suggestions of what this progressive stance could look like are made in the recommendations section below.

This is perhaps a tall order as it would require wholesale cultural change, a concern that I now discuss.

3 Incentives and Culture

As seen in a number of previous cases, there are places at which important information is not considered, not made available, or considered too late. This points to a much larger problem around concessionaire and financier incentive structures and culture that needs remedy. Given that financial organisations are keenly lending into the development agenda, wholesale cultural adaptation and mindset change is needed such that operations teams will think beyond a culpability tick-the-box model (and insist that their client companies do the same) to one that considers the leverage and power that DFIs and companies have for progressively and creatively realising safeguarding standards through early prevention.

Obviously, closing the many lacunas in the governance framework for development projects urgently requires companies and financiers to see human rights as part of their core activities – there is nothing new about this general observation. However, what is new are the suggested methods through which early due diligence on land and indigenous peoples can be seen as good for business and a sensible proxy for stable investment. In this regard, investors should be asking specific questions to companies on how their internal incentives and behavioural culture delivers on these issues prior to committing funds. Answering these questions would require companies to critically reflect on how these issues affect their work, where these risks integrate into contractual and management systems and decision processes and determine who, at corporate level, has responsibility for them. This means grappling with difficult and expensive issues. Specifically, these include scheduling of decisions; conflicts of interest; over-reliance on privately appointed experts appointed by the company and paid for by the lenders; and documentation that ignores local realities, misapplies FPIC requirements or treats communities as business stakeholders. Clearly, this approach is at odds with the short-term ideology of financiers and companies who are only answerable to their shareholders. Nonetheless, these incentives require attention and I discuss further recommendations for this in Section 4.

As the preceding chapters have illustrated, there is also a correlation between the legal nature of the domestic and international legal framework and the extent to which corporations and financiers will take these issues seriously within their operations. So, something more needs to be done to address the lacunas in the legal framework which can, in turn provide the legal threat needed to motivate behavioural change and trigger specific actions within the governance framework.

4 Ecosystem of Remedies

Throughout the book, I have made a case for an approach that emphasises integrative efforts between judicial and non-judicial processes in order to fill the regulatory deficits that are a hallmark of this field. Criticisms to this approach might include the inability of private actors to move from a short-term to a long-term lens in which profit will be relegated to issues of human rights and fair outcomes ('Is this realistic?' and 'It sounds expensive'). Other arguments against the approach include the practical inability of the state to force these changes through using targeted regulation, or that a focus on private mechanisms encourages private power and the privatisation of public law issues.

These concerns only demonstrate the urgency and complexity of the problem that indigenous communities face when confronted with the growing phenomenon of development projects. In real terms, these projects show no sign of abating given the current sustainable development agenda. There is, therefore, a need to think creatively about state, non-state and hybrid processes through which the gaps in the legal framework surrounding large development projects can be plugged. Making systemic legal changes to plug international and domestic law's inability to directly regulate private actors in the slippery and conflicted circumstances of resource and infrastructure development is essential, but so is exposing and then constructively engaging with the private contracts, financier policies and related behaviours that permeate this field and show no sign of disappearing. In this spirit of realism, the following recommendations think about complementary changes across an ecosystem of judicial and non-judicial processes that could promote fairer and more equitable outcomes for indigenous communities in these circumstances.

5 Proposed Remedial Agenda

Many changes to the existing framework for transnational development projects are required to make it clearer and fairer for indigenous peoples. It is important to keep in mind that given the level of fragmentation, powerful vested interests and regulatory deficit in the field, the quest for a perfect solution is, in practice, somewhat illusive. Nonetheless, some progressive engagement across state, non-state actors, NGOs, policy-makers and academics for addressing the automated power imbalances and legal hierarchies in this field through changes to formal and informal mechanisms, domestic and international law and subsequently, behaviours, could bear fruit.

5.1   Legal and Regulatory Oversight

1. *Special legislation that recognises the special vulnerability of land-connected people in the context of transnational development projects.*

Far more attention needs to be given to the upstream, that is, pre-construction stages of development projects and the ability of communities to say no to a project prior to land incursion. To this end, as a core minimum standard, national legislation should require that early in a project life cycle (before the grant of any lease or licence, and not after project design), no land clearance can take place and that a development project conflict prevention assessment is undertaken. This type of assessment process can form the basis for a new type of consultative licence permit that is delivered by a state department and is a compulsory requirement for any concessionaire. Companies should be required to deliver the assessment with their licence application. Crucially, the law must stipulate that if during this assessment process, the community decides that they do not want the project to go ahead, the state and companies must respect this decision regardless of wasted costs, thus giving communities a veto right.

That assessment must address the layers of issues that could contribute to building trust, reducing conflict and risk reduction for concessionaires and could include the following legal strategies.

2. *Measures targeting the stage prior to grant of the mining permit/concession.*

The assessment would need all of the key actors at the table (including the state and the concessionaire) for an extended period of time.

During that time companies must disclose, on an ongoing basis, the ownership structure of the project, including the identity of the project shareholders (plus all beneficial owners), financiers, and who the company has contracted to conduct any land clearance processes. This information must then be made publicly available on the website of the relevant ministry.

The legal expectation should be that all land claims (irrespective of formal legal recognition) are mapped as part of the assessment and made publicly available for consultation. The assessment must contain information on these claims, proposed processes for local mediation, FPIC strategies that evidence corporate involvement with local context and land legacy issues (if any), and a heads of terms for a future negotiated process, all of which must also be made public or anonymous, on community request. That heads of terms must set out basic principles for mediation and concrete measures to support FPIC and related rights to access land and water throughout the project duration, for instance.

This is a clear way to translate aspects of the formal legal framework for good faith consultation and trust into the governance framework. Importantly, the above process must carry the legitimacy of communities and require the concessionaire to consult with and include indigenous peoples in project design prior to construction. Suggestions for the funding and independence of this process are made at point 7. This assessment (or redacted versions thereof) should then be appended to the concession as part of a state permitting requirement. The concessionaire could then be required to immediately deliver this information to any prospective lenders through, for instance, the preliminary information memorandum (PIM) mechanism and provide written acknowledgement to the relevant ministry from a lender as evidence of delivery.

Taking these steps prior to construction are vital for a UNDRIP compliant approach. Given the lack of state incentive in taking these domestic measures when it is a project shareholder, DFIs can use their leverage to advocate for this type of legislation or, failing that, formulate a code of practice stating that they will not provide financing for a project without evidence of the above assessment. In this regard, they can require that any prospective client deliver this type of information within the PIM mechanism. Crucially, DFIs can exert leverage on the borrower's contractual framework stating that any future loan agreement cannot allow the waiver of this part of the permit. Whilst it would be difficult to regulate for these requirements at the state level because the loan is between private parties, this could form part of a code of practice, discussed below.

The above recommendations would begin to address the current practice of the concessionaire conducting a retroactive gap analysis *after* resettlement has occurred due to the later entry of DFIs, which for many communities constitutes a legal and governance failure.

3. Communities must have the legal right to say no to a project before land is disturbed and regardless of a company's wasted costs.

States are well aware of the polarised starting points of many communities and concessionaires and thus have a clear role to play as more private actors go into developing countries, some of which have fragile and post-conflict contexts. In this area it cannot be the sole domain of the private sector to solve fundamental domestic legal issues through an independent accountability mechanism or contractual mechanism. Laws are required that clearly target development projects as detailed in point 1 and those laws must contain a veto mechanism. If political will for this is lacking, the state can take softer actions that encourage and facilitate early pre-construction meditative practices involving good faith attempts to resolve ongoing local legacy issues around land within the proposed project area. Simply put, more government is needed.

Again, DFIs have a role to play in this regard. Constituted of member states they have unparalleled access to state decision-makers and can exert commercial pressure and discipline on prospective clients through their policies. If they, along with concessionaires, are willing to invest billions of capital into a fragile or developing country, the prior planning, time and costs required for early consultation are a price they, and the state, must pay. Using the shield of a non-political legal mandate to deny any role for dealing with these issues in a preventative manner is, in the context of their enormous financial gain, unacceptable.

4. Legal obligations requiring project documentation and contractual terms to formally recognise competing land claims.

If the community agrees that the project can go ahead, domestic laws (with pressure exerted from DFIs) could require, by default, that all future concession holders formally recognise competing land claims within their contractual arrangements and those arrangements do not contain features that can displace those rights. Furthermore, a general state-level mechanism for independently scrutinising state-negotiated contractual documentation such as the PPA/concession from a poverty reduction and fairness angle is required and time needs to be built into the project design to allow for this review. For a PPA arrangement for instance, mechanisms could provide for the electrification of poorer households within the concession. Others could require that all project costs are made public and that any cost savings made by the company in negotiation with the lenders are shared with the government buyer so that government tariff payments reduce. Clauses should also ensure that the buyer has the right to approve key project contracts in order to ensure the incentives are fair, as ultimately the buyer is paying financing costs within the capacity charge. One way to ensure all of the above is to require that PPAs are debated and approved by parliament and civil society representatives. Practices around state provision of financial guarantees during the construction period, for instance, or a separate host government support agreement containing a non-discrimination clause, and the impact of higher interest rates during construction also require independent examination from a poverty reduction angle.

This is a bold proposal and for states that lack this commercial technical capacity, it would require support from development institutes such as the International Development Law Organisation[2] and UNDP to fund such a mechanism perhaps through an independent legal fund. Through this facility, commercial lawyers can work on these issues on a reduced fee or pro bono basis. For this to work, DFIs would also need to apply pressure on their clients to disclose contractual provisions, perhaps with suitable confidentiality undertakings.

5. *A legal requirement that the concessionaire deposit funds for resettlement into a specially designated bank account.*

Some mineral laws require a licence holder to deposit funds equal to a percentage of its environmental budget for a particular year. A similar mechanism could be made for land- and resettlement-related issues. This then links with the suggestion on trusts discussed below.

6. *Permits and grievance mechanism*

Given that complaints frequently come through DFI grievance mechanisms after the project is operational, there is a need to think about making the identification and establishment of suitable project-specific grievance mechanisms part of the state permit allocation process. The identification of a suitable grievance mechanism can then be entrenched within the project documentation at specific points such as within the PIM and the loan agreements as a condition to initial disbursement and as specific covenant on the borrower, which lenders cannot waive. Ongoing covenants in the loan agreement can require the company and financiers to cooperate with the designated grievance mechanism as well as any general DFI ombudsman mechanism, if one becomes applicable to the case.

---

[2] The IDLO is currently looking at conducting this type of programme.

7. Trusts

In order to facilitate the above national conflict assessment processes, a national-level basket trust can be set up to appoint the independent anthropologists and specialised lawyers needed to audit the mapping of communities, represent local communities and provide certificates or opinions. Local inside mediators that are more typically used in conflict resolution could also be valuable as they are not external consultants but come from someone within the community, understand existing decision-making structures and already hold trust.

To complement this national arrangement, DFIs could set up a type of institutional-level blind trust, evidence of which should also be delivered under the debt instruments (as discussed in the code of practice recommendations below). This sees the lenders initiate and co-fund (with the concessionaire) a trust mechanism but have no control over the actions taken within the trust and receive no reports from the trustees while the blind trust is in force. An independent institute would then act as a trustee and have a large amount of discretion over which experts to appoint for representing the community in all aspects (the latter being the trust beneficiaries). This type of arrangement theoretically breaks any link between the lenders controlling how the trust money is used (who is appointed with it for instance), thus potentially avoiding conflicts of interest in the now normal delegation practices illustrated in the case studies. A blind trust structure could be used for hiring a local mediator, project social consultants and evaluators that are appointed by civil society and academia, and a community approved local lawyer, rather than the current over-reliance on company-hired private experts. All costs relating to the creation of the blind trust, appointment of experts for agreement-making and resettlement can then feed into the debt agreements as project costs. This allows for the earmarking of funds for these issues within early design and closes the gap on this issue in current PF documentation, which fails to include resettlement costs as a line item in project costs.

8. Promoting state-based non-judicial mechanisms

At the international legal level, more publicity is needed around the presence of state-based non-judicial grievance mechanisms for mobilising the recognition and implementation of indigenous land rights in development project contexts. For example, the Optional Protocol to the ICESCR could be a useful advocacy tool for individuals or groups to directly lodge complaints with the Committee on Economic, Social and Cultural Rights regarding specific domestic human rights violations. This could have been a potentially useful additional mechanism for the herders in the Oyu Tolgoi project, as Mongolia has signed the optional protocol; however, herders were not aware of this mechanism as a potential advocacy tool.[3] Similarly, there is the possibility for individuals or groups to lodge applications to the UN Committee on the Elimination of Racial Discrimination under article 14 of the ICERD. This could be a particularly useful advocacy strategy given that the ICERD recognises that racial discrimination can apply to the right to own property individually or collectively with others: a provision that was relied upon in the seminal *Mabo* case. Yet no indigenous group has advanced a claim through the article 14 procedure which reflects the overall weakness[4] of these petition systems to serve as a remedial tool. States and advocates need to do more to promote these mechanisms known as a potential advocacy tool for cases involving development projects, the state and private actors. Complementary to this would of course be a general legal aid scheme within the UN. This could be achieved through international cooperation. The proposed establishment of an international fund to provide for legal and financial aid for victims under the draft binding treaty on business and human rights could be a model.

5.2   Codes of Practice

These can tie with the above suggestions and require the following:
1. *Changes to the contractual governance framework*

Financiers and concessionaires should see the special purpose vehicle legal structure commonly used in asset-based lending, as a blank sheet and thus an ideal opportunity to introduce changes for better engagement within the existing contractual governance framework.

As discussed, DFIs can use their leverage to encourage companies to channel the information it has provided for the permit to the prospective lenders within the PIM. The common terms agreement could also contain a specific contractual covenant that the company provides the lenders' global facility agent with all ongoing details regarding land and indigenous

---

[3] Reference is made to interviews and conversations with resettled herders in October and November 2015 (translated from Mongolian to English).
[4] T Van Boven, 'The Petition System under the ICERD: An Unfulfilled Promise', in Alfredsson et al (eds.), *International Human Rights Monitoring Mechanisms: Essays in Honour of Jakob Th. Möller* (2nd edn., Martinus Nijhoff Publishers 2009).

issues and information on any project-specific grievance mechanism that has been established, at regular periods throughout the life of the loan (monthly or quarterly, for example). Given that the facility agent charges a fee for its work it is possible to include these progressive features if mindset and culture changes.

Changes can be made to existing loan instrument clauses for rights implementation at specific vulnerability hotspots. One measure could be to target the initial condition precedents preceding disbursement of a project loan. For issues of land, embedding specific provisions into a loan agreement is vital as initial disbursement of funds is typically required to finance construction. The company could be required to deliver a representation stating as follows: at the time of depositing its request for funds, it has carried out an independently verified process with an expert acceptable to the community for determining the presence of indigenous communities in the project area; has the communities' consent; and has commenced FPIC-compliant processes of early community participation, negotiation of land access and benefit sharing, compensation and mediation practices. Of course, if national legislation provides for the type of conflict assessment suggested above, evidence of company compliance should be a specific condition.

At this stage it would also be good practice to require, as a condition precedent for initial drawdown, that the company deliver any publicly available heads of terms for a company–community strategy which sets out general principles through which consultation strategies will be implemented. The local legal opinion on land and indigenous issues, commissioned by the borrower as a result of any pre-permit assessment, must also be delivered to the lenders at this initial pre-financing stage. As we can see from the Panama project, the failure to deliver this information should signal a red flag and a no go for investment. A code of practice would flag exactly this type of issue.

The debt contracts should remove the ability of lenders to waive the borrower's contractual duty to deliver information about the implementation of performance standards. Lenders would never agree to waive the underlying licence that is salient to its commercial due diligence, so why should they agree to waive social components? Indeed, this is absolutely imperative from a human rights–compliant approach, as without it the entire process can be overridden. Clearly, the gold standard would be for national law or regulations stating that no development can take place without community consent, as discussed in the first section. In the absence of this political will, companies and financiers can do more to

consider these issues further upstream in project design. From a governance perspective, these types of contractual changes can discipline a
concessionaire towards taking these issues seriously and at the most
meaningful and rights-compatible points within the project governance
architecture.

Other changes to the finance documents could include that the global
facility agent requires the company at the time of requesting its first
drawdown of funds, to deliver evidence that it has implemented a
grievance-mechanism policy, which it has publicised and made available
to communities in ways that align with local context and traditional institutions. This should be complemented by an ongoing covenant requiring
the company to deliver information on all complaints to the facility agent.
Delivery of evidence that the trust mechanisms suggested in Section 1,
have been set up, should also be a condition to first disbursement.

Other suggestions include a carve-out to the payment of delay-related
liquidated damages by the construction contractor if construction delay is
caused by land disputes. Provisions could also be included in the construction contract requiring the contractor to report any local tensions to the
company, which would then through the loan mechanisms, be delivered to
the lenders through the global facility agent. The blind trust mechanism
discussed in Section 1 could then provide an independent mechanism for
appointing a local community agreed mediator to help resolve the dispute.
A further suggestion is the addition in the project completion certificate of
a specific independent certification confirming that resettlement impacts
and strategies for obtaining FPIC, such as mediation and agreement-
making, have been developed and are ongoing.

Given that many of the contractual arrangements are English law–
governed, the above practices could be supported through a good practice guidance note from the Law Society of England and Wales highlighting some of the salient risks around investing in transnational
development projects and alerting lawyers to the fact that contracts
might contribute to those risks and in increasing vulnerability. Flowing
from the development of the business and human rights movement, the
Law Society of England and Wales has begun to discuss how lawyers
need to give attention to issues of human rights when advising clients. In
this light, a specialised note on large projects is a fitting addition.

2. Companies need to be sensitive to social context

Senior managers must make changes in incentive structures and
address the systemic project governance failures illustrated in the

preceding chapters so that land, indigenous and vulnerability issues are considered in context, further upstream and within contract negotiation, as suggested earlier. Facilitating this cultural change and sensitivity to context could be achieved through, for instance, training senior company managers to undertake mediation and financiers to insist that companies use those practices. Other general strategies could include the engagement of independent specialists within a company that have a mixture of technical expertise from the fields of anthropology, contractual negotiation and sustainability, and mediation that can advise and oversee these practices. Again, DFIs can insist that companies use those practices and are transparent about them. Another suggestion is for companies to make it policy to take seriously instances of state non-recognition of groups that claim indigenous status within a project. For companies, non-state recognition ought to be another red flag for investment and a code of practice could stipulate this.

The obvious tension with all of these recommendations is that context, early intervention, project design change and mediation, costs money and hits against incentives. In this regard, government development agencies, NGOs and ombudsman panel members can exert more pressure on project developers and financiers to see these as inevitable project costs that must be budgeted for by a company and its investors that stand to make millions from an investment. One method of potentially overcoming these tensions is to push for a type of social impact incentive in which payment structures are directly linked to specific social impacts. Once that impact is verified, a retroactive social incentive payment is triggered which pays companies for impacts achieved. The Swiss Agency for Development and Cooperation is pioneering this model for smaller agricultural projects but applying the principle to larger development projects could be considered depending on the types of funders involved.

3. Changes to direct agreement-making

Should communities agree to an agreement, companies should realise the value in grounding the contract in recognition of customary land title regardless of the underlying domestic law as a method of building trust. The use of the term stakeholder should be de-coupled from its corporate context, both in spirit and in paperwork practice. This can be worked towards holistically, for instance, by engaging with communities prior to construction, drafting a heads of terms of agreed principles for conducting consultation, showing that they will not continue with the project if a community says no and through methods for correcting underlying power asymmetries which should be considered obligatory in this field. This can include the provision of independent counsel and anthropologists chosen by the community and possibly in consultation with academics and NGOs.

The company should also consider making formal apologies within the agreement along with commitments to ongoing consultations prior to land incursion, continued land and water access rights, compensation for economic and, specifically, cultural loss of land and other good neighbour benefits. Companies should also consider the long-term benefit of engaging with local government structures in a tripartite structure, always using traditional decision-making practices and being more transparent about the details of any ongoing mediation processes they are involved in and contracts that emerge (should communities also agree to transparency). DFIs can exert pressure on its clients to use all of these strategies.

4. *Export credit agency contractual terms must include human rights provisions.*

5. *Financiers should reassess the provision of funds to Category A projects.*

6. *Separate mediation mechanism*

Whilst most DFIs now have safeguarding experts working within loan operation teams, there is still a need for more specialist people with anthropological expertise as well as skilled mediators all working as part of the safeguarding teams that can encourage a preventative approach. One suggestion is for DFIs to create a stand-alone mediation mechanism that is separate from the accountability mechanisms. This would be staffed with independent local mediators from the country in which a project is based and have the legitimacy of the community. The point is for those mediators to work with the community from the start, as part of a conflict-prevention assessment process and prior to the filing of any complaint with the ombudsman. There are obviously huge cost and logistical consequences to this. Another suggestion would be the creation of a mechanism whereby a community can seek independent advice on which form of accountability mechanisms – judicial or non-judicial – would, in their interests, be most suitable for their specific complaint.

7. Companies should take stock of the current legal framework and strategies that apply to this field as delineated in Chapter 3. Whilst lacunas do exist, companies should recognise that legal activists can

and will creatively cross-fertilise and develop these cases and strategies in future legal proceedings.

5.3   Research and Advocacy

Research and advocacy can facilitate all of the above as follows.

1. More research and advocacy attention around how the types of governance interfaces discussed in the preceding chapters matter for those concerned with indigenous rights to land and vulnerability studies generally. This is especially the case for the pre-construction phase which, as I have argued, constitutes a vulnerability hotspot for indigenous communities. Equally, more awareness should be given to the current practice of conducting a 'gap analysis' in resettlement contexts and the late entry of DFIs. Exposing the numerous contractual interfaces and behaviours that impact on rights recognition, perhaps linking these issues to the effectiveness of IAM mechanisms and how to conduct better due diligence in development project contexts is also required. More scrutiny needs to go into the methods for appointing ombudsman panels as an important measure for determining their independence from the relevant DFI. As discussed, some mechanisms score better than others in this regard.

2. NGOs might wish to dedicate a stream of research into PPAs for hydropower projects to conduct research and policy analysis that interfaces their contractual mechanisms and structures with poverty reduction and the sustainable development agenda.

3. There is an overall deficit in research and policy thinking about the special vulnerability of land-connected communities to development projects particularly in non-settler colonial contexts. A way of addressing this is for more research that translates FPIC standards to the context of transnational development projects involving the indigenous movement globally. This is because the attraction of FPIC lies in its ability to articulate the distinctive core of the indigenous movement: vulnerability and discrimination stemming from a community's special relationship to land; a vulnerability that is transnational and non-specific in time and space. Such contextual efforts could develop the legal framework in this field in a more inclusive and rights-compatible lens by increasing the visibility of land-connected groups as a transnational movement that is inherently vulnerable to powerful development projects in a variety of geographic and historical contexts. This could add to strategic litigation efforts to protect

indigenous rights to land and territories in the diverse geographical contexts within which development projects take place and push the legal framework around compensation for non-economic losses. The latter point is important given that it is quite clear that concessionaires will, as a baseline, follow formal law on this issue.

4. Research and advocacy is needed for the international regulation of agreement-making which might set out some fundamental principles for this practice. This could be spearheaded from the UN level and provide guidance for matters such as addressing power asymmetries, and suggestions for a blind trust structure in this setting for appointing community legal representation. Furthermore, international guidance could be produced around what a due diligence framework in this field could look like that takes into account the legal, contractual and policy issues raised in previous chapters.

5. Agencies involved in development such as DFID, the Commonwealth Secretariat, USAid and the UNDP must recognise large development projects, their legal and behavioural framework and potential impacts on vulnerability and conflict as a serious part of the development agenda. In this regard, research should be undertaken into the building of technical capacity and regulatory policy within government institutions around these issues, the identification of local mediators and the renegotiation of existing contracts, where practicable.

INDEX